SNO-ISLE REGIONAL

012.

P9-DVN-584

WITHDRAWN

0 A MAY 21 1992ATE DUE			

Sno-Isle Regional Library System
Marysville, Washington

Wilfully retaining public library materials
after notice in writing to return the same
is a misdemeanor.
Excerpt from RCW 27 12.340.

ALSO BY TIMOTHY EGAN

The Good Rain

Breaking Blue

BREAKING BLUE

by
Timothy Egan

ALFRED A. KNOPF
NEW YORK
1992

THIS IS A BORZOI BOOK
PUBLISHED BY ALFRED A. KNOPF, INC.

Copyright © 1992 by Timothy Egan
All rights reserved under International and Pan-American
Copyright Conventions. Published in the United States by
Alfred A. Knopf, Inc., New York, and simultaneously in Canada
by Random House of Canada Limited, Toronto. Distributed
by Random House, Inc., New York.

LIBRARY OF CONGRESS
CATALOGING-IN-PUBLICATION DATA

Egan, Timothy.
    Breaking blue / by Timothy Egan. — 1st ed.
        p.   cm.
    ISBN 0-394-58819-3
    1. Murder—Washington (State)—Pend Oreille County—
Investigation—Case studies. 2. Police murders—Washington (State)—Pend Oreille County—Case studies. 3. Police
corruption—Washington (State)—Pend Oreille County—Case
studies. 4. Bamonte, Tony. 5. Ralstin, Clyde. 6. Conniff,
George, d. 1935. I. Title.
HV6533.W2E36   1992
364.1′523′0979721—dc20   91-27848
                                                         CIP

Manufactured in the United States of America
First Edition

To Joni, for the time

There ain't no sin and there ain't no virtue.
There's just stuff people do.
                JOHN STEINBECK, *The Grapes of Wrath*

The following story is true, based on public records, newspaper and archival material, and the recollections of people who lived through the summer of 1935 to tell about it in the last years of their lives.

Contents

Contents

EPILOGUE

MAY 1990

Acknowledgments

Prying this story from people who were around in 1935 was not nearly so hard as was tracking down the most basic of police documents from that era, most of which have disappeared. For help in the tracking, I am grateful to the staff at the Cheney Cowles Museum in Spokane, to the Newport Historical Society, and to Joan Egan. I owe much to Jon Landman in New York, who has the best eye for storytelling of anyone on West 43rd Street. I'm grateful to Carol Mann, for insight and guidance. At Knopf, my thanks to Ash Green, Melvin Rosenthal, and Jenny McPhee.

ONE

THE LAST ACT
OF LIFE

SEPTEMBER 1989

1.

Judgment Day

WHEN IT CAME TIME for Bill Parsons to die, he crumpled into his wife's arms and started talking about the things cops seldom share with the women in their lives. She ran her fingers through his hair, this silver thatch, and felt the faintness of life: a tired and congested heart following a directionless beat, torn-up lungs gulping from the plastic tendrils of a metal appendage, a body in full retreat. Here it was, an Indian-summer morning in a valley cut by the Spokane River, and he couldn't take a breath of cool air. The wind blew down from the Selkirk Mountains, carrying a scent of the year's final hay-cutting and apples pressed to cider; his oxygen came from the pharmacy, bottled.

The doctors could keep him from dying, but they could not make him feel alive. After thirty-five years of service to the city of Spokane, Washington, the former chief of police had a first-rate pension and medical plan, but it seemed to amount to nothing more than an open ticket to see more urologists and respiratory therapists—the young men in running shoes waiting to stick something new up his ass or down his throat. Retirement was supposed to be about poker games in the light of a campfire, hip waders instead of tight shoes, chasing elk through huckleberry thickets, not about chrome trays and hospital

3

gowns and a daily breakfast of color-coded horse pills. He seldom left the doctor's office feeling any better, just more burdened with stuff. The bottled oxygen, the stimulants and slow-you-downs—all this *crap*—for what? To sit in a trailer park, on the fringes of a city whose laws he'd once enforced, waiting for Oprah to come on the tube?

From his office beneath the Gothic tower of police headquarters, he used to look away and imagine a salmon fly floating down the Spokane River below, taking the bend in slow motion until— *thwap!*—a big brownie rose to snap the line. On the river that carried snowmelt from two states to the Columbia rode the retirement dreams of the former chief. In the inland Northwest, where the great coastal ranges blocked the rainstorms from the Pacific and the land was ripe with the kind of wildlife that most of America has lost, the outdoors was the only place for honest work and decent play. Ten minutes from the center of town, downstream from the raging falls, an old man could be Huck Finn again, lost in the eternal flow of the Spokane River.

Life was supposed to ebb away, like the river. But Parsons's body answered to its own schedule, throwing in a heart attack and emphysema, payback from earlier years. Physical pain he could tolerate; the toll on his good name was something else. Suspicion, half-truths, a vague and unfinished story about corruption and death from another era—that was not the sort of thing a person wanted to leave behind. The body would not go cold before the gossip would harden to gospel.

A rancher's son, born when followers of Chief Joseph of the Nez Percé still dreamed of driving homesteaders from the ponderosa pine forests and alfalfa fields of the inland Pacific Northwest, Edward W. "Bill" Parsons had seen the length of the twentieth century, only to have one incident, the worst mistake of his professional life, come back at him now. He started in police work at a time when bootleggers and Chinese numbers rackets could provide a patrolman with a healthy income on the side, and he got out just before crack dealers and the state lottery commission made a mockery of the Depression-era enforcement routine. When he retired, plotting a good life in the woods, serving on citizen boards and honorary panels, the chief thought he had escaped with his reputation intact. Baby-faced Bill Parsons, rookie cop in 1935, silver-topped dean in 1970, leader of the state police chiefs' organization, past president of the Fraternal Order of Police. But where were his brothers now, when he needed them? The secret Parsons had carried with him his entire career was coming out: people were whispering; it was in the papers, on television. And it wasn't even *his* secret; yes, he was its custodian during his years on the force, but once he retired, he had passed it on—or so he thought. The damn thing belonged to the Spokane Police Department, an institutional responsibility. Why, he wondered in these last days of his life, should he have to answer for it? It wasn't fair! Parsons had held up his end of the Blue Wall, keeping a silence that is the bond of his profession. Never, never, never had he spoken a word.

Confined by the limits of his collapsing body, Parsons longed for company, a few fellows who Knew What It Was Really Like. He used to go down to the Police Guild lounge for a snort and a memory blast. But, over time, most of the faces were unfamiliar, the common ground faded. Jerie asked some of the old boys from the station to visit her husband—"Just give the chief an hour of your time"—but few people came around to the trailer park on the fringe of town. It seemed obvious, though it took some time for him to believe it, that perhaps his popularity was entirely dependent on the uniform he had worn half his life. Now, he was so lonely it sometimes felt like physical pain, a powerful ache. In baggy clothes, no longer chief, Bill Parsons sat through his last year as a bored and pained bystander.

A few months shy of his eightieth birthday, nothing seemed to work but his conscience, the nag. Jerie held him, a frame of soft skin and weak bones. The prettiest man in the police department still had his eagle's crown. He closed his eyes and fell back to 1935, when he was a rookie patrolman, natty in blue and tight collar, a .38 strapped to his side, polished boots, with a regular salary and a degree of respect few men could command during the darkest days of a time when everything seemed to have fallen apart, a low, dishonest decade, as the poet W. H. Auden had called it. In whispered words and broken cadences, he started telling Jerie about that other September fifty-

four years earlier, and the truth about a story that was just now starting
to emerge.

THE MAN who had stirred Parsons, lighting fires under the dead and
the near-dead, lived alone in a decaying three-story brick building—
a former office, his home—about seventy-five miles north of Spokane,
in the border hamlet of Metaline Falls. Anthony G. Bamonte had
spent the last year thinking about September 1935. He was reasonably
sure that he knew what Parsons, and much of the Spokane Police
Department, had been trying to hide for more than half a century.
A few questions remained, though, to keep him awake. Bamonte was
forty-seven years old, trying to rebuild a life pained by a pending
divorce and the political pressures of his job. More and more, he
retreated into obscure books and yellowed newspapers from sensa-
tional times. His world was falling apart, his wife gone, his boy es-
tranged from him, his job in jeopardy; but when he worked the past,
everything he touched came to life.

Bamonte was pursuing a master's degree at Gonzaga University,
the old Jesuit college that was built on the banks of the Spokane River
at a time when most of the people who lived near its shores were
native Spokane or Coeur d'Alene Indians. A logger's son, raised in
canvas tents and backwoods cabins without plumbing or electricity,
Bamonte had a passion for history, perhaps because the stories of
rough-edged men wrenching a living from a land so recently undraped
from its glacial period were not that far removed from his own early
years in the inland Northwest. Bamonte could look at a meadow above
the Pend Oreille Valley, a country where he built fifteen log homes,
and he would see a tribe of Kalispel Indians gathered to spear salmon
and swap pelts with the Hudson's Bay Company. The past was not
dead, he believed, and the dead were not powerless.

When he enrolled in the master of organizational leadership program at Gonzaga, his thesis idea seemed unique to the professors.
He wanted to do a history of all the sheriffs in Pend Oreille County
(pronounced "Pond-O-Ray," the name was a legacy of French-
Canadian fur trappers, a reference to the shell ornaments, *pendants*

d'oreille, worn in the ears of the natives) and the major crimes of their times. Except for his tour in Vietnam in the early 1960s and a few years in Spokane, home for Tony Bamonte had always been the Pend Oreille, where nine thousand people live in a county half the size of Connecticut. The land is crowded with tall pines wrapped in jigsaw pieces of red bark, holding to the rumpled spine of the Selkirk Mountains. Grizzly bears, among the last of the biggest land mammals left on the continent, still roam the woods, occasionally tearing up gardens or chasing farm animals. Although the Coeur d'Alenes, the Spokanes, the Nez Percés, the Kalispels, and visiting Blackfeet and Crows hunted elk and pulled chinook salmon from waterfalls, the human presence is recent, and negligible. Washington's only significant populations of moose, caribou, and wolves live in the county. What they have in the Pend Oreille is a vastness where time is never forced. The valley was not settled by whites until the mid-1890s, when a sawmill was stitched to the banks of the river on the Washington-Idaho border. A hard town of loggers, miners, saloonkeepers, and chow merchants formed around the mill.

In the early stages of Bamonte's graduate research, one particular case—the crime of the century in the wilderness county, some called it—was a chapter full of holes. So little was known about it that Bamonte wondered how he, an amateur historian, wrestling with words, unsure of his academic ability, could explain this lapse to his professors. At one time Bamonte thought he might have to write around it. But then something extraordinary happened, a convergence of conscience and coincidence: the lost years came to life. The archives, police records, and newspaper clippings told nothing more than the usual details of blood, grief, and mystery. What Bamonte found was a living time capsule; he broke into it, and was now in the process of rearranging the pieces.

From his home in the Pend Oreille, he phoned Parsons and explained what he was looking for. "Just hoping you can help me out with a few details about what happened in 1935, Bill—"

The older man cut him off; he knew all about Bamonte and the case that had become his obsession. "I wondered why you didn't call earlier," Parsons said, speaking in a halting and whispery voice. Bamonte could hear the strained breaths, the sucking of oxygen. "You come by," Parsons said. "I'll be here."

SET IN A GRAND BREACH sliced through the basalt layers of the upper Columbia Plateau, Spokane was a town of cumbrous secrets, where the jazz artist Billy Tipton lived most of her adult life disguised as a man, and the worst rapist in the city's history turned out to be the son of a leading citizen, the managing editor of the afternoon newspaper. Butch Cassidy, leader of the Hole in the Wall Gang, is said to have spent the last third of his life there, living off the earnings of his nineteenth-century bank robberies as a quiet citizen with an impeccably neat lawn. Though historians had maintained that Cassidy died in a Bolivian shootout in 1909, his sister, Lula Parker Betenson, said in a deathbed interview in 1970 that her outlaw brother lived on in Spokane until 1937. "The law thought he was dead and he was happy to leave it that way," she said. "He made us promise not to tell anyone that he was alive. It was the family secret. He died peacefully in Spokane."

From the outside, Spokane looked as orderly as mathematics and just as sedate—a well-groomed town on a tight leash. City leaders referred to their town as the center of the "Inland Empire." But the city's worst critics, natives who left and swore never to return, sometimes referred to it, in a swipe at the century-old booster slogan, as the hub of the "Ingrown Empire," a reservoir of buried personal histories.

There are millennia-old glaciers in the North Cascades, to the west, that move faster than the pace of change in Spokane; and that was just fine with Parsons and thousands of other citizens who lived all of their lives in the biggest city between Minneapolis and Seattle. Spokane offered the security of a routine as reliable as the dawn. From 1929 until the mid-1980s, the city was essentially frozen. Outsiders—from the radical labor unions whose members staged free-speech marathons to the defeated Indian tribes from Montana and Idaho who held occasional rallies in town—were dealt with quickly and violently. During the early part of Bill Parsons's career, crime was tolerated so long as it was the right *kind* of crime. Bootlegging. Cathouses. Gambling. Wife-beating. Gun-running. No harm there. Like other cities in the American West, Spokane was built virtually overnight on the wealth of abundant natural resources. And when the silver veins dried up or didn't bring enough money to pay for the cost of transporting men underground, and the market for white pine from Idaho and wheat grown in the rolling hills of the nearby Palouse collapsed along with the rest of the economy in the 1930s, Spokane reverted to its frontier roots. Breadlines brought out the devil. For all but the most serious of crimes, the law was nothing more than what a given police officer said it was.

Thinking about those first days now, Parsons would have preferred to dwell on the small triumphs: a shootout that he walked away from, a winning footrace with a fleeing felon, a burglary ring cracked. He focused instead on a flick in a lifetime, knowing very well that this one asterisk, unearthed by Bamonte, could well define him in the years to come.

When Bamonte arrived at Parsons's house, he found a man as thin as broth, pale and gaunt, attached to an oxygen machine. Jerie told the visitor that her husband was dying of emphysema. Parsons peered through thick black glasses, blinked as if startled by a headlight, and extended a hand. He said a few words, but his voice was so weak that Bamonte had to move his ear next to Parsons's face to hear him. Now that the interrogator was in his home, Parsons seemed relieved. He wondered how this younger man could possibly understand the Depression, a time when you could not trust tomorrow.

"You're making a lot of trouble for everybody," he said.

"I just have a few questions, Bill," Bamonte said. "Trying to get to the bottom of this thing."

Parsons told his visitor about police work in 1935. The job wasn't about law enforcement, it was about survival. An honest policeman during the Depression was a loser and a loner. Parsons knew, because he started out as one.

"What kind of stuff are we talking about?" Bamonte asked.

Parsons took several pulls from his tank, removed the black glasses, wiped his eyes. "Burglary," he answered. Also, theft. The officers, men in uniform, stole food, turkeys, radios, small change, jugs of oil, he said. Try feeding a family on twenty-seven dollars a week during the Depression. Even when the money was better, a sergeant's salary plus perks, who could keep the peace without keeping a piece for himself?

"Robbery." They took from people they didn't like, with impunity.

Bribery was common.

"What kind? How big, Bill?"

"Chippy stuff," Parsons said. "Ten-dollar bills."

For much of his life, Bill Parsons had convinced himself that he was different from the other officers. They were dirty. He was clean, the respected community leader. By the 1950s, Parsons believed that that crowd, from the 1930s, was out of his life for good; and so he thought the secret they had shared had left town with them. They could have hurt him in 1967, when he was named chief of police, but he heard nothing. Every decade further buried the story of what had happened in September 1935, until the truth was very deep and very distant.

"What else, Bill?" Bamonte asked, his voice a gentle prod.

Parsons looked into the eyes of his wife of forty-five years. Then he told Bamonte what he had just told Jerie.

"That killing from 1935 . . . we all knew about it. It was . . . one of us."

To Jerie, who had long ago stopped asking her husband what went on inside police headquarters, the revelations of the last fifteen minutes were astonishing—not so much for what he said as for the fact of his saying it at all. There was natural law, there was man-made law, and then there was Cop Code. As every police officer knew, only one of these was absolute—above all, the commandment "Thou shalt never snitch on a fellow officer." More than half a century after Bill Parsons's initiation into the fraternity of lawmen, he was breaking the trust.

What's more, he was naming names, dates, details. Bamonte's tape recorder was running, and he took notes as well. His interest in the case went beyond historical curiosity, for he was also the sheriff of Pend Oreille County, where the 1935 killing remained an unsolved homicide in his jurisdiction. By 1989, it was the oldest active murder case in the nation, a probe that had occupied the time of three sheriffs and the director of the Federal Bureau of Investigation. Thus, as Bamonte's graduate project entered its last phase, he was not just blowing dust from a corner attic of Washington while pursuing an academic degree. He was looking for a murder suspect in his county. Bamonte the scholar, reading microfiche until his eyes blurred and his head ached, was attempting to alter a small bit of history—the private motive of many tellers of the past. Bamonte, the Pend Oreille sheriff, was attempting to extract some measure of justice from it.

That same week in September 1989, there had been a story in the paper about drug gang members from Los Angeles moving to the Northwest; they would kill one another over the color of somebody's hat, the story said. Imagine. But Parsons now recalled a day when one man would shoot another over a few pounds of stolen butter.

TWO

THE FIRST ACT
OF DEATH

AUTUMN 1935

2.

The Need for Butter

IN 1935, something happened to parts of the American West and midsection that only God in the foulest of Old Testament moods was supposed to be capable of causing: the land died. Green never came to those prairies and river valleys and meadows and former sea bottoms and high-elevation soil beds which had always brought forth grass and fields of knee-high perennials. Instead, barely a half-century after the first white farmers cut the ground with plow blades, the earth dried up and gathered itself into amber clouds of airborne dust. Some days, though the sun burned high overhead, much of the sky was dark, blackened by raging dust clouds. Streams disappeared; cows choked to death or went blind; corn curled and collapsed; leaves blighted and withered; trees stopped and surrendered to beetles and locusts. When the anemic spring alfalfa fields were exhausted and the reserves of hay depleted, there was nothing to feed the livestock. In Fort Worth, Texas, six hundred thousand head of cattle were shot, firing-squad style, and buried. Parched and emaciated, they were deemed not even fit enough to feed those thousands of Americans who found themselves without homes or hope in the Southwest.

This drought had begun in 1934, when the winter rains never came, and the winds carried soil from state to state, until there was a wall that could be seen a hundred miles away. A curtain of dust blew east across the Great Plains, dumping twelve million tons on Chicago, and then on to the Eastern Seaboard and out to the Atlantic Ocean, where the soil that was supposed to produce food from seed fell to the sea. By early 1935, the winter wheat, planted out of optimism and little else a few months earlier, came forth stunted and brown; there had been only a trace of snow during the cold months. Plow it under, the farmers were told; five million acres of winter wheat were destroyed. Start anew. But with what?

In the cities, where money could be made out of other money or from serving those who had it, the depression had started with the stock-market collapse of 1929. In ten weeks, the market shed half its value, and shareholders lost $40 billion—more than eight times as much as the entire federal budget of the time. Life savings were wiped out; pension funds disappeared; banks folded like cheap tents in a gust. Earlier that year, Herbert Hoover had been sworn into office with the boast that "Americans are nearer to the final triumph over poverty than ever before in the history of any land."

In the new farmlands of the West, hard times had hit well before 1929; the economic drought arrived just after the end of World War I, when there was a surfeit of farmers and food. While city dwellers practiced the silly sophistications of prosperous life in the 1920s—flapping and flagpole sitting and bathtub-gin parties—farmers suffered through one inexplicable disaster after another. There were no Roaring Twenties, no New Era, no giddy exploration of leisure's edge for those who tilled the ground. By 1935, the worst agricultural depression in this country founded by farmers was in its fifteenth straight year.

The railroads and real estate promoters had lured the parents and grandparents of these farmer families from the old land in Ohio, Pennsylvania, New York, and other states with promises that the new land was virtually free and would come to life with little more than a few years' care. It was an arid stretch of rumpled land, from Texas and Oklahoma on up through Colorado, Utah, Idaho, Montana, and the eastern halves of Oregon and Washington; but all that was needed to produce a crop was perhaps fifteen inches of rain a year, the promoters said. "Muscle is the only capital needed!" went one slogan. "This is by far the best money-making country in America" was the banner across the Northern Pacific Railroad Company's milk-and-honey depiction of Montana, Idaho, and eastern Washington.

So the first of the farmer families came, immigrants and Civil War veterans, staked off small homesteads with barbed wire, put potatoes in the ground, grazed a few head of cattle, and turned over the bunchgrass. Always, the wind blew. For a few years, the soil responded well. But then this land, which had fed the natives for centuries—the natural sod nurtured bison and grouse and brought forth edible bulbs—turned to powder. Without the root structure of the short grass to hold the soil down, it disappeared.

By early February of 1935, the great dust clouds had started up again, a return of the tantrum from the year before, and kicked across the land, ripping up the carpet of what had been spared from the previous year's drought. Dust blew into unpainted frame homes and covered everything—dishes, lamp shades, family bibles—and it stung the eyes and lacerated the skin. One storm in March scooped out twice as much soil as had been dug to create the Panama Canal. Through Colorado and Nebraska and Kansas (where a train was derailed by a fierce blow), the sky rained dust. Through Texas and Oklahoma and Arkansas, cotton fields blew away; orchards browned and weakened and collapsed.

By spring, the new land was leathered; even the cursed tumbleweed, Russian thistle, could not grow in 1935. Near the end of the year, more than 850 million tons of topsoil—enough to layer 6 million acres with an inch of dirt—had been ripped from the surface of the new land. In Texas and Oklahoma, four million acres were abandoned. A million people left their homes. Farm prices fell to the lowest point in history, then climbed as food became scarce. Those who had held on by diversifying their crops, or lending their muscle out for hire, gave in. On their heels came swarms of grasshoppers and men from the banks, carrying promissory notes. A farmer who could barely stay alive on rural subsistence now found himself on the road and unable to afford the food he hadn't been able to give away a few years earlier.

Food riots broke out in several cities, mobs clamoring for something to eat; they were dispersed, in some cases, by riot police with tear gas. Families that had studied the hard face of a half-dozen acres for a generation now packed themselves into a house on wheels and set out for land where the rain was said to be reliable and life-renewing. Throughout 1935, they poured into California, Oregon, Washington, and Idaho. By train, they arrived in Spokane, the railroad and commercial hub of four states covering two hundred thousand square miles. Like the streams that fed the Columbia River from distant draws, desperate families channeled into the valley of the Spokane River.

With just under 120,000 people, Spokane in 1935 called itself "the Queen City of the Richest Empire in the Western Hemisphere." The city was an infant, barely fifty years old, built around a triple-tiered waterfall that dropped through a rock canyon. It was isolated from the rest of the world by a fence of mountains: the Cascades to the west, the Selkirks to the north, the Bitterroots, the Coeur d'Alenes, and the Rockies to the east, and the trench of Hells Canyon to the south, where the Snake River cut the deepest gorge on the continent. Spokane's ceaseless promoters, whose grandfathers had grabbed the valley from the Indians after a terror campaign that consisted of summarily hanging the native leaders, slaughtering all their horses, and burning caches of winter food, billed their town as a diamond in the Depression rough, the center of that Inland Empire which produced a third of the nation's lead, a fourth of its silver, a fifth of its apples, a tenth of its wheat, a fifth of its water power. The biggest stands of white pine—cut down to make matchsticks—were just across the border in Idaho, as was the biggest silver mine in the world, the Bunker Hill tunnels into the Coeur d'Alene Mountains.

The farmer families had clambered aboard trains, packing pots and pans and bits of dried food, dodged the head-busting goons, and then emerged from week-long journeys in the rail yards east of Spokane. They considered themselves lucky; many train-riders never survived the trip. On one line alone in 1935, the Northern Pacific, more than

150 people were killed while trying to hop aboard. Every day brought families, some wearing everything they owned, to the Hillyard section of town. A generation earlier, these railroads had deposited Italians, Germans, Swedes, Jews, and Irish, most of them with a little stake. For $350 a family could buy a home and twenty acres. Now the railroads brought to Spokane a new breed of passenger, a reluctant hobo: the American farmer.

When they arrived in the valley of wheat and orchards in a city whose fine stone buildings were built with money from farmers in the Palouse and silver miners in the bordering mountains, they found what they had left behind: a land sick with thirst. Spokane's September of 1935 was the driest in half a century. The sky was clouded by smoke, drifting in from the forest fires that raged in the surrounding pine forests. When the fires weren't started by lightning, they were started by hungry men looking for work. President Franklin D. Roosevelt was looking to find jobs for the 13 million unemployed—one out of every four Americans of working age. A fire on national forest land meant a fire crew on a federal payroll would be dispatched to the woods. So there was always somebody who made sure the pine forests of the Inland Empire were burning. Governor C. Ben Ross of Idaho used National Guard troops to patrol his state's forests against arsonists, but the big pines continued to burn.

And where was all the water that was synonymous with the Pacific Northwest? Certainly not on the east side of the Cascades. Instead of black earth and plump streams, the migrants found dust devils of whirling wind and parched irrigation ditches. In Green Acres, the orchards outside Spokane, brown fruit rotted on trees, spoiled by sun spots. West of town, in the treeless sage country, coyotes, jackrabbits, and rattlesnakes roamed across farm fields gone fallow. In Idaho— where the suicide rate had gone up 600 percent since 1930—a mob of farmers dynamited a dam whose reservoir of irrigation water was siphoned off for the exclusive use of a few large landowners. Governor Ross declared martial law and threw the farmers into jail. A local jury refused to convict them. Deep inside Idaho's Sawtooth Mountains, another group of angry men blew up a dam on the Salmon River that blocked chinook from spawning at the end of a nine-hundred-mile journey from the Pacific. In the Northwest, during the worst of times, there were always king salmon to keep people alive; the saboteurs justified their action by saying they preferred wild fish to breadlines.

Around Othello, in the heart of eastern Washington's wheat country, land prices fell to thirty-five cents an acre—and still there were few takers. Without water, the soil was worthless. In 1935, for the first time in memory, America imported wheat.

And where were all the jobs? The mines limped along, with skeletal crews scraping out silver, ore, and lead which sold for dismal prices. With few people building new homes, demand for timber was anemic. The most visible product of the "richest empire" was apples, and they moved, sold by sad-faced street vendors on every corner in downtown Spokane, for a nickel apiece. It was a form of charity.

One morning in August of 1935, a headline in the Spokane *Chronicle*—one of two daily newspapers in town owned by the powerful Cowles family—told readers what many already knew: SPOKANE BUTTER SHORTAGE LOOMS. "Creamery men report that a serious scarcity of butter is developing in Spokane territory," the story said. With farms folding and the land dying, even butter was scarce in the new land. Prices reached forty cents a pound—more than double the cost of one year earlier. For the poorest of working families, those who labored cutting cords of firewood for a dollar a day or picking apples for five cents a bin, a week's supply of butter, if they could find it, meant handing over a day's wages.

Worse, much of the butter that had been stockpiled was now being taken in a series of creamery burglaries. In the dead of night, thieves backed up trucks to creamery entrances, broke into the buildings, and hauled away huge loads of butter, cheese, and cream. Nearly half a dozen such burglaries took place in August and early September. Who would steal butter from farmers? the local people asked themselves, aghast. Although police had few leads, they had some ideas. In the rail yards, the new arrivals, the farmer families, had been stealing coal to keep the fires and stoves in their cardboard and tin hovels warm at night. Everybody knew how desperate they were.

Throughout hamlets of the rural West, there was serious talk of violent revolution.

And there was a saying, muttered around campfires in the rail yards east of Spokane, the city's own Hooverville, where upwards of two hundred and fifty people a day arrived from the Dust Bowl: "An empty stomach does not recognize the law."

3.

Cop Code

FRESH ON A JOB that promised not only a guaranteed salary of twenty-seven dollars a week but clean clothes as well, Bill Parsons was given a leather strap, brass knuckles, an oak billy club, and a six-chamber, five-inch-barreled, .38-caliber Smith & Wesson, and was introduced to the routine of a lawman in a town staggered by the sixth year of the Great Depression. Outside the city limits, creameries were getting knocked off. Nobody had ever seen anything like it, a series of quick strikes. Inside the city, cafes and diners were broken into and large quantities of butter taken. Some merchants believed that one gang was behind the dairy heists; they seemed systematic.

In 1935, the most common crime in Spokane was vagrancy. As defined by Washington state law, a vagrant was a person without visible means of support; and in the middle of the decade that was supposed to bring an end to poverty, nearly half the adults in the inland Northwest were technically criminals.

There was a simple order to this universe of broken families and uniformed enforcers in Spokane: a policeman was prosecutor and judge, jury and executioner. It was up to the patrolmen and detectives to decide who should be rousted out of the cardboard shacks and canvas tents along the river's shore—who should be plucked from the ranks of emaciated migrants, banged across the head, and made into a usual suspect—and who should not. Gypsies were jailed for telling stories, and union organizers were hustled away from small rallies and sent packing with nothing but bruised shins to show for their visit to Spokane.

Vagrancy was the nightstick of the foot patrolman, wielded freely against the outsiders whose presence was so threatening. It was not uncommon for a judge to give somebody a six-month prison term for vagrancy. The problem was, the city could throw you in jail, but once you were there it couldn't afford to feed you. Although more than twelve hundred arrests were made every month in Spokane for a variety of crimes, the city budgeted no more than three hundred dollars a month to feed all the prisoners. It was cheaper, and certainly more expedient, to squeeze a suspect—extorting sex, food, change, or the grocery scrip that had been substituted for money—than to bring him into jail to starve or survive on potato sandwiches. By one official estimate, more than $100,000 a year was spent bribing Spokane police officers in the mid-1930s—twenty-seven times the annual amount spent on jail food.

Around the city, posters had advertised a $15,000 reward for information leading to the capture of John Dillinger, the bank robber who'd been wending his way through the West. Holding a submachine gun in one hand and a pistol in the other, Dillinger presented a formidable challenge in the poster. When word had it that he was passing through Spokane, every cop on the 120-man force was drawn into the manhunt. They found not a trace of Dillinger, who stood only five foot four inches tall but was a giant of the type of diversionary crime that kept so many American minds off their hollow stomachs. The feds finally caught up with him in Chicago—a city whose most prominent soup kitchen was funded by its most prominent gangster, Al Capone—where he died in a shootout. The reward money went unclaimed.

Young Bill Parsons was advised that more reliable money could be found elsewhere. As a policeman, he was told, he had certain privileges. For starters, there was legitimate moonlighting. Foreclosures, one of the few growth industries in the 1930s, relied on off-duty policemen to provide force for the hated banks. A third of all the legal work at the time was in taking back property. And it wasn't just failed mortgages that led to foreclosure; many people couldn't pay for the most basic of services. One woman lost her home because she was behind on a twenty-four-dollar sewer bill. Old and sick, she begged a pair of Spokane policemen to let her die in her home. Attempting to cut a deal during her eviction, she promised to leave her house to the city if they let her live her last months inside. The city took the home and kicked the woman out.

As a hub for miners, lumberjacks, fruit-pickers, railroad workers, and assorted farmhands who'd lost their tenuous link to the land, Spokane had always been a town where the most urgent of vices—sex and booze and gambling—were well serviced. Just before the start of statewide prohibition in 1913, there were seventy-eight saloons within the small downtown area. Nearly twenty years later, in the dying years of the dry era, a newspaper survey found eighty-six illegal liquor joints. Chinese workmen, who had stayed long after the railroads were built, set up a thriving lottery business and sold opium to regular customers. Farm girls who couldn't make it on tired fields found easy work hopping from laptop to laptop of saloon clients. At least forty-two Spokane establishments burned the red lampshade of the brothel in their windows after dark. The toils of liquor-consuming and ass-chasing went on almost exclusively in a ten-block section downtown, on the south banks of the river, across from the falls. The gentry—those families enriched during the boom years around the turn of the century—lived above all the riffraff, on the South Hill, in elegant mansions shaded by thick oaks. They promoted their town through annual marketing reports, issued by the *Spokesman-Review*, the morning daily; they produced an official version of city history that was like a Christmas card from a fractured family, omitting all mention of the bruises or beatings. The paper trumpeted the virtues of a city with 156 churches, a "negro population of less than one-half-of-one percent," a place where "white and native-born people far exceed the general average."

Just south of the crashing torrent of Spokane Falls, at the center of the vice factories, was a six-story stone building erected in 1912: headquarters of the police department. When Bill Parsons first walked out of that building in 1935, he beamed, wearing a uniform of navy blue, a cap with a badge atop its brim, polished leather shoes, and the confidence of a young man who'd found secure job footing amidst an economy where the earth had moved. Before the Depression, everyone seemed obsessed with how much his neighbor made; after 1929, the talk was of how much he had lost.

Hundreds of men applied for the five openings in the police department that year. They didn't need a high school degree or any knowledge of law enforcement or particular skill at shooting a pistol. What the department was looking for were men who could kick butt and walk away from it, men who wouldn't burden the pension system with their broken noses, back problems, bad teeth, or flat feet.

Pictures of the new officers ran in the *Spokesman-Review*, five young patrolmen whom the civil service commissioner labeled "as fine a bunch of men as I have seen in a long time." Each face stared out sternly, already wearing the sphinxlike visage of the cop—except for Bill Parsons. He was a stunning looker, with perfect teeth, smooth skin, thick, dark hair, and sleepy, half-lidded eyes that in a later time might have been compared with those of Elvis Presley. His cap was half-cocked, on the side, and he smiled in a jaunty, got-the-world-by-the-tail look.

Parsons weighed in at nearly two hundred pounds; his upper body was knotted and hard, his hands shiny from calluses. Before moving to Spokane, he had labored in the forests of northern Idaho, fighting fires, building trails, sawing through the four-foot-thick waistbands of Ponderosa pines. Parsons was not afraid of the raw elements of the rural West. What's more, his confidence was bolstered by a moral code forged in the woods. A guy had to be loyal. A guy had to be fair. A guy couldn't cheat another guy out of something that was rightfully his. So when twenty-five-year-old Bill Parsons first walked out of the stone building as a Spokane police officer, he found his philosophy inscribed on a statue of Abraham Lincoln looking west from a perch above the falls. The words read:

> Let us have faith
> That right makes might

And in that faith
Let us to the end
Dare to do our duty
As we understand it.

As Parsons understood it, his duty was to walk a beat, fists and billy club ever ready, looking for vagrants, miscreants, petty thieves, drunks, and Reds. He was to respond when a good citizen asked for help. More important, he was to watch for outsiders—suspicious characters looking for trouble. The city seemed to be full of such individuals in 1935. For months, the transit workers had been on strike, complaining they couldn't feed their families on their meager wages from the city. Spokane's political leaders would not budge. There was no money to fill potholes, no money for jail food, no money for parks, no money for the zoo, which closed its doors and gave away the animals, and no money for city workers. After several months, they began to hire scabs from the ranks of the farmer families pouring in from Oklahoma and Texas. The striking workers went on a rampage, smashing windows at transit headquarters and blowing up one transit car with dynamite. During a riot, the entire police force was called out to smash heads and arrest strikers.

Then there were the new workers from the East, blacks mostly, who'd been sent from such places as New York, Philadelphia, and Chicago to Spokane for three-dollar-a-day government jobs. In 1935, Roosevelt introduced the Works Progress Administration—the centerpiece of his New Deal job program. The West was treated like a long-neglected yard, ready for chores. The newcomers from the East were put to work building a road to Mount Spokane, north of the city around Deadman's Creek. They slept under big tents or assembled shacks of their own. By day, they were given picks and shovels and told to plow their way up the mountain. At night, many of the men came in for a drink at Jimmy Young's, a second-floor walk-up just two blocks from the police station, or for a dance at the Cotton Club, on First Avenue, a few blocks the other way. Too often, a Saturday night's relaxation turned into a vagrancy charge.

The city leaders had a particular distrust of anyone who attempted to disrupt the political order. For the first three decades of the twentieth century, Spokane enforced laws that made free assembly, public speaking, and certain demonstrations illegal. Since the Cowles family controlled both newspapers—a profitable monopoly—the hardy perennials who held office were invariably Protestant Republicans approved by the paper's editorial board. The raw political energy down below, where the vice pits and shantytowns clustered along the river's shore, was feared, and not easily cornered. It could spring from the compost of discontent—a beer parlor, a union hall, a Civilian Conservation Corps hiring camp—and quickly take hold. The city's solution was to outlaw certain types of free speech.

Spokane had changed very little since the most famous fight over free speech. In 1908, members of the Industrial Workers of the World labor union, known as the Wobblies, converged on the city to stage a public-speaking marathon. Several hundred Wobblies who were trying to organize timber and mining camps had been arrested, charged with being union rabble rousers. To protest the arrests, thousands of Wobblies came to Spokane from all over the West. They arrived with soapboxes and took up positions on the street, where they proceeded to advocate revolution, unionism, one-worldism, and a host of other utopian ideals. The city council promptly passed a law prohibiting street speeches, and when the Wobs held forth from their soapboxes as usual, they were arrested. The jail was so full that a nearby high school had to be opened up in order to hold all the street orators. The Salvation Army took exception to the new law, so the council passed a loophole, which outlawed free speech in public places except that with musical accompaniment. In response, the Wobs starting singing their slogans. They were still arrested. Even in 1935, long after most of the Wobblies had faded away, the official yearbook of the Spokane Police Department recorded dozens of arrests for speaking without a permit or handing out flyers without a license.

Bill Parsons made his rounds, a bit confused by the rules he was supposed to enforce. His baby face had a way of drawing raised fists. In two months of police work, he picked up more cuts and bruises than he did during years of tramping in the woods of northern Idaho. Around the police station, he was starting to hear things. How could the sergeant afford a new Buick—a five-passenger sedan priced at nine hundred dollars—on his salary, with two kids and a wife to support? What was the night-shift captain doing in the Cotton Club, after hours, with the town's biggest bootlegger? There was a lot of talk about liquid cash, trade secrets, payers and players. The words were barely concealed. Surely, nothing spoken within the stone fortress of police headquarters would ever leave the building.

Outside, the natural world seemed to be falling apart, from dust storms in the Columbia Basin to forest fires in Idaho to earthquakes in Montana. The man-made world was no better, with lines of hungry people snaked around the block of the big soup kitchen at Sacred Heart Hospital, and the streetcars unsafe to ride for fear of a striker's bomb blast. But inside police headquarters, one thing had not changed: the Cop Code. The worse things became, the more the tribe of the Spokane Police Department closed ranks, for mutual gain and mutual defense.

The way a rookie cop learned the job was to follow a journeyman around. There was no police academy. No rudimentary introduction to the law. No courses in when to fire a weapon or in legal rights. During his first months on the force, Parsons was introduced to Dan Mangan, a patrolman six years his senior. Most rookies were afraid of Mangan, with his big hands, his lightning scowl, and his small eyes glowering behind wire-rim glasses. With a select bunch of friends, he was a cutup. Angered, he was a terror. Mangan was one of only a handful of officers to be hailed as "physically perfect" during the annual physical of 1935, something that he never let any of the muscularly inferior officers forget. Mangan told Parsons that being a policeman presented all sorts of opportunities. Just watch.

Liquor came from one of several gangs that made hooch in town and retailed it to the clubs, or from a connection in Canada. The repeal of Prohibition in 1933 did nothing to change the way Spokane's speakeasies did business. The states could still enact their own laws. Washington allowed beer parlors to operate, providing suds with no more than 3.2 percent alcohol; but it was illegal to sell liquor by the glass. So many clubs, which specialized in moody piano music and healthy shots of bourbon for a quarter, continued to flourish throughout the thirties. There were actually more bootleggers in town after Prohibition was repealed than there were during the dry years.

One big-time mover, Albert Commellini, used to buy corn sugar by the truckload. When Parsons was introduced to him, the rookie asked him what he did with all that sugar. "I make good pies," Commellini replied. Mangan howled. Commellini was a swell guy—a regular, Mangan said. At first, Parsons didn't understand what he meant by that. A regular? In his inaugural months on the street he had heard the story about the big shipment of whiskey that arrived one day from Canada, an attempt to horn in on well-marked territory. It was hijacked by a Spokane police officer and promptly delivered to Commellini.

Every six months or so, the newspapers would call for an investigation, and the federal prosecutor would make alarming sounds in front of a grand jury. Then the clamor would die down; among the clients of some of the best-known and most profitable clubs were assistant prosecutors, defense lawyers, and reporters. By day, they professed to be shocked—*shocked*—at what was going on in the queen city of the self-proclaimed richest empire in the Western Hemisphere. By night, they warmed regular seats at the Cotton Club or at the second-floor speakeasy of Jimmy Young.

The night shift, midnight to eight, was Mangan's most lucrative time. Making the rounds, he could count on at least one envelope from a club—the usual price of doing business. Sometimes, Mangan told young Parsons, you could double your salary just by knowing which way to walk. Parsons was appalled. He wanted to tell somebody what he'd seen and heard. But of course there was no one to tell.

On duty, Officer Mangan was especially good at working with his hands. He knew how to pry open a slot machine and was quick enough that he never got caught. He could crack virtually any lock with a flick of a small tool—a skill that came in handy at a butcher shop on his beat. Mangan and his circle of police friends and hangers-on ate well during the dark days of 1935. Another shop, a candy store north of the river, was also a favorite target of Officer Mangan. He knew how to loosen a back window so it would pop open, allowing him enough space to crawl through. Inside, he would find sugar, butter, tools, occasional cash. Back at the station, Mangan made no effort to conceal the fruits of his labors; he shared the booty with his regular friends and boasted of how he had done it.

The small-time merchants Mangan was stealing from were people living on the edge, working twelve- and fourteen-hour days to take home thirty dollars a week. In a year when 40 percent of the state's citizens were without steady income, it burned in Parsons's gut to think that a cop, whose salary was paid by their taxes, was taking from the few people trying to hold on. He didn't consider himself a snitch. You could call a guy an Okie, a Red, a nigger, a bindle stiff; but to be labeled a snitch was a death sentence. Turning away from the talk among other officers, Parsons was determined to do legitimate police work, something to make him stand out, to justify his selection above the hungry hundreds who wanted his job. When the civil service commissioner included him as one of the "fine . . . bunch of men" upholding the laws of the city of Spokane, Parsons wore the compliment like ranch initials engraved on cowhide.

Walking his beat in the summer of 1935, the rookie wondered what he could do about the surge in burglaries. Across the state line, in Idaho a young sheriff's deputy was celebrated as a hero when he caught somebody in the act of stealing beans and wheat from a farm. The thief was loading up a truck with food in the middle of the night when the deputy nabbed him. The arrest spurred talk among the merchants and creamery men: if only they could get a similar break in the Spokane area. . . . Parsons was ambitious. To catch the butter thief—that would be a coup.

But what Parsons was learning from veteran cops had very little to do with police work. The other officers were starting to turn away from him, keeping their secrets in a circle which broke up when Parsons came near. They had nice clothes to change into when the shift was up, cars that could make a fellow proud, and cash for food, whiskey, a hunting rifle. Parsons took home his twenty-seven dollars a week, but after paying for rent and food and giving a bit to his family, he had very little left. The rap on Parsons, early on, was that he wasn't a go-along-and-get-along guy.

By contrast, William Harrison "Hacker" Cox, who had joined the department just before Parsons, was already deemed one of the boys and had become a drinking buddy of Mangan's. Cox was chunky and loud, in a patronizing, back-slapping way. While waiting to be hired by the police department—he had scored high enough on the civil service test to be ranked near the top—Cox had been arrested for bootlegging and brawling in a hotel room one night. On his way to the station, he told Officer Clyde Phelps that the arrest would ruin his chances of joining the force. So he was booked under the name William Harrison, and when his number came up for hire at the police department and he was asked if he'd ever been arrested, he shook his head, knowing his real name wouldn't be connected to the bootlegger who'd been picked up a few months earlier. Phelps, Mangan, and a few others knew his secret, but that was the nature of the department—a conspiracy of small corruptions.

The Spokane County prosecutor, Ralph Foley (whose son, Thomas S. Foley, would, many years later, become Speaker of the United States House of Representatives), knew how badly compromised the Spokane Police Department had become. When he wanted to raid one of the Chinese gambling dens downtown in Trent Alley, he by-passed the city police and used cops from the county sheriff's office. After the raid, Foley's name was shit inside the stone fortress. Most patrolmen and some of the detectives felt they were getting more consideration from the bootleggers and the club owners—at least they were respectful, treating an officer of the law like somebody who mattered.

On duty one night in midsummer, Parsons saw a truck loading from a rear entrance of a garage on Riverside Avenue, about ten blocks from the police station. Cases of whiskey, scotch, bourbon, and vodka were being transferred from the rear to the unmarked truck. Parsons jumped out, ordering the men to stop.

"Who are you?" came a gruff reply.

"Parsons. Spokane Police."

"Don't recognize the name."

Parsons was asked if he knew Officer Mangan, or Officer Cox, or perhaps Detective Clyde Ralstin. Yes, of course, Parsons knew them. The connection established, the men continued loading the truck.

Parsons persisted. They asked him if he was a troublemaker. "You want to settle this," said the man who appeared to be in charge, "go across the street, get Clyde Ralstin."

Parsons looked to the other side of the street, at Mother's Kitchen, an all-night diner where Ralstin, Mangan, and other cops hung out. Parsons felt alone, a man without a tribe.

"Here," the liquor-loading foreman said, stuffing a pair of ten-dollar bills into an envelope and handing it to Parsons. "Take this and run along."

Parsons stared at the envelope, the truck, and across the street: Mother's Kitchen was lit up with warmth and camaraderie. It radiated a glow of security, of belonging. The train whistle blew; another load of people with long faces, empty stomachs, and the resolve to find a job in this hub of the richest empire stumbled out of boxcars.

"Take it," said the bootlegger.

Parsons stuffed the envelope into his pocket and walked across the street to Mother's Kitchen. He was alone no more. Near the end of his shift, back inside the Stone Fortress, Mangan called him buddy.

4.

Mother's Kitchen

THROUGHOUT the first two weeks of September, people from distant towns and dusty fields continued to funnel into Spokane, and the sun burned hot and ceaseless as never before. Monday, 92 degrees; Tuesday, 97; Wednesday, 95; Thursday, 97; Friday, 97. Here was the weekend, seven days to the start of fall, with the sky bleached and shapeless, the wheat fields limp and rusted. The forests smoldered as one fire embraced another. What came from overhead was not rain but ashes, the fine residue of burnt pine needles. The Spokane River, carrying the last collection of mountain water sucked from the summits of the Coeur d'Alenes, forced itself through the ancient channel from the Idaho border, passing the beige orchards on the way to the falls of the city, where the torrent had shrunk to a trickle, exposing the polished skin of big rocks.

It was the scent of jobs and water that had lured these families to the inland Northwest, stirred by President Roosevelt's dream. The largest of the Roosevelt's WPA projects was the Grand Coulee Dam, a scheme to subjugate the Columbia River, mightiest waterway in the West, and fill an ancient, dried-out coulee ninety miles east of Spokane with water. The idea was to deliver, through irrigation, the basic lubricant of life to a high plateau that was then the domain of sage and rattlesnakes. Spokane newspapers blasted the project as a

33

"socialist scheme," but their criticism meant very little outside of the South Hill and the Spokane Club. As Will Rogers said at the time, "If Roosevelt burned down the Capital we would cheer and say, 'Well, we at least got a fire started, anyhow.' "

On a tour of the region, Roosevelt said, "There are many sections of the country where land has run out or been put to the wrong kind of use. Out here, you have not just space, you have space that can be used by human beings—a wonderful land—a land of opportunity." In between feature screenings of *G-Men*, a James Cagney crime picture picture of 1935, newsreels around the country showed surveyors and engineers running along the length of the future dam site—the Great Pyramid of our times, it was called, the biggest construction project in history.

But when the new arrivals, their legs stiff and their necks sore, departed trains in Spokane and looked around for work or water, they were told the Grand Coulee wasn't hiring yet and wouldn't need an army of excavators for some time. Like the tumbleweeds that whisked across the Columbia Plateau, they were supposed to blow away, move on to some other place. But for many of them this was it—the end of the road in the far corner of the country. Stuck in Spokane, the migrants were shooed away from the rail yards east of town, the dense village of other broken families living off what could be taken from boxcars or pulled from the river. They were told they might find shelter at the Hotel de Gink, a former brewery which had shut down during Prohibition and was now a concrete warehouse for temporary residents of Spokane. Only men were allowed in the Gink; it was a place of knife fights and alliances based on accents. Some men who had spent time in the old brewery said they preferred jail to the filth of the hotel. Other families ended up downstream, just below the falls, where the mid-river band of the Spokane Indians had once gathered for a month of spearing the hefty chinook salmon. There, on the north bank of the river, beneath the thousand-foot arch of the Monroe Street Bridge, another village arose. A steep path with a wire cable for guidance led down the rock-and-earthen bank to a squatters' settlement at the river's edge. Some of the newcomers found work in the woods, at three dollars a day, which was enough to bring home food and maybe keep a little hidden for particularly lean weeks. If they stopped for a drink on the way home, the path to the river was particularly hazardous. Oftentimes, a man would lose his footing, stumble down the embankment, and drown. The city leaders did not like these transplants; they were an embarrassment, one councilman said, a nest of Reds and Okies and drifters. And so it was proposed that the transient village be doused with gasoline and set afire.

INSIDE MOTHER'S KITCHEN, on Riverside Avenue, midway between the Hotel de Gink and the Stone Fortress, the world maintained a certain routine, directed by a tight circle of men who had found a way to profit from hard times. The diner's doors never closed. There was a long bar near the kitchen, the stools invariably occupied by at least one man in uniform. Mother's fed and watered the working policeman, free. In turn, the working policeman made sure that no harm came to Mother's. Much like the Stone Fortress, Mother's was a safehouse for police secrets—where food and drink went with furtive sidelines and black humor, deal-making and payoffs. The restaurant was no place for scruffy Civilian Conservation Corps trail-builders from the East—more than twelve thousand men, each given two blankets and outfitted in leftover clothes and boots from World War I, now filled the camps and shelters of the inland Northwest—or migrants looking to spend half a day's wages on what was arguably the best steak in town. Because the town was so full of strangers, the regulars at Mother's Kitchen grew more defensive of what they had. Some of the city's most important bootleggers had regular booths there, in part because a budding bootlegger, Virgil A. Burch, the manager and part-owner of the place, lived in a room in the back, with his latest wife and a wood-eating parrot.

Burch came from Montana, where he'd been imprisoned for cattle-rustling on what he said was a bum rap. Making his way west, he was arrested in Idaho for bootlegging, but avoided a prison term. Arriving in Spokane, he learned the plumber's trade and worked throughout the area. But he despised pipe work, the grease and green-rusted toilets and no respect; it only made him feel more insecure.

He married five women during his life, and even during his younger days he needed the constant attention of a new bride. When he walked across the Monroe Street Bridge and saw the broken families huddled by the river's shore in the canyon below, it made him shiver. He would ride in his new Hudson up to the Tudor mansions on the South Hill, passing a long line of the defeated who waited for soup and bread at Sacred Heart Hospital. Life's losers, he called them. He would rather die than fall among their ranks.

Burch had accumulated enough of a stake from an old mine in Montana to become a partner in Mother's Kitchen. But even when his restaurant became the hottest ticket in town for mid-level deal-makers and all-night grazers, Burch wanted much more. It was one thing to have a diner; it was another to be the center of a self-manufactured world. He was especially enamored of the police detectives who drove new cars, wore tailored suits, and told everybody else how to run their business.

Burch scoured the city looking for women. He liked them young, attractive, vulnerable to his manipulations. Burch himself was fair-skinned, bulky but not fat, with cinnamon-colored curly hair; he could not easily have been described as handsome, but that is how he thought of himself. By mid-September 1935, he had twenty-nine women on his payroll—the best-looking girls in town, he bragged. Some waitresses at Mother's seldom served food; they were hired to be part of the scenery. They would appear at booths out of nowhere, smiling between main course and apple pie to ask if everything was swell. The customers were allowed a wink-and-pinch tolerance that went so far, depending on how wobbly Burch's ego was on a given day.

Just as the garage across the street was a fender-fixer by day and a liquor-warehousing operation by night, Mother's Kitchen had a dual purpose. Under the hand of Burch, ex-con and cattle-rustler, boot-legger and plumber, Mother's trafficked in products that were in short supply. In August and September, Burch sold great quantities of butter and cream which seemed to come out of thin air. Cars would come and go at night, bringing in deliveries of butter. So, throughout the driest summer of the maturing twentieth century, when butter reached its highest price in decades and was rationed by the few wholesalers who could get their hands on normal supplies, Mother's Kitchen had a surfeit. Burch let the word leak out around town to other restaurants that if they wanted creamery products, he was willing to sell. At first, some merchants balked. They were suspicious and angry: how come Mother's Kitchen had such a bounty? But when they walked in to see the product, or talk price, or snoop around for evidence to use against Burch, they saw cops—at least a pair in uniform, ingesting a free meal, and always one detective in a three-piece suit: a tall, rock-fisted man named Clyde Ralstin.

A young patrolman, acting on the suspicions of merchants, walked into Mother's Kitchen to investigate the butter surfeit; the probe ended when he saw Detective Ralstin. People either feared Ralstin or worshipped him. And some worshipped him out of fear. Those who looked up to him gathered at Mother's to hear his stories of bedding women and besting challengers to his boast of being the toughest man in town. At just over six foot three inches tall—with a fifty-four-inch chest—Ralstin towered over all but one man at the Stone Fortress. He had a long, pointed nose, green eyes, and showed dimples when he smiled. In silk vest, pressed fedora, gleaming shoes, he didn't look like a man who earned forty-two dollars a week. He was the best marksman on the police force, and certainly the best-known fighter. Several times a week, he took on contenders inside the Stone Fortress. Nobody ever pinned him. But as strong as Ralstin was physically, his real power came from psychological intimidation. He knew a little bit—the right information—about everybody who might have some control over him. He traded in these small secrets, the shadings of character that could determine a career or break a marriage. It was, until the late summer of 1935, his black-market specialty.

By 1935, after seven years as a cop, Ralstin seemed to have enough ammunition on his police colleagues to see him through the roughest of times. He needed it, because his career was then in decline, and his marriage, to Monnie Elliott, was falling apart. When he liked another woman, he simply went after her. By the mid-1930s, he liked a lot of women, most of them introduced to him by his best friend,

Burch. When Monnie objected, he blew up at her: it was none of her goddamn business what he did outside the house. After a while, he rarely came home or made any pretense about monogamy or trying to stay together.

But he adored his wife's daughter, Ruby. She was barely a teenager when Clyde introduced her to liquor, taking her into a speakeasy and ordering her a whiskey sour. She coughed; he laughed. "Swallow it, kid; it'll make a man out of you." He seldom mentioned anything to his stepdaughter about police work, unless something had happened that he found funny. He told her once about an acquaintance of his, a fellow cop, who would spend the first part of his shift walking down one side of the street, drinking a pint of whiskey; in the second half, he would walk down the other side, consuming another pint. His doctor told him he was going to kill himself if he continued this routine. So, rather than give up drinking and patrolling, the cop went home and blew his brains out. Clyde nearly fell to the floor from laughing as he told the story to his stepdaughter.

When Ruby was in her early twenties, she married. Ralstin hated his new son-in-law, a car salesman. On a November night in 1934, Ralstin went over to their house, a few blocks from his own home on the North End, and started slapping around Ruby's husband, a much smaller man. Clyde dragged him out into the street, knocked him to the ground, and kicked his head against the pavement. Blood poured out of one side of the young man's head; his face was smashed in and he could no longer resist. In the midst of this pummeling, a gas station attendant, Monte Adams, who had just ended his work shift walked by. Seeing the younger man on the ground, attacked by a windmill of fists, Adams screamed at Ralstin to stop. Ralstin told him to back off, mind his own business. Neighbors peered out from behind drapes. Lights came on. Fearing that Ralstin would kill the man, Adams jumped atop Ralstin, who threw him to the ground. While they wrestled, Ralstin's service revolver fell out. Adams grabbed the gun and pointed it at Clyde.

In a few minutes, a patrol car arrived. When the two officers stepped out, they immediately recognized Detective Ralstin. "He tried to kill me," Ralstin said of Adams. Pointing to his wounded son-in-law on the ground, Ralstin said that the boy was drunk and had been beating his wife. The gas station attendant and the young man were arrested and charged with disorderly conduct.

At their trial, they were found not guilty by a judge who said there was no evidence to back the charge. "The man who was most guilty and was the cause of the disorder was not arrested for some reason," the judge said in dismissing the case. He knew the reason, of course—no Spokane cop was going to arrest a brother, no matter what the offense. But the judge went no further than his comments from the bench.

The fight enhanced Ralstin's reputation among fellow officers and at Mother's Kitchen, where he spent most of his time while on duty. To his renown as a wrestler and marksman was added the designation as a man with an undefeated pair of fists.

Ralstin and Burch were the closest of friends. They told each other they had the best women, the best food, the best booze, and the best clothes in a bad time. They shared a hunting cottage near Superior, Montana, not far from the old placer mine Burch had picked up. Ralstin loved to kill things—in season or out. He and Burch shot deer, elk, cougar, grouse, marten, even an occasional buffalo. They shared women from the talent pool that Burch brought through Mother's. And they shared a vision, born of failed schemes, that the needs of hungry people could bring untold riches to a plumber and a cop.

WITH EVERY NEW DAY of the drought, Spokane's butter shortage grew worse. Mother's controlled one of the largest local supplies of the scarce commodity, and they were selling it as fast as they could bring it in. Nearly two thousand pounds of butter from different creameries had moved in and out of Mother's Kitchen in late summer of 1935—appearing by night, from some furtive connection. Now, two weeks into September, they needed a fresh load. Burch knew of a creamery in Newport, forty-seven miles north of town on the Idaho-Washington border. He had worked on the place as a plumber and was familiar with the doors, the locks, the volume of creamery products moved in and out. It would be a piece of cake. They could take

Saturday night, service a couple of women Burch knew in the neighboring timber town of Priest River, and then hit the Newport Creamery on the way home. It would be one of their biggest butter heists.

They could keep some of the butter at Mother's and store the rest of it at Ralstin's ranch, south of Spokane near Hangman's Creek—so named as the site where defeated Indian leaders were hung from pine boughs in 1858 after they came to Colonel George Wright seeking terms of surrender. In 1935, some citizens were urging that the original name, Latah Creek, be restored—a proposal that was shot down by Spokane civic leaders, who said it must remain Hangman's Creek "to remind us of when the Redmen were cowed," as one local politician put it.

As Burch and Ralstin discussed the rough outline of their plan, Burch noticed that somebody was listening—a woman named Pearl Keogh. A late-night regular at Mother's Kitchen, Pearl was short and very pretty, with intense blue eyes and dark curly hair, which she usually wore to her shoulders. After midnight, when Pearl got off work from Sacred Heart Hospital, where she was a nurse, she went down the hill to Mother's. Her sister, Ruth, worked there as a cook and later as night manager. With three children, and a husband sick with tuberculosis at a sanitarium, Ruth needed every nickel she got from Mother's. Pearl was a bit more footloose. She flirted with cops at Mother's and told jokes that cracked the boys up. Some nights, she would sit and chat with Ruth, nursing coffee, listening to the radio. Walter Winchell's weekly round of rapid-fire news, launched from table 50 of New York's Stork Club, was a favorite ("Good evening, Mr. and Mrs. America and all the ships at sea. Let's go to press . . ."). Everybody was talking about Huey Long, the Kingfish, former governor of Louisiana, then a senator, who could coax a snake onto an iceberg. "Every man is a king, but no man wears a crown," the Kingfish would say. His call to take money from the wealthiest people in the country and give it to the poorest, in the form of a five-thousand-dollar homestead fund for each family, was well received in much of the West. But in September, an assassin's bullet effectively buried his plan.

Mother's Kitchen

Before she moved to Spokane, Pearl had a temporary job in Idaho doling out bullets to out-of-work miners and timbermen living in tents along the Saint Maries River. Governor Ross's idea of relief was to encourage hunting. But some of the broken men couldn't even afford to buy bullets for their rifles. Pearl was given boxes of cartridges by state officials and assigned to parcel out a ration of bullets to each family she could find along the river. One of eleven white children raised at the Saint Ignatius Catholic Mission on the Flathead Indian Reservation in Montana, Pearl was living a near-subsistence life in Idaho when the Depression hit. But having grown up around Flathead natives who lived in tepees, snagged fish with dip nets, and hunted game by horseback, Pearl Keogh was no stranger to extracting food from the land. She fished and hunted and sassed back men who were twice her weight.

When she moved west to Spokane, she was hired as a nurse at Sacred Heart. Pearl was happy to have the job—except that the hospital couldn't afford to pay her. Her salary was a weekly allotment of scrip, which she could redeem with merchants for food. She worked a second job in the day as a nurse for a doctor who gave tonsillectomies to schoolchildren, who paid a quarter for the operation.

During the endless hot nights of the final days of summer, Pearl joined the regulars at Mother's in all sorts of diversions. Some nights, they piled into Virgil Burch's Hudson and went out for a whirl and a gulp of cool air. But during the second week of September, the usual mix of loose humor, smart talk, and open deal-making seemed to be missing at Mother's. Pearl felt the tension. When she asked Ruth about it, her sister put her finger to her lips and looked around. Something was up, she told her sister on Friday night, September 13. The boys were planning something.

Burch caught the sisters looking his way; he snapped at Ruth. "You wanna keep this job, you stay out of other people's business," he said.

Clyde Ralstin snickered; the idea that some little girl from Montana could hurt them was laughable.

A third man, a goose-necked ex-con from Mississippi named Acie Logan, a regular at Mother's, was also in on the talk. Tall and muscular, with gray eyes and floppy ears, Logan was covered with tattoos and scars, sketches on a body at war with the world since he had dropped out of school in the fourth grade. Nude women intertwined with snakes and cows on both forearms. On his chest an American flag was wrapped around a dagger. Logan had once challenged Clyde Ralstin to a fight. After Clyde whipped him, he became an acolyte, looking up to the big detective, impressed by his absolute confidence. King Clyde seemed invulnerable; nobody in the Stone Fortress or at Mother's Kitchen could touch him.

Logan, who'd served time in five different jails since leaving Mississippi in the early 1920s, was afraid of returning to prison. He used to talk about his last address in a Washington State institution, the damp stockade at Monroe in the forests of Snohomish County, northeast of Seattle: he swore he went nearly thirty days one winter without seeing the sun. Logan had been in on at least two other butter heists, but the plan to knock off the Newport Creamery seemed to bother him. The dairymen were up in arms, angry and trigger-happy, talking about organizing posses and hanging the sons of bitches who were stealing their food and their source of winter money. The job might not be as easy as Burch and Ralstin made it out to be, Logan said.

The radio squawked of war talk between the Italians and the Ethiopians. Sipping her coffee, Pearl Keogh tuned out the news and listened to an exchange between Logan and the two friends who ran Mother's Kitchen. Burch's parrot was starting to chew on the wooden bar.

"What if somebody's there?" Logan asked in his muddy drawl. "What if we get caught—what do we do then? I won't go back to the joint. I won't, goddamn it!"

"It ain't gonna be a problem, Acie," Burch answered.

"What the hell do you know that I don't know?"

"I know we got experience."

"Yeah?"

"We got Clyde here," he said, slapping Ralstin on the back. "And he's no virgin."

5.

The Night Marshal

WITH ITS wood-planked sidewalks and saloons thick with sawdust, the town of Newport, population 1,400, made no effort to paint a promotional gloss over the haggard look it acquired during the Depression. Some days, when smoke poured from the chimneys of rawboned frame houses and a single car driving down the main street was enough to raise a cloud of dust, the town looked like it might well slide down the bank into the swift hold of the Pend Oreille River, and the valley would be better off without it. The river, one of the few in North America to flow northward, drains the timber and mine country of western Montana, northern Idaho, and eastern Washington. Like the towns of Ione and Usk and Metaline Falls and Priest River and Bonners Ferry, Newport existed because the nearby mountains were full of silver, lead, and gold, and the forests were thick with cedar, Douglas fir, and white pine. In 1935, Newport had not a single restaurant, no gas station, two banks, one small hotel, a grocery store, and a few bars, including one where patrons could wrestle with a live bear. On the Idaho side of the river, the Diamond Match Company maintained a sawmill, though it sputtered during hard times. Perhaps the most valuable enterprise in Newport was its commercial creamery, on the edge of town.

The job of Marshal George Conniff, Sr., was to protect the creamery and the handful of other businesses in Newport. He was fifty-three years old, stumbling through the worst losing streak in a life of fine adventure. The marshal had sandy hair, blond on the way to gray, and a cleft chin. He was not happy walking a night beat for the town of Newport; after four years as police chief in the town of Sandpoint, just across the Pend Oreille River in Idaho, he'd sworn off this line of trench-level law enforcement. At Sandpoint, he'd been shot at, kicked, punched, cursed, chased—and underpaid for all of it. He fought Indians and Finns drawn to liquor and the Pend Oreille fish runs, and tangled with tanked-up lumberjacks and tough-guy boot-leggers. With his three children grown, George Conniff figured that it was time to get back to the land, as he'd long planned. This job in Newport, protecting merchants with a pistol and a badge, was sup-posed to be a one-year affair. His plan was to make just enough to finish the cabin he was building on acreage in a meadow facing the mountains, and then settle in for a better life. By September, he had only one month left, and then he would quit—done with law en-forcement forever.

In the broad valleys and flat meadows of the Pend Oreille country, winter lingered too late and the first frost came too early for growing fruit or seed crops. But geologic tumult had endowed this land with good soil for alfalfa, one of the basic foods of dairy cows. When an ice and earthen dam in western Montana burst more than twelve thousand years ago, it unleashed the greatest flood ever known, a force of more than five hundred cubic miles of water pushing through the mountains and scraping coulees out of the basalt and forested high country of eastern Washington. Gradually, as the water retreated to the bigger channels, including the Pend Oreille and Spokane rivers, it left behind thick sediment, thirty feet deep in parts. Most years, a farmer could get several cuttings from a small hay field, which provided enough to feed a herd of milk producers. In those days before hay was baled and stored under tin-roofed barns, it was har-vested by horse-drawn mowers and piled into hooded mounds ex-posed to the weather. During the mid-1930s drought, cinders from nearby forest fires torched many a haystack, further depleting the supply.

Farmers whose cows were not starving brought their milk into the cooperative in Newport, where cream was separated and processed into cheese or churned into butter, and the remainder was kept in large urns and sold to retailers. Every week, the creamery ran an ad in the Newport *Miner*.

Newport Creamery Co.
A Community Industry.
Highest Market Price Grade A Butterfat.
Honest Weight. Correct Tests.

The creamery had more than enough business in the Pend Oreille country without having to sell in Spokane. A few years earlier, many of these same dairymen had been forced to dump their milk because prices were so low that they lost money on every gallon sold in a glutted market. As Americans moved to the cities in the 1920s, farmers for the first time became an object of contemporary caricature; they were laughed at, called hicks and hayseeds. Now, milk, butter, and cream were gold; the Newport Creamery was a regional Fort Knox, and the derision was more discreet. As hay became scarce and dairy supplies dwindled, the farmers who took their milk to the Newport Creamery felt the paws of a hungry land. There was a national shortage as well, with milk selling at ten cents a quart, but demand for at least thirteen million more quarts than farmers were producing. At Washington State University, in Pullman, students bartered for tuition with crates of canned peaches; a dozen jars could buy a student one semester of college. Wheat silos were being robbed. In 1935, the first year America ever had to import wheat, the price rose to its highest level in a decade. At the same time, Mussolini's moves into Ethiopia with the Italian army helped to drive up the price. The notion that a European dictator's thrust into Africa could provide enough incentive for thieves to break into wheat silos in the inland Pacific Northwest was an indication to some farmers that the world had become too small, too fast.

Just after seven-thirty Saturday night, the fourteenth of September, the sun ducked behind the western edge of the Selkirks, where the valley floor of the Pend Oreille rose in forested waves of green. A few of the aspen and larch trees at higher elevations were in the early stages of the slow turn to gold. The saloons were roaring as usual—piano music blended with laughter—and full of timber beasts and part-time miners and firefighters and government road-builders and prospectors. Darkness quickly drained the air of heat, but it didn't lessen the aroma of forest fire smoke. Marshal Conniff kept away from the wild life in the beer halls and made his rounds in the alleys and back streets of Newport. Small-town America in this part of the rural West was no more idyllic than Al Capone's Chicago. A month earlier, the town marshal of Rosalia, just south of Spokane, had been killed by gunfire from a trio of bank robbers. A year before that, Conniff's predecessor as Newport marshal had nearly died of head wounds from a beating he suffered at the hands of food thieves. He had been kicked, pistol-whipped across the head, and left for dead.

For women, suffering with husbands who saw their pride dwindle away with the drought and Depression, the times were particularly harsh. In a town of shuttered gossip and diminishing hope, Saturday night would bring Marshal Conniff into the homes of women bleeding from the fists of their spouses. The marshal made occasional arrests, but the courts were not much help. As one judge in Spokane said in dismissing the divorce suit of a wife, "There is probably no greater cruelty which may be inflicted upon a man than that which is inflicted by a contentious, unreasonable, and nagging woman."

An hour after sunset, the sky turned dark, the moon and stars disappearing under a sudden cloud cover. Winds pushed the warm air south; the rustle of pine boughs was a precursor to a storm. Conniff had checked the two banks in town and was on his way to the creamery. The forest fire smoke, which had hung in the air for most of summer, was a reminder of Conniff's misfortune, the fire that had gutted his house.

One of fourteen kids raised in Montana, Conniff left home at age thirteen, joined the merchant marine, and saw the world. But his overseas adventures were cut short by a freak accident: a load of ballast was dumped atop his head, breaking his back. Though he never regained full strength, he worked some of the most demanding of muscle-powered jobs—cutting ice blocks from mountain lakes for shipment to California, hauling timber from distant sites.

Later in life, Conniff found a forest-and-meadowed slice of valley twelve miles south of Newport and proceeded to set up a homestead. Conniff's son, George junior, made friends with a native elder who one summer took him into a tepee where a ceremony was held. The Kalispels, whose name means "eater of camas," had always lived on salmon and bulbs of the blue flower for which they were named. Although whites had built roads and set up villages and plowed many of the camas fields into hay farms, there were still hundreds of Indians whose lives were tied to the migrations of fish and elk in the rivers and woods north of Spokane. Well into the twentieth century, the natives set up traditional seasonal camps along the shore of the Pend Oreille or the Spokane, dip-netting fish and drying them for winter storage. Every July, the natives would hold a powwow, out of habit more than need; most trading was done with white merchants. If the name Spokane came up, it was often as a cautionary tale, the story of the utter betrayal of man and his homeland.

This inland empire was the last big section of mainland America to be seen by whites. On their return in 1805, Lewis and Clark had followed the Columbia east to its juncture with the Snake River near the present Oregon border, but they had not come near the high country to the north. A trading post, Spokane House, was established in 1811 by David Thompson, a trapper of great charm and endurance. He claimed the land for England. After Spokane House folded, a victim of its isolation, the Hudson's Bay Company became the regional European presence with its operation at Fort Colville, northwest of the Spokane House location. Food was never a problem. "The natives have an abundance of the finest salmon in the world," wrote one Hudson's Bay Company official. "All within a hundred yards of their door, and plenty of potatoes and grain if they like it." A young native, his Salishan name changed to Spokane Garry, befriended the traders and was sent to England to study Christianity and the new language of commerce. He was the eldest son of Illim-Spokaneé, chief of the

Sin-ho-mas-naish, or salmon-trout people, who became known as the Spokanes.

When Garry returned from overseas, he could read and write, speak English and French, and he knew which fork to use for salad and how to defer to a lady. He was given two wives by his tribe, the middle band of Spokane Indians living near the river. As sketched by artists in the 1850s, Spokane Garry had sharp, wide-set eyes, a regal nose, and a full head of thick hair, which he wore past his shoulders. He set up a missionary school to preach the new gospels of agriculture and Christianity. The Spokanes took to neither.

Garry, trusting men in uniform and those who said they represented God, thought the three thousand people who lived near the river would be left alone. But then gold was discovered near Colville, and a steady stream of hard-rock miners followed. When a white man was killed by an Indian in 1858, a cavalry brigade of 164 troops came north from Fort Walla Walla and was ambushed. It was never clear how many Spokanes took part in the skirmish; but that made no difference to Colonel George Wright, who led a punitive force north to avenge the loss. Wright became to the natives of the inland Northwest what Sherman had been to Georgians in the Civil War. Armed with new, long-range, rapid-fire rifles, Wright's six-hundred-man army crushed the tribes as he drove north to the Spokane River and east into the Coeur d'Alenes. When the natives scattered in defeat, he sought them out, intending to burn their food supplies and kill their leaders. Chief Owhi and his son Qualchan came forth to discuss terms of surrender; Wright had them summarily hanged. East of Spokane Falls, in late September, Wright rounded up eight hundred of the natives' horses and had them shot, one after another. All night, the shrieks of bleeding animals filled the valley as they were mowed down by round after round of gunfire. Some of Wright's officers later wrote that it was the most sickening spectacle they had ever seen. But Wright wasn't finished. He had fifteen other natives hanged. Moving east, he burned storage sheds full of grain and winter food, and he shot cattle.

When Wright at last withdrew, he left a starving and defeated band of people in the rich empire. Spokane Garry, who had signed the terms of surrender after Wright forced him to grovel in tears, was given a homestead and the promise of a small pension every month from the federal government.

During the latter half of Garry's life, the town of Spokane took shape around a flour mill by the falls. Silver was discovered in the east, gold in the north, and wheat farms blossomed in the rolling Palouse country to the south. The railroads fed the new town thousands of immigrants every year. Garry still tried to live a dual life: as a property owner on his homestead and as a traditional gatherer of food near the river. One day, while he was fishing, a white family simply appropriated his farmland, claiming he belonged on a reservation. Garry retreated to a tepee near the site where other Spokanes had been executed by Wright. Schoolchildren taunted Garry, a curious, shrunken old man with a half-blind wife. His pension stopped not long after his homestead was stolen from him. In his last years, he made occasional trips on his white horse to the fast-growing town. He survived off charity and the earnings of his daughter Nelly, who made a living washing clothes. When he died in 1892, his entire estate consisted of ten horses, all of which were later stolen from his widow.

The Conniffs worked with Indians—the Kalispels and the Spokanes—but did not share the gloom the natives had inherited from their fathers and mothers. The Spokanes were left with a small reservation far downriver from the falls, and the Kalispels were placed on forty-five hundred acres hugging the east bank of the Pend Oreille River—the smallest Indian reservation in America.

After felling the trees on his sixty-acre homestead, George Conniff blasted the stumps away with dynamite—a curious form of cultivation to the Kalispel and Spokane, but common in the early years of the twentieth century, when settlers like Conniff were called stump farmers. He planted potatoes and wheat and killed an occasional deer. The hope of Conniff and his wife, Alma, was that the garden, plentiful venison, and bartering would provide them with enough to get by. They raised three children in a drafty wood-frame house without indoor plumbing. Some winter mornings, it was so cold that frost formed on the inside of their home. But the stump farm was not enough, so Conniff took the job as lawman in Sandpoint. It was difficult work—seven-day weeks, wrestling with woodsmen and itinerants. He quit the job after four years and made plans to become a full-time farmer, perhaps branching out with dairy cows. After traipsing around the world carrying loads of grain, ice, or logs for meager wages, and then keeping the law in the timber town of Sandpoint, he was ready to go to work for himself.

Conniff's dream collapsed in a fire that burned the family home to the ground. When he went to collect the insurance money, he was told he had nothing coming to him. How could this be? He had paid the premiums, faithfully, for years. Yes, but he now found out that those premiums had not been turned in to the company. George Conniff was left without a dime to compensate for the house that had been destroyed by fire.

Broke, their house in ashes, George and Alma took up residence in an apartment in Newport, and he accepted the night marshal's job—for one year only. At the same time, he worked furiously to build a new home, a log cabin, to replace the one gutted by fire. In the hours before his shift as night marshal, Conniff and his son cut logs and notched them together, the foundation of the place in which he hoped to live out his remaining, and better, years.

On Saturday night, as George Conniff walked to inspect the Newport Creamery, the cabin was half-built, and the marshal had given notice that he would be off the job within two weeks. It seemed as if his luck was starting to change. A few days earlier, he had received some wonderful news: the Washington State Supreme Court had ruled against the insurance company for failing to compensate Conniff for his fire loss. It ordered the company to pay the family $1,000.

ON THEIR WAY NORTH in Detective Clyde Ralstin's REO Flying Cloud, the boys from Mother's Kitchen talked about their own dreams. Women, of course. Clyde had his eye on one of the waitresses at Mother's—a real looker, he said. Her name was Dorothy. Hunting was another favorite subject. Ralstin and Burch were plotting their next trip to the cabin they shared on the Montana border. They knew the creamery heists could not go on for long—for one thing, they were running out of places to rob. Their ambition was to get out of the petty stuff and move on to something big. The pay of a Spokane police detective, Ralstin said, was pitiful. He'd been on the force seven years, had risen from patrolman to motorcycle cop to sergeant to detective, and still he made only forty-two dollars a week—an insult. "I don't know why I even put up with it," he would say.

It was bad enough that he wasn't being paid what he thought he was worth; now Ralstin had to deal with hostile politicians and prosecutors. The year had begun with a city council investigation of police graft. They didn't find anything on Clyde; he was too well insulated by his personal stockpile of other men's secrets, the politicians and lawyers and police captains whose liquor came from the bootleggers who counted Detective Ralstin as a close friend. But the constant corruption probes were a headache. Clyde was tired of it all; he wanted a windfall.

Logan, the veteran con, had his own sketch of the big time. Everybody in the joint had a plan; mostly it was just talk, word stuffings to fill a day. But finally, in 1935, somebody had pulled it off: a con's dream had come true. Big time was the Weyerhaeuser kidnapping, a crime that was hatched in Spokane. A pair of low-level cons, William "Swede" Dainard and Harmon Waley, and Harmon's bride, Margaret, were killing time in a Spokane apartment when Margaret read something in the newspaper about the Weyerhaeusers. The family, one of the wealthiest in the nation, had millions of acres of private timberland in the Northwest and enough money to fill bathtubs with twenty-dollar bills. The cons drove to Tacoma, where the family lived in regal splendor among the small circle of timber barons. In the light of mid-afternoon, Harmon and the Swede kidnapped nine-year-old George Weyerhaeuser while he was on his way home from school. They took the boy to logged-over stump lands east of Seattle, blindfolded him, and dumped him into a deep pit, three feet wide and six feet long, covered with tin. A ransom note was mailed to Philip Weyerhaeuser, the father. Though he tried to keep it secret, word of the kidnapping leaked out; after flashing around the country, it became one of the biggest stories of the year. George spent several days in the pit; then he was removed, locked in the trunk of the kidnappers' Ford coupe, and driven 280 miles east to Spokane. There he was chained inside a closet in an apartment. After the $200,000 ransom was delivered, George was driven back across the state and released. Waley and his wife went to Salt Lake City, where they were arrested after Margaret tried to buy a pair of stockings with a bill whose number had been recorded. The Swede got away. He was traced to Butte, Montana, but slipped through a police dragnet. As of September, he and his $100,000 share of the kidnapping loot were still missing.

Black-market butter would not make Logan, Burch, and Ralstin rich on the scale that the Swede had pulled off, but it brought in plenty of money—enough, at least, to fuel the next dream.

Just after 9:30 p.m., the car backed into an alley entrance to the Newport Creamery. It was dark, and nobody was there. Piece of cake, just like Burch had predicted. The lock popped, the door opened, and there it was—hundreds of pounds of fresh butter, cartons of cottage cheese, and containers of cream. They stacked enough to load up the trunk and part of the floor in the back. Spokane was an hour south, giving them enough time to get the dairy products into storage before they would spoil.

Just as the door was closing, the squeak of hinges and the sound of footsteps on gravel attracted Marshal Conniff. He moved closer to the creamery, a single-story, cinder-block building, and shined his flashlight. "Who's there?"

The burglars were in the dark; the marshal was under a light.

As Conniff edged forward, he saw the car, the stacks of butter, cream, and cottage cheese. When he reached for his pistol, a gun was pulled on him. The night air, full of smoke and heat, now had gunfire—at least four shots from the butter thieves.

One bullet passed through the marshal's left wrist.

Another shot hit his right arm and lodged against a bone in the shoulder.

A third bullet ripped through his groin and shattered his hip, knocking him down.

As he lay bleeding on the gravel floor of the alley, a final shot pierced his heart, tearing open an inch-and-a-half-long gash, then penetrated his right lung.

The gunmen entered the car and sped away. Across the street, two boys who heard the shooting ran toward the creamery. The mayor of Newport, who lived nearby, also rushed to the crime scene. One bullet had entered his house. They found the marshal in shock, still clutching his flashlight, gagging on blood, his gun beside him. There was no blood near the creamery door. The butter thieves had escaped unscathed.

GEORGE CONNIFF lived for another ten hours, awake for most of it, conscious that his life was draining away. He never got a good look at the people who shot him—just two men with guns, he said. One of them was a big guy, well over six feet tall. The other man was smaller. Never saw a face. As his wife and three children gathered around him, he told his boy, George junior, to look after his mother.

Throughout the night and into the dawn of Sunday morning he lay on a bed in Newport, pain overwhelming his body. Just after sunrise, when the whistle of the Diamond Match sawmill summoned the morning shift to work across the Pend Oreille, Conniff was loaded into an ambulance to be taken to a bigger hospital in Spokane. He cried out as they carried him into the car; his body was on fire, the wounds open flames. The ride to Spokane was torture, a jangling, jarring route, Conniff's body leaking pus and blood; the fever pushed ever higher. Alma stayed with him, but he couldn't force any words out to his wife. By the time the car arrived at Saint Luke's Hospital in Spokane, George Conniff was dead.

The creamery had lost several hundred pounds of grade-A butter, and the slender book of local history, a record of the white man's brief attachment to the Pend Oreille country, was given a new chapter. During the second week of the driest September in memory, a little boy named Harold Chase drowned in the river, the Indian dipnet fishermen at Kettle Falls said the salmon run was the worst they had ever seen, and the Newport night marshal was killed by butter thieves. On Monday morning it rained.

6.

The Search

WITHIN AN HOUR of the shooting, the roads leading into Spokane, south of Newport, were barricaded. There were only two real escape points for the butter thieves: they could race down the paved road toward Spokane, then blend into the city, or they could try their luck in the woods of Idaho, east across the Pend Oreille River in the other direction, perhaps sit it out and wait for things to cool down. Only a few, familiar faces passed through the Idaho border. At the other blockade, the entrance to Spokane, a steady stream of cars came into the city; each was stopped and inspected by two officers.

Nothing angered a lawman, even a corrupt one, more than the shooting of a cop. Life was a war; the bad guys could gain the upper hand, or retreat, but if they took out a foot soldier in uniform, somebody from the other side had to die. As news of the shooting spread, police from all over the inland Northwest volunteered to help track and find whoever had murdered Marshal Conniff. Hard times had brought a surge of lawlessness to the West: robberies, rapes, assaults, drunkenness, burglary—the new America was frightening. But even then, homicide was rare. In all of 1934, not a single killing happened in Spokane. The previous year there had been only two murders. Now, not quite nine months into 1935, two cops had been shot—the

55

town marshal of Rosalia, south of Spokane, and Marshal Conniff in the village to the north. Bursts of anger and outrage came from the Spokane mayor, the chief of police, the sheriff, the United States marshal, and the county prosecutor. They would spare no expense, in manpower or resources, to find the killers. This was not the Old West, they thundered, but a civilized area, the richest empire in the Western Hemisphere.

On Monday morning, September 16, Bill Parsons joined several other Spokane police officers in a search for the marshal's killers. At roll call, the basic plan was outlined: they would surround the city and move in toward the center, squeezing the dirt out. Eventually, they would find the cop killer. Officer Dan Mangan led a patrol of men out to Hillyard, the rail yards east of town, where hundreds of homeless people camped. They were told not to return unless they came back with a suspect.

The transient village, Spokane's biggest Hooverville, exuded a stench of campfires, garbage, and clothes worn for weeks without washing. Everybody smelled of fire, the children especially. They were used to being kicked around, the farmer families who picked hops and apples or cut wood by day and then returned to the camps at night. But they had rarely seen anything like the ferocity of this search, aided by billy clubs. Mangan swatted heads and kicked rib cages. The tall, bespectacled cop was on a tear.

"Anybody here see two guys show up in a car last night?"

No, sir.

"Butter? How 'bout it? You bindle stiffs seen a load of butter moving around here?"

Butter? Nobody in this gulch of despair had seen butter for months, and if they had, word would have spread. Folks in the camp were living off brown apples and potato soup. They boiled water in tin cans and cleaned what they could in the river. Butter? No, sir. Not in this heat wave. It wouldn't keep any longer than a Popsicle on pavement.

Then it was on to the boxcars. The officers went through the cars one by one, looking for the hiding, sniveling bastards who had gunned the marshal down and then put a final bullet into him as he lay on the ground. Seven rail lines came into Spokane from all directions, bringing in silver, wheat, timber, apples. But the most common cargo of 1935 was the broken men and women from the dry lands of the West and the Plains. Searching the boxcars, the patrolmen found tiny, urine-fouled homes in darkened corners. How could people live like this? This town was going down the toilet.

Empty-handed, the police search team headed for the Hotel de Gink. Perhaps the killers were trying to blend in with the rest of the Okie trash, as they called the inhabitants of the former brewery. They searched rooms where hollow-eyed men awoke to the light of another hot day and a Monday-morning hangover. The Gink smelled worse than the boxcars. People had made small fires in their rooms to cook. The cots were yellowed and flat, stained by moonshine and love-making. An Italian immigrant was found with a gun; they slapped him around and chained him to a post while they looked for other suspects. There was plenty of hooch in most rooms of the Hotel de Gink; plenty of gambling slips from the Chinese lottery game. But no butter. "The Indian did it!" one man said in desperation. "Yes," a friend seconded, "check the Indian!" The officers rousted an alcoholic native, red-eyed, mumbling when they woke him. He was chained next to the Italian. By day's end, the search had produced a handful of warm bodies: a smart-mouth, a troublemaker, a goddamn Okie with an attitude, the Italian, the Indian. There was nothing to tie any of them to the robbery of the Newport Creamery or the killing of Marshal Conniff. But it was enough to get the officers back into the station without a tongue-lashing from the shift captain.

VIRGIL BURCH had showed up at Mother's Kitchen early Sunday morning, just before dawn. He looked terrible, nervous and frayed. Pearl Keogh was still there, waiting for Ruth to get off work. She had never seen Virgil so tense. When she asked him what was up, he yelled at her to keep quiet. A few police officers, the usual contingent of uniformed stool-dwellers, were still at the diner. Burch went to a back room, and when he reappeared nearly an hour later his face was pale. He paced behind the bar, walked around the restaurant, un-distracted by the familiar banter.

Just after dawn, Detective Ralstin appeared, a sight better than the sun. He looked clean and well kept, his green eyes clear, and never more commanding. Virgil rushed over to him, but Clyde made a motion with his hand, like a master slowing down his overanxious pup. Clyde flashed a grin at Pearl, ordered coffee.

"You heard about the shooting?" Pearl asked him. Even before it hit the papers, the cops who spent most of their shift at Mother's Kitchen had spread the word.

"What do *you* hear?" Clyde asked, his voice as slow as crankcase oil.

"The marshal," she said. "Somebody gunned down the Newport marshal last night. Shot him in the back."

Clyde stared at Pearl, an interrogatory hold with his eyes. At six foot three, he was a full head taller and a hundred pounds heavier than the nurse from Montana. "And . . . ?"

"That's all I heard," she said.

Clyde sat down, holding back a smile. He looked up at Virgil and winked. "Relax," he told his buddy.

"So they shot the marshal?" he said to Pearl, flashing his teeth, showing his dimples. "In the back, you say?"

"That's what the boys are saying."

"Shouldn't ever turn your back to anybody."

Now Virgil eased up a bit. Clyde was so commanding. "Shouldn't ever turn your back to anybody," he echoed.

"What kind of smokepole he use?" Clyde asked.

"Smokepole?" Pearl asked.

"A rifle? Forty-five? What?"

"Didn't hear."

Clyde sipped his coffee, checked his watch, and turned to Virgil. "I'm going out of town for a few days," he said.

"I'm going with you," Virgil said.

"No, you're not. It wouldn't look good."

"You can't leave me here, Clyde."

Ralstin told Burch to calm his nerves and settle his heart. He would be gone for only a day or so—just enough to establish his whereabouts this weekend. His brother Chub had a place down by the Snake River in the traditional home of the Nez Percé Indians, not far from where Ralstin was raised. If anybody asked, Clyde was hunting with Chub. Gone the whole weekend.

He didn't want to be away from Dorothy, the waitress at Mother's, for too long. Now in the process of shedding his wife, Clyde had been sampling some of Virgil's talent, as he called it: the redhead from Idaho . . . the blonde with the big lips. And now he was moving closer to Dorothy.

"What if somebody comes to see me?" Virgil asked. "Starts asking questions?"

"Nobody's gonna ask you any questions, Virgil."

Clyde whispered something in his ear. Virgil seemed to relax. Clyde always made him feel good. Nothing could touch him as long as the big detective was around.

On his way out the door, Clyde tipped his fedora to a pair of uniforms sitting in a booth. He slowed to wink at Pearl. When she looked away, his face turned hard, an instant threat. Pearl was afraid, but she tried not to show it. Clyde squeezed Pearl's arm and motioned toward her sister. She had three kids to support, right?

Yes, Ruth had three little ones at home.

And no husband?

He was in the sanitarium, under treatment for tuberculosis.

"Wouldn't want anything to happen to those kids," Clyde said to Pearl.

"My God, no! Clyde Ralstin, what on earth are you talking about?"

He loosened his grip, smiled. "Just keep your mouth shut."

THE DOCTORS removed three bullets from the body of George Conniff. A fourth slug, which had passed through the marshal, was found in the side of the creamery building. Two of the bullets had soft-nosed casings and two were harder, made of steel. They all looked as if they came from a .32-caliber pistol. It was possible that all four were fired from the same gun, since it was not unusual to load a single weapon with both steel and lead casings. In any event, the bullets were placed in evidence, with the intention of sending them to the crime lab for precise analysis on what sort of gun had fired them.

George Conniff was buried on Tuesday afternoon, September 17, at the Greenwood Cemetery in Spokane. The funeral procession was led by a motorcycle brigade from the Spokane Police Department. The sky was full of clouds, and light rain fell on the mourners at the cemetery. Alma Conniff, left now without a home or a husband, was helped by her three children. She had no idea what she might do to survive this hard year of 1935, no idea where to go, even. The house had burned down, and now George was dead. In Newport, merchants suspended business for one hour in the afternoon to commemorate their slain marshal. Everybody said it wasn't fair. Conniff had worked so hard. He was a good man, honest, who'd hit a patch of bad luck and had been trying so hard to put himself back together. He was building the log cabin, the new family home, and he was going to take things a bit easier. Conniff had very few enemies, even after his years as police chief in Sandpoint. He was good with people, fair. He understood that mean times made people do things they wouldn't normally do. But killing a man over butter? What animal would stoop so low?

When members of the Conniff family asked Elmer Black, the sheriff of Pend Oreille County, about the progress of the investigation, he assured them that the killers would soon be found. Police from eastern Washington, northern Idaho, western Montana, and southern British Columbia were checking all the railroad depots, the major roads, the hobo camps, the Hoovervilles, the jails, the bars, the union halls, the fire camps. The four bullet casings were on their way to a lab for forensic analysis. Before long, the sheriff expected, he'd know exactly what kind of gun had been used, and its year and make. Already a few leads were starting to trickle in. The killers would screw up, he told the family—they always did. Something would leak out; somebody would make a wrong move. Nobody killed a cop and got away with it.

The Search

*   *   *

ARRIVING IN SPOKANE three days after the shooting, Black told reporters he was visiting tailors to check on a promising clue. Somebody had pawned a pair of fine wool, handmade trousers in Newport on Saturday night, an hour or so before the killing. Why would anyone sell his own pants, Elmer Black theorized, if he weren't planning to leave town quick or if he weren't desperate for money? Although an identification tag had been ripped out, most likely the pants belonged to one of the killers, he said. So Sheriff Black made the rounds of tailors in Spokane, pawned pants in hand, trying to find someone who could remember them.

He also brought to town a door removed from a garage in Priest River, Idaho, a mill town eleven miles east of Newport. A few hours after the shooting of Marshal Conniff, a green sedan had been stolen from the garage. The door to the garage had been covered with grease to deaden the noise of the break-in. Sheriff Black turned the door over to Spokane police, hoping they could lift fingerprints from it. The stolen car had been found in Spokane Sunday morning, abandoned, with a few half-eaten groceries in the backseat. "The theory that the stolen automobile may have been used by the bandits seems good," the *Spokesman-Review* reported. "Priest River is only a few miles from Newport and it would have been relatively easy for the thugs to reach the town after the shooting."

Black was under tremendous pressure. The sheriff was short and heavy, with a reputation for slow thinking and sloth. He was fifty years old, with wire-rim glasses and a fleshy double chin, a Republican who didn't like the New Deal trail-building camp in his county and thought the world would return to normal if everybody just worked a little harder and the government minded its own goddamn business. Conniff had been a beloved figure in Newport, as evidenced by the memorial service at the Methodist church. Several hundred people crammed into the church; the room overheated with talk of vengeance. In the northern part of the county, in the mining town of Metaline Falls, members of the Rod and Gun Club talked of organizing a posse. The Conniff killing, coming one month after the

61

Rosalia shooting, fed a fire of vigilantism. Nobody felt safe. Anything of value—a creamery, a bank, a wheat silo—was vulnerable. More than half the people in Pend Oreille County were out of work. Those who could hold on, selling their dairy products through the Newport Creamery, now felt they were under siege. If two men were desperate enough to kill a marshal over butter, what might they do next?

Elected in 1934, Sheriff Black promised to bring order to an area where beer halls outnumbered churches and 90 percent of the county had never been penetrated by roads, let alone lawmen. His jurisdiction, the last county to be established in Washington, had more than eight hundred thousand acres of forest, and mountain peaks that reached heights of nearly eight thousand feet. With only a few thousand people, Pend Oreille County was broke in 1935; all services had been cut back except the most basic—enforcing the law. Fights with fists or knives were so common among workingmen of the Pend Oreille that the sheriff was seldom called to the scene unless somebody had been seriously wounded. At Kelly's Tavern, Newport's most popular bar, patrons in a fighting mood could wrestle with the black bear kept in a cage inside.

NOBODY IN SPOKANE recognized the pawned pants. After striking out with the tailors, Sheriff Black began searching the transient camp a mile south of Newport. A riverfront Hooverville, the camp was an outdoor version of the Hotel de Gink. Men who had worked as farmhands or built houses during the go-go years of the Roaring Twenties took refuge there, hoping to snag day jobs, scratching together enough money to stay alive. They were paid fifty cents a cord, plus board and free work gloves, to cut and load firewood onto freight trains bound for Spokane. Black had his suspicions about this camp: it could provide easy camouflage for somebody running from the law. But a search of the camp, and a check with a few informants, produced no hint of butter thieves or anybody who had boasted of a recent windfall.

The shooting had been so quick and precise that Black thought the killers might be convicts. Most thieves, when caught in the act, will merely run off in panic. It's the rare person who holds his ground after a warning and then guns down an armed lawman. Black set up a dragnet through the mail, firing off letters and telegrams to neighboring police departments. To Seattle police, he mentioned the name of an ex-con who had recently been picked up for shoplifting and was known to have been in Newport. To the sheriff in Ellensburg, a farm town east of Seattle, he wrote a query about three men in custody: "Could you give these young fellows a good working over in regard to their whereabouts on the night of the 14th?"

An Internal Revenue Service investigator based in Idaho sent a letter to the sheriff in response to Black's investigation. Suspicious of a convict in his state, the not-quite-literate IRS man wrote: "This bird is at St. Maries now and he is capibel of aney crime u mite name."

The tips went nowhere. But Black still had the bullets; with lab results, he hoped to trace them to the murder weapon.

DETECTIVE RALSTIN'S confidence was infectious. A few days after the killing, Acie Logan was feeling up to snuff again, thanks to Clyde. The ex-con had disappeared on Sunday, but by midweek he was back at Mother's Kitchen. Nobody had seen Clyde, either, for a couple of days, but then he showed his face at Mother's. Virgil Burch still seemed edgy. Logan, who'd known Burch ever since they'd tried to scratch riches from an old mine in Montana years earlier, wanted to discuss a new project. The butter from the Newport Creamery had moved faster than anybody had expected. Cached at Clyde's ranch and at Mother's, it was rewrapped and distributed to buyers around the area.

The creamery robberies were bringing in a couple hundred dollars a pop. Logan was also trying to move cigarettes and shoes, stolen from boxcars during the month of September. But nothing else was as easy as butter. He knew of a creamery in Stevensville, about four hours' drive east of Spokane, in the mountains of western Montana. It was a big one, a distribution center for dairy products from farmers in the isolated valleys of the Bitterroot Mountains. Logan had a friend from his days in the Idaho State Penitentiary, a short, curly-haired man named Warden Spinks who was twenty-seven, nine years younger than Logan. Spinks had helped Logan break into the boxcars to steal shoes. Now Logan enlisted him for the creamery burglaries.

Bringing Spinks in was fine with Clyde and Virgil. The Newport Creamery robbery had been just a little too much excitement for Burch. He could not get over how unfazed the big detective seemed by all the heat that followed the Newport killing. Clyde loved to ride an adrenal surge. But it was only smart to put some distance between the procurement end of the operation and the payoff.

During the next two weeks, Logan and Spinks, at times aided by a third man, brought in more than a ton of butter to Spokane. They made several quick trips to Montana, to Stevensville, and to another creamery on the Montana-Idaho border, breaking into the buildings in the middle of the night and then fleeing with a fully loaded truck. They were stalled only by the shortage of creameries. The robberies, of course, only heightened the butter crunch in the inland Northwest, thereby driving up prices for the product that Burch and Ralstin were starting to monopolize.

The drought held on as September faded. October was the hottest and driest on record in Spokane. And with each day that passed after the killing, Ralstin and Burch let their guard down a bit more. As Clyde said from the start, they would walk away from one of the biggest crimes in the inland Northwest. Sitting at the bar of Mother's Kitchen in early October, Pearl Keogh heard the two friends talking about the killing. Not really talking—laughing. They developed a routine, which worked to soothe Virgil's nerves. When Clyde would stroll into Mother's Kitchen, Virgil would say, "Who'd you kill today, Detective?"

"Can't remember," Ralstin would answer.

They had the best-tuned ears into both sides of the law. Clyde kept up with the progress of the Conniff investigation through his fellow officers at the Stone Fortress, so he was always a step ahead of the latest speculation. Sheriff Black, in Pend Oreille County, wasn't anything to worry about. Let the fat little lawman bring in his greased doors and pawned pants. The trousers, in particular, brought a howl to the gang at Mother's Kitchen.

It was only when a Spokane policeman started to check one end of the case, an accidental discovery, that Clyde went on full alert. Clyde was troubled by the bullets that had been recovered; they could be traced to the murder weapon.

During the first days of October, nearly three weeks after the killing, Clyde walked into Mother's Kitchen and saw that Burch's face had gone flat. His parrot, having chipped away at much of the bar, was now on the ceiling, working over the wooden molding.

"Clyde!" Burch motioned the detective to come behind the bar. "They got Logan."

"You sure?"

"Logan, Spinks, and two women. They picked 'em up this morning."

"Who picked 'em up?"

"Your own people. Here in town."

7.

Stone Fortress

BURCH THOUGHT it might be time to disappear, to fold the operation and head for a hideout somewhere in the Bitterroot Mountains or the Salmon River drainage. In early October, Dutch Schultz, the gangster whose racketeering empire reached its peak during Prohibition, was gunned down by a rival after returning from the restroom in a New Jersey tavern; Greta Garbo opened as the tragic heroine in the film *Anna Karenina*; and the National Geographic Society sent an exploratory party up the distant reaches of the Salmon River in central Idaho. New York's most famous racketeer and the enigmatic beauty Garbo were well known to most Americans, but parts of the Pacific Northwest remained unnavigated and unseen. It was into the mountains above the chasm of the River of No Return that Ralstin and Burch went to hunt elk and bighorn sheep and black bears. In the alpine country at the waistband of Idaho, a person could disappear, and only those who knew the country could ever hope to return.

Ralstin held firm: he told Burch, the former cattle rustler, that they didn't need the cover of wilderness—not yet, so long as they had the protection of Ralstin's bag of other men's secrets. When he nearly killed his son-in-law on that November night in 1934, beating and kicking him until blood poured out his ear onto the street, and then escaped arrest and prosecution, or even minor reprimand at the department, Ralstin proved to his rivals in the Stone Fortress what he had long boasted of at Mother's Kitchen: the law did not apply to him. At Mother's, Pearl Keogh heard Clyde's boast: "I am the law."

Acie Logan and Warden Spinks were picked up because they were acting stupid, Ralstin explained; it shouldn't be contagious. The two ex-cons had been sitting in a dust-coated sedan in downtown Spokane, in between creamery heists, snuggling up to a pair of young women. Logan was feeling rich, having brought in nearly two tons of butter in the previous thirty days. On the black market, the butter was fetching nearly fifty cents a pound—the highest price anyone had ever seen. Logan and Spinks and the two women were just easing into a full night when their car was spotted by Detective Charles Sonnabend, a Spokane police veteran, somewhat of a loner on the force. Checking the license plate, he found the car was listed as having been stolen in Montana.

The two butter thieves and their dates got out of the car and walked into the World Hotel, where they had been staying. Sonnabend and his partner followed. Once inside the hotel, Logan and Spinks were arrested. The detective found two loaded pistols in the room: a .32 and a .38. Now, Sonnabend thought he was on to something bigger than a pair of car thieves. He slapped Logan around, grilling him about the weapons. The guns alone made the tattooed ex-con a parole violator, guaranteeing a return to jail. With the stolen car, he could be facing a long lockup. But Logan kept quiet, as did Spinks. The two women said they were just out for a good time. They were arrested for vagrancy.

Searching the stolen car, Sonnabend found butter wrappers from a creamery in Stevensville. When he opened the trunk, there was the unmistakable whiff of bacon—another black-market specialty of the gang from Mother's Kitchen. There were also dozens of new shoes.

Charley Sonnabend, a rounded, lumpen man who liked to work with his hands, had been on the Conniff case, in a peripheral way, from the beginning. It was he who found the car that had been stolen from Priest River around the time of the shooting—a find that later proved to be a false lead. Sonnabend was known as a good detective, somewhat slow and deliberative, who approached each case like a new house: the foundation had to be solid or the walls would not stand. His face was puffy and his jowls were loose, the exposed flesh of a 280-pound body just over six feet tall. Although he was now a short-timer, with only a few years to go before retirement, his work pace did not slow with age. Some of his friends considered him too stubborn for his own good, a hard-ass; he did not back down from a fight. Because he was never around when the handouts and envelopes from bootleggers came to the Stone Fortress, many of the other officers did not trust him. One detective had gone so far as to tell Charley Sonnabend to watch his step: A fellow who wouldn't go along was no good to anybody. They were all brothers. Sonnabend shrugged and went about his work. Threats came and went. He knew what real danger was all about, for he had once been in a shootout and had stood motionless, firing his gun while bullets zipped by him.

When Logan and Spinks and the two women were brought into the Stone Fortress, paraded through police headquarters on the ground floor, and then taken upstairs in an elevator to jail, a great fuss and commotion was made over them. A long night of interrogation produced enough material about the butter burglaries so that by morning the police announced they had found the creamery thieves —and possibly nabbed Conniff's killer as well. A shift captain told the press that Logan and Spinks had taken a thousand pounds of butter from a single creamery, in western Montana; the police weren't sure what had become of the stolen creamery goods. They also said the two men had taken two hundred pounds of ham and bacon, which they had sold in Spokane for sixty-four dollars.

Inside the Stone Fortress, everyone wanted to have a lick at the cop killers. As vowed by hundreds of officers throughout the inland Northwest, nobody was going to kill a policeman and get away with it. The *Spokesman-Review* ran pictures of Logan and Spinks, puffy-eyed and battered, staring out in befuddled despair. Their mug shots appeared under a headline that read: SUSPECTED OF NEWPORT MURDER KNOWLEDGE. The story said Spokane police believed the two men "[knew] something about the murder of George Conniff, night marshal at Newport." The two loaded guns that had been found in the World Hotel were sent to FBI headquarters in Washington, D.C., where, the papers said, J. Edgar Hoover himself would help solve the crime of the century in the wilderness county south of the Canadian border. The FBI was going to do a ballistics comparison with bullets taken from the marshal's body.

Logan looked particularly promising, and not just because of the guns-and-butter evidence. When he was arrested, he was a fugitive, wanted for state and federal parole violations. All along, Sheriff Black of Pend Oreille County had said they were looking for a con, because only someone desperate, someone with the career criminal's disregard for human life, would gun a man down over a few hundred pounds of food. As he lay dying, Conniff had whispered that one of the shooters was tall, well over six feet, and the other was smaller, about five foot seven—the exact height of Acie Logan.

The son of a Mississippi sharecropper, Logan had quit school after the fourth grade and left home as a teenager. A stint in the army ended in the barracks at Fort Leavenworth, where he did twenty-three months on a desertion charge. He wandered all over the West, testing the laws of every state he visited. In the Washington town of Snohomish, he was convicted of having sex with a little girl, a felony for which he served a year in jail. In Idaho, he did two and a half years in the state prison for bootlegging. In Louisiana, he did time for beating a man up. In Spokane, a year before the Conniff killing, he was arrested for vagrancy and spent ten days in the city jail. Only over the last year, when he fell in with Burch and Ralstin at Mother's Kitchen, did his luck begin to change. The money was good. Burch lined him up with plenty of women, even though the waitresses at Mother's found him a hard man to like, a lizard-faced con with a stare that seemed to stretch to the Great Plains. He was thirty-six years old when Sonnabend picked him up at the World Hotel.

Logan did not expect to be sent to Walla Walla for butter crimes or to hang for the Conniff killing. In fact, he did not expect to be spending much more time on the top floor of the Stone Fortress under the fist-aided questioning of Charley Sonnabend. The detective was sure he had the Conniff killer in his hands; all that was needed to make the case was a little added persuasion. But Logan would not talk. He kept bringing up the name of Detective Ralstin—his buddy, Clyde.

"Get a hold of Clyde," he said.

"What for?"

"Just get him."

Any minute, Logan expected, the king of the Stone Fortress, the master of Mother's Kitchen, would stroll into jail and get this cop off his back.

"Wait till Clyde shows up," he told the detective.

AT MOTHER'S KITCHEN, Ralstin was trying to soothe his partner. Burch wavered from spontaneous confidence to whiny panic, depending on his proximity to Clyde. Logan knew everything, of course; and loyalty was not one of his character traits. If he talked to Sonnabend, everybody else could fall. But Ralstin did not seem worried. He ordered Burch to get rid of all the butter from the storage cooler at Clyde's ranch and at Mother's Kitchen. Take a loss, dump it, just get rid of it, he told his friend. Then he and Burch set out to contact all the members of the fence, a loose network of go-betweens and petty thieves who had helped them sell butter on the black market.

Then Clyde went to the Stone Fortress, not to see Logan but to see what his colleagues had on Logan. Sonnabend told him that Logan had wanted to see him.

Ralstin laughed. Fucking con. Clyde said he'd busted Logan's head once. A loser, no doubt about it. But he couldn't imagine what Logan wanted of him. Sonnabend said Logan was part of a gang of butter thieves who were using Spokane as their base. Somebody other than Logan—the detective didn't know who—was the mastermind. Logan wasn't being very cooperative. Sonnabend expected to make his case as soon as the FBI came back with the gun report, and then the skinny loser from Mississippi was going to hang for the Conniff killing.

When Ralstin arrived back at Mother's Kitchen, he looked edgy for the first time since the killing. Pearl Keogh saw a big, bold man who had lost his strut. Ralstin and Burch argued. Something had to be done with the gun: not the loaded .32 that had been found in the World Hotel—Ralstin knew that gun had no link to the bullets that ended the life of Marshal Conniff—but another gun, another .32-caliber revolver. A bullet leaves the barrel with exit marks unique to the gun from which it was fired; in that sense, it can be traced like a fingerprint. Ballistic experts try to determine which gun fired a particular bullet by examining the grooves inside the pistol. In the 1930s in Spokane, whenever a cop arrested somebody, he was entitled to take and keep the criminal's weapon, one of many small perks. The officer had only to register the gun with the department, noting the serial number of his new possession. Clyde Ralstin had kept a .32 pistol from an arrest a few years earlier. It wasn't his favorite gun; the piece was too small for his use—practically a toy, he used to say. But because of its size, it fit nicely in a holster inside his suit without causing so much as a ripple in his jacket. Now, if Logan broke down and told Sonnabend everything he knew, they would want to check Clyde's .32, which he had left in the Stone Fortress. If the gun matched the bullets from Conniff's body, and Logan told everything he knew about Clyde's involvement, Ralstin would be the one facing a noose at Walla Walla.

Detective Ralstin's solution was simple and direct: the .32 had to be buried. Now. But how to get rid of it was a bigger problem. The pistol was at the Stone Fortress, where Logan was under intense, round-the-clock questioning. Not to worry, Ralstin assured Burch. He had a lot of friends at the Stone Fortress.

"WHY ARE THE ITALIANS invading Ethiopia?" Pearl Keogh asked Ruth.

"The dictator, Mussolini," her sister replied. "He's hungry."

In the last week, the sisters had talked openly of everything except what they had seen and heard at Mother's. So much had transpired in front of them that they were starting to feel like accomplices. Ralstin had been so confident of his control over all who sipped coffee and passed the time at Mother's Kitchen that he had not bothered to be very discreet. The sisters from Montana had heard the whole thing

—talk of the shooting, fretting over Logan's arrest, the order to get rid of all the surplus butter and alert everybody who had some connection to the gang. They were ready to tell the police—a move that might cost Ruth her job. With her husband in the sanitarium and jobs scarce, Ruth would be left without a way to support her three children. How would she stay alive? Pearl had no money; the hospital paid her in scrip for her work as a nurse. Ruth feared that she might have to join the long line that stretched from the soup kitchen at Sacred Heart around the block and down the hill. Going to the police could mean her children would go hungry and she would lose what dignity her wages at Mother's Kitchen had brought her.

Pearl and Ruth were Catholic, raised in the Jesuit tradition in Montana, but they weren't lily-white by any means. Pearl liked to party and flirt, and she occasionally let her pride get the best of her. But no matter how many minor lapses there had been, she had tried to keep her soul free of the big sins—the ones that could anchor a spirit in hell. A mortal sin meant eternal damnation, if the offense wasn't first wiped away by confession. The worst sin of all was to take another human's life. And to know of such a crime and do nothing was no different than carrying that very stain on your soul. After a long night of discussion, which spilled over into another hot early-October dawn, the sisters decided it was better to risk hunger and have a clean conscience than to keep quiet and hold on to a job in a place run by men who seemed at times to be the devil's soldiers.

So, they would go to the authorities and tell them everything. Their evidence consisted of what they had heard and what they had found. "We've got proof," Pearl told her sister by way of shoring up a tenuous decision. "And we owe it to that marshal's family."

They thought first of going to the Spokane police, but Ralstin and his close associates at Mother's Kitchen *were* the Spokane police; they might as well call up Clyde and say they were about to turn him in. Pearl couldn't shake the image of Detective Ralstin and his routine with Virgil Burch: the strut, the smirk, the line "Who'd you kill today?" What about the sheriff from Pend Oreille County, Elmer Black? It was his jurisdiction. No, Pearl said; he was too close to the Spokane police. Every time the papers mentioned something about the Conniff investigation, it was always Black working with Spokane detectives.

They decided to go to the Spokane County sheriff, Ralph Buckley. His men seemed to be clean. When Ralph Foley, the prosecutor, had raided the Chinese gambling and opium dens earlier that year, he had used county cops.

Sheriff Buckley listened to everything Pearl and Ruth told him about the goings-on at Mother's Kitchen. He acted very interested, jotting down notes and names, nodding and encouraging. After an hour or so, Buckley showed them out the door, and said they should not breathe a word of this to another soul. The sisters had thought of going to the FBI, or maybe directly to the prosecutor, but Buckley assured them such steps weren't necessary. They had done the right thing. He would personally take control of everything they had told him. One last thing: he asked if they were sure about this big fellow, Detective Clyde Ralstin. Oh yes, the sisters answered. Clyde's the one. When Pearl started to describe him in detail, Buckley cut her off. He knew Detective Ralstin.

ON HIS THIRD NIGHT in custody, Acie Logan was hungry, tired, and angered at the absence of Clyde Ralstin. He had not told Detective Sonnabend anything about the killing or the Newport Creamery robbery. But he was feeling betrayed. Chain-smoking, he went back and forth with the big cop about what he knew and didn't know. As they spoke, Sonnabend assured him that the entire operation—the black-market butter schemes, the fencing of shoes and bacon—was about to collapse. Other cops were out in the field, rounding up members of the gang.

"You will hang, Acie," Sonnabend told him.

Better to tell the detective everything. Cut a deal. Maybe Logan could still keep his long neck out of a noose at Walla Walla.

Exhausted, Logan fell asleep, slumped against the wall on the sixth floor of the Stone Fortress. His partner Spinks was good for very little. Sonnabend told the papers that Logan was the one with knowledge.

From the top floor of the Stone Fortress, the Spokane River looked like a black snake, slipping around the big rocks just below the falls. The water that pushed through the ancient channel was tired. If the river could hold its flow through this drought, make it till the November rains, things might return to normal. The woods still smoldered, and some said only winter snow could snuff the big fires. Further downstream, beyond the point where the Spokane fed the Columbia, engineers were blasting through basalt, looking for places to anchor the foundation of the Grand Coulee Dam. When the Columbia was finally harnessed, the water would back up for hundreds of miles, burying centuries of human life and bringing green to the high desert. Then, the parched inland Northwest would have all the water it ever needed, no matter what the capricious moods of fire or weather. Man would control water, the master architect of the Northwest.

The first light bled out of the eastern sky, and a flutter of color lit the thin falls of the river. Logan was asleep, fresh bruises on his dirty face. A new day, and the police were so close. Detective Sonnabend, the carpenter cop, felt the foundation of this case was in place, the house was framed, and they might very well top it today.

A reporter knocked on the detective's door, loaded with coffee and questions. A familiar face around the Stone Fortress, the newsman asked Sonnabend about the Conniff case.

"It will be solved within twenty-four hours," he replied, and the reporter thanked him for the headline.

8.

To the River

THE POST STREET BRIDGE spans the midsection of Spokane Falls, where the water gathers after tumbling over one of three drops. From the bridge, the torrent looks impossible to descend by canoe, kayak, or raft; yet people have thrown themselves into the swirl in an act of bravado—or a moment of despair. As the water slides through the rock cliffs, en route to the Columbia and the Pacific, the river powers turbines that light the streetlights of Spokane. A few years after the city was incorporated, in 1881, the river brought light to downtown streets; it was one of the first waterways in the world to be harnessed for electricity. During the mid-1930s, when Spokane had to close its zoo and pawn the animals, electric power—even that which came from the perpetual flow of the falls—was considered a luxury, and so the city removed nearly four hundred streetlights, and much of Spokane was dark at night.

The police station was a long block south of the Post Street Bridge. The span was a place for private talks and solitary strolls. At peak flow, the roar of the falls was so loud that two people could not hear themselves speak. But in early October, when the surface of the land was hard and dry, and little water fed the falls, the sound was a weak cry in the background of a clattering city, dominant only when Spokane slept.

In the darkness of night, Dan Mangan and Bill Parsons stood above the falls on the bridge. Their police car, a Pontiac with a radio inside, one of five patrol cars used on each shift, idled as Mangan stepped out. They were both in uniform, on duty, upholding the laws of the city of Spokane. Mangan was carrying a package, a bundle of newspapers wrapped around a gun. Parsons was confused. The rookie, still on probation, was paired with Mangan that night because Dan's regular partner was off. Parsons was still trying to make a name for himself as a decent policeman. On a recent night, while Officer Mangan had been breaking into a restaurant called Dorothy's and stealing what he could get from inside the diner, Officer Parsons had recovered a stolen typewriter, and he was written up in the newspaper for this notable bit of police work.

Mangan usually operated on the other side of the law, and 'most everybody at the Stone Fortress knew what he was up to. When a particularly dirty job had to be done, Mangan was summoned. It was that reputation that led to his arrival on the ledge of the Post Street Bridge, carrying a package. In addition to burglaries, break-ins, and shakedowns, Officer Mangan drew a regular income from bootleggers, who delivered his payoff in envelopes—usually ten dollars at a time, but sometimes more. Although Mangan was constantly reprimanded, he was never seriously disciplined. His personnel file was stuffed with suspension and warning notices for actions labeled "disgraceful" and "conduct unbecoming an officer."

Mangan would show up in the cold house he kept in the east part of town drunk and smelling of perfume; if his wife, Helen, ventured to raise even the weakest line of questioning, he would knock her to the ground or put his fist to her face. Often, she was kicked around in front of her children, who were jolted awake by the noise of the drunken patrolman returning from a binge. The next day, nursing a black eye or a swollen lip, Helen Mangan felt helpless. And when friends would seek to console her, she would wonder aloud, "What am I supposed to do—call the police?" Because he considered himself a good Catholic, Mangan would not allow his wife to divorce him.

Mangan's regular partner was Hacker Cox. Cox had picked up his nickname because of his habit of hacking at prisoners in the elevator on the way up to jail. On the short ride from the ground floor of the Stone Fortress to the top-floor jail, Hacker Cox could change a man's appearance.

Cox and Mangan were perfect for each other; they also occupied regular stool space at Mother's Kitchen and aspired to be in the close orbit of Detective Ralstin. In early October they were given their chance. Just after Sonnabend announced that the killing of Marshal Conniff would be solved within twenty-four hours, Mangan was called in to see Captain James "Ed" Hinton, one of three shift leaders in the Spokane Police Department. Fat-faced and balding, with deep circles under his eyes and cheeks shaped by an habitual scowl, Hinton moved in a slightly higher circle than Ralstin or Mangan, spending late hours at the finer speakeasies in the company of the city's other mid-level leaders. Early in 1935, which had opened with the Spokane *Chronicle*'s call for a full inquiry into corruption at the Stone Fortress, there came rumblings of a grand jury investigation of the department. As soon as Captain Hinton heard about the prosecutor's action, he fled to Canada. He later reappeared, back as the shift captain, when the legal thunder died down. Hinton wanted to be chief, and it was that career goal which kept him on a leash held by Clyde Ralstin. Clyde would not have minded seeing Hinton as the top man of the largest police department between Minneapolis and Seattle.

When Captain Hinton called Mangan into his office, he did not look the patrolman in the eyes.

"Shut the door," he said.

"What's up?"

"Ralstin's in trouble," the captain said. "He needs a favor."

"What kind of trouble?"

"Cox will tell you."

"He's off today."

"I know he's off. Go to his house. He's got something for you. Who's your partner today?"

"Bill Parsons."

"Take him."

"You sure about Parsons?"

"Take him. He's okay now."

Mangan and Parsons drove to the northwest part of town, to the home of Hacker Cox. Mangan was silent most of the way. When he pulled up in front of the house, he kept the engine running. He returned in a minute with a package wrapped in newspaper.

"What's that?" Parsons asked.

"A favor."

"What kind of favor?"

"Ralstin's in trouble. We gotta get rid of this."

Mangan turned the Spokane police car around and headed south, for the river. He did not say a word during the drive.

WHEN DETECTIVE SONNABEND went to round up the other members of the butter gang, he discovered that most of them had left town. The loot also was gone. Shoes, bacon, butter—it had disappeared. How could this be? They had Logan and Spinks in custody, and they knew about most of the operation, where the butter had come from. Sonnabend was livid; almost overnight, his case was falling apart. How could he get a conviction without the evidence?

Back at the Stone Fortress, a young officer approached him, somebody who had been in Mother's Kitchen a few days earlier. He took Sonnabend aside and told him that everybody involved in the black-market ring had been tipped off by Clyde Ralstin.

"Ralstin? Detective Ralstin?"

The detective had leaked the latest information from the Stone Fortress to his partners in the fence—his *partners?* That's right, the officer said. And Ralstin was their leader.

Sonnabend had heard plenty of stories about his fellow detective. Most of them, he couldn't give a damn about; but this was a new low. Not only was Ralstin sabotaging a murder investigation; he might have had a hand in the killing.

Sonnabend stormed into the office of Ira Martin, chief of police. Martin, the first chief to hold the job for any considerable amount of time, was particularly good at curbing public outrage during the periodic calls for wholesale firings and grand jury investigations. He was known as an efficient administrator, not particularly cunning or well connected around town. Above all, he believed in the institution; after a tumultuous decade of graft, and then five years of hard times, the very survival of the police department was at stake.

When Sonnabend told him that Detective Ralstin had leaked inside information to the very criminals who were under investigation, Martin at first tried to calm him. Sonnabend's face went red, and he waved his callused hands around. Whose side were they on, for Christ's sake? Ralstin had sabotaged his case! He should be arrested—prosecuted! Fired at least!

The chief was well aware of the complaints about Ralstin. This latest information did not seem to surprise him so much as it left him looking helpless. He couldn't bring the hammer down on Detective Ralstin because it would damage the entire department at a time when it was under siege from the newspapers, the federal prosecutor, the county. And Ralstin could do more than seriously tar the reputation of the Spokane Police Department. If cornered, he could end careers, force men into jail, break up families. Is that what Sonnabend really wanted—to ruin the lives of other policemen?

AT THE Post Street Bridge, high above the falls, Officer Mangan opened the door of his police vehicle and walked to the rail. The Great Northern Railroad clock tower, an Italian Renaissance–styled spire, was anchored to the riverbank, a place where saw and grist mills used to crank out the elemental products of the infant town. The biggest Hooverville was not far from the railroad tower, upriver, and the little squatters' camp at the base of the falls was less than a mile the other direction, downstream. In accordance with the wishes of Spokane's political and business leaders, the smaller homeless village would soon be doused with gasoline and burned to the ground. Upriver another twenty miles or so was the graveyard of the eight hundred horses slaughtered in 1858 by Colonel George Wright. Some of the bodies had floated down the river. But a number of skeletons, the bones bleached white by the sun and then decayed to an overcast gray, had remained in clumps at the site of the mass shooting. It became known as Horse Slaughter Camp, a designation that Spokane's promoters tried to discourage; Wright's animal massacre was not a historical image that merited further scrutiny. By the early part of this century, most of the bones had been reduced to ash and had washed downstream, the river hiding the last physical traces of the mass killing. Only the memories of cavalry soldiers, preserved in diaries describing the "whinnying cries" of the panicky animals, remained as proof of the night Colonel Wright executed eight hundred horses.

Long ago, in other days of early October, nearly ten thousand natives used to gather to spear fish and talk trade and swap products at the base of Spokane Falls. The original Spokane people believed that a benevolent god had created this breach to funnel fish into the hands of the hungry. When most of the natives and the fish runs had died, and the new city rising around the falls wanted to distinguish itself, civic leaders hired the Olmsted Brothers, the landscaping firm from Brookline, Massachusetts, to create something of lasting value in Spokane. The brothers, whose father had helped design New York's Central Park, said the city needed only to protect and highlight the great natural waterfall in its midst. "Nothing is so firmly impressed on the mind of the visitor to Spokane as the great gorge into which the river falls near the center of the city," the brothers wrote.

The river's course was first altered by humans in the mid-1880s, when the south channel was dammed to make a pond for a sawmill. By 1890, the ten-year-old city had a hydroelectric plant just below the wood planks of the first Post Street Bridge. During the next four decades, the river's wild character was forever changed. The swift flow was used to power electricity for silver mines in the Coeur d'Alene Mountains and to run the streetcars in Spokane. Riverbeds that had been untouched by sunlight were suddenly exposed, and banks that had not felt the overlap of water since the retreat of the last ice age were buried anew. Lakes were formed with backwater, and orchards and vegetables flourished with irrigation water. The salmon were killed off after Washington Water Power constructed a dam in 1906 at the site of an ancient Indian fishing village.

Standing above the river, Officer Mangan wanted only to bury a weapon and be gone. He wound up and tossed the bundle into the falls, watching the package descend until it hit the foam of the re-grouping water. The falls were lit up by lights below, so even at night Mangan could see that the bundle he had been told to dispose of had gone to the floor of the Spokane River.

He turned and got back into the police car, where Parsons had watched the whole thing.

"What the hell did you throw in there?" the rookie asked him.

Mangan said nothing, and they drove off. Mangan whistled, staring straight ahead.

Again, Parsons asked him what he had done.

"We threw a gun in the river," he said.

"We?"

"Yeah. You and me."

ACIE LOGAN remained in police custody for three more weeks and then was released to federal authorities, who allowed him to plead guilty to a charge of interstate theft. He was already in violation of parole and would have faced a much longer sentence as a habitual criminal if he had not pled. In November, he and Warden Spinks told a federal judge that they had stolen forty-two pairs of shoes from a train car. The judge sentenced Logan to four years at the McNeil Island Federal Penitentiary in Puget Sound. Spinks was given three and a half years. They were never heard from or seen again in Spokane.

The same day Logan was sentenced, Officer Bill Parsons was taken off probation. He would stay on the police force for thirty-five years, retiring in 1970 as the chief of police.

Dan Mangan, his partner for a single night on the Post Street Bridge, stayed on the force until 1946, when he was forced to resign after he attacked his wife, nearly killing her with his fists and feet. When fellow policemen arrived at the Mangan home after being summoned by neighbors, they found Helen Mangan on the floor. She had been choked and punched and kicked by Sergeant Mangan, who was drunk at the time. In a police report Helen Mangan was quoted as saying, "I asked him who he had been laying up with, and

he hit me. He knocked me down and I don't know what all happened."
She said her son had jumped atop his father. "If it wasn't for the kids,
he would have killed me." Mangan was never prosecuted. He moved
to Hungry Horse, Montana, where he opened a bar—the Dam Town
Tavern. For years, his annual Fourth of July party in Hungry Horse
was the best-attended social event among members of the Spokane
Police Department.

Virgil Burch continued with Mother's Kitchen for a few more
months, though the volume of food moving through his all-night diner
declined considerably. In late January 1936, Burch was arrested and
charged with attempting to bribe a government witness. He had tried
to pay $500 to one of the butter gang members to keep him from
testifying. "Of all the beefs I've had with the law, this is the bummest,"
Burch said at the time.

In February, Burch was acquitted. The prosecution's case fell apart
when its witnesses lost their memories and their tongues. Burch sold
Mother's Kitchen, married another woman, and moved to Portland,
Oregon.

A few days after the gun was thrown in the river, a small story
appeared deep inside in the *Spokesman-Review*: POLICE OFFICER
GETS DEMOTION. The story said that Clyde Ralstin had been relieved
of his duties as a detective and assigned to the ranks of uniformed
patrolman, on night duty. "The action was said to be the result, in
part, of recent indiscretions of the officer, including tipping off information in an important case," the story said. Before he started his
new duty as a beat cop, Ralstin was suspended for six days. A few
months later, in early March 1936, Ralstin was given a much greater
suspension—four months, for actions described by Chief Martin as
"infractions which cannot be tolerated." The story did not elaborate.

A year later, Ralstin resigned from the police department. He said
to his stepdaughter, Ruby, that he was leaving town and did not know
if he would ever see her again. He deserted his wife, Monnie, and
told friends he was off to find his fortune in South America with
Dorothy, the waitress he'd met at Mother's Kitchen. They would be
far from the drudgery of police work in a town that couldn't afford
to pay its best marksman and its toughest cop any more than forty-

two dollars a week. At the time of his resignation, while turning in his police gear, he reported that his .32-caliber pistol was missing.

The murder of Marshal Conniff remained unsolved. Eventually, the case was forgotten, a distant killing from a dishonest decade. The Spokane River returned to normal in the late 1930s, rainfall and snowmelt filling mountain creeks; and a thick vein of water once again coursed through the center of the biggest city in the inland Northwest, a town that was back on track with the business of empire-building.

THREE

PSYCHIC DUEL

1989

9.

The Student

THE STUDENT had sandy hair, the skin of his southern Italian ances-
tors, and the type of muscled forearms and chest that a weightlifter
could never create in a body shop. A lifetime of outdoor work—
cutting trees and skinning logs, clawing inside mine shafts, and pouring concrete—had given Anthony Bamonte a look of lean utility. He
was forty-six years old when Professor Michael Carey at Gonzaga
University's Graduate School of Professional Studies in Spokane asked
him for some elaboration on his master's thesis. Sitting in a basement
classroom in Colville, a timber town seventy-five miles north of Spokane, where the Jesuits ran an off-campus program, Bamonte seemed
ready to spring from his chair. The pace of academia, the slow whit-
tling of ideas to a fine point, was a poor fit for a physical man. Bamonte
answered in his usual tone, a voice barely above a whisper, Clint
Eastwood without the snarl. The other students—a couple of wheat
farmers, a pastor's wife, a small-town newspaperman, a teacher, two
sawmill workers, a city manager—took notice; they were never sure
what might come out of Bamonte. One day he might bring a crude
weapon to class or pictures of autopsies; another day he would arrive
with news from his latest interview inside a jail cell. During class
discussions, he would sit quietly, then toss an odd thought or a jarring

anecdote into the usual discourse on how to use computer-drawn pie charts to enhance a career.

His idea was to do a history of Pend Oreille County. Not the story of settlers breaking the back of the wilderness and tacking the rough carpet of civilization to the sod; in the Pend Oreille, where fewer than ten thousand people shared a million acres of mostly roadless forest land with grizzly bears, mountain lions, and the last wild caribou herd left in the United States outside of Alaska, that story was obvious and still unfolding. No, Bamonte was after a peculiar history, a study of law and order in Pend Oreille County. He wanted to dredge up all the major crimes in his county, solved and unsolved, to see if most bullies ever got caught, if victims found justice, if mistakes of the past meant anything to succeeding generations. And he wanted help from the ages, a few lessons from a near century of awful behavior, something he could use to get him through the middle years of his own life.

He would not be relying on footnoted tomes or museum archives for most of his raw material, he explained. With little choice, the information had to come from marginally literate men whose job it had been to record the pained facts of assault, rape, robbery, incest, theft, arson, murder. The police reports (there were stacks of them from the last eight decades, stored in odd locations throughout the county) seldom voiced an opinion on what the observer had seen. Just the facts, often misspelled: Bartender shot in dispute over six-pack. . . . Prosecutor wounded in ambush attempt. . . . Convict tries to cut head open by scissors.

Pend Oreille County had been in existence for seventy-eight years (it was the last county formed in Washington State) when Bamonte began to research his thesis, sifting through a compilation of pokes and stabs, kicks and gunshots, accidents and acts of God. The bare facts, loosely assembled by chronology, were full of storytelling holes; the motives, and in some cases the culprits, were left out. The open mysteries alone could keep a researcher—or a cop—busy for a lifetime. But it was not Bamonte's intent to solve ancient crimes or discern human motivation beyond the obvious.

The life story of one county, in its raw form, came to him like this:

40 homicides (7 of them unsolved), 130 drownings, 87 fatal industrial accidents, 153 fatal auto accidents, 71 suicides. From this short stack of misery, Bamonte would seek to earn a master's degree in organizational leadership.

"A compelling idea," Professor Carey told his student. "But it must be something more than a basic history."

"Oh, it will be," Bamonte replied, trying to sound confident, although he doubted his ability to finish such an undertaking. Never a good student, forced to repeat his senior year in high school, Bamonte became interested in academics well into his adult life. And then he was insatiate. "You don't think this is a dumb idea or anything, do you?"

No, the professor assured him, it was not dumb. Odd, perhaps.

Rather than focus on a single pattern of misdeeds, Bamonte's approach was to examine history through each of the eleven sheriffs of the county—a life and crimes of the Pend Oreille as seen through the enforcers of legal conduct. History is usually written by the victors; in this case, it would be written by a grunt in a ceaseless war.

"Every crisis ends in resolution, good or bad," the professor said. "Those who learn from it move on to something higher. Those who don't are stuck. Tell us if they learned anything. Why did some sheriffs succeed and some fail?"

Bamonte promised coherence in the chronology. He would seek to pass on some wisdom from how the eleven sheriffs dealt with local government. For example, was there a pattern to first sheriff Ben Gardiner's fight with the county over a livery fee—the twelve hundred dollars a year it cost taxpayers to feed the department's horses—and a more recent complaint by a sheriff—who parked all the police vehicles until his budget controllers agreed to release more money for gas?

The thesis would begin with Gardiner, who was born in 1866 and never had a first name until "Ben" was bestowed on him later in life, and end with the eleventh and current sheriff—Tony Bamonte himself, a Democrat, serving his third term as chief lawman of Pend Oreille County. There was an inherent conflict in writing about himself, but Bamonte hoped that the last chapter of his thesis would serve as a demonstration of what the latest of the county sheriffs had learned from the others. It was also an unusual writing technique for an academic project: after pages of passive, third-person storytelling, the narrator would come alive in the last pages.

WHEN BETTY BAMONTE called her husband to bed, the student looked at the clock—well past midnight—and said he wasn't ready yet. She rolled over and tried to sleep. They lived on the third floor of an old brick building in the atrophied mining town of Metaline Falls, eight miles south of the Canadian border, forty miles north of Newport, eighty-seven miles from Spokane. Betty was small, attractive, with hair the color of polished oak. Easy to laugh and slow to anger, she was a calm counterweight to her impulsive husband. Tony adored her; she was the only person who came close to understanding him, he felt. But of late, their life together was full of tension. Tony blamed himself for most of it—his fits of despair, his lack of self-esteem, a job that demanded all his time and held him up as a target for the ills of Pend Oreille County. He challenged every bully, whether it was a tavern tough or an arrogant bureaucracy, and took it personally when he lost. The county newspaper was constantly attacking him for trying to shake up the old ways. He saw the master's degree as an escape from those pressures, a challenge of bringing order to musty chaos, without the usual obstructions.

"Just a few more minutes," he called out, but Betty was asleep, and he was elsewhere, thinking the curse of historians: what might have been. Working on a thesis was certainly easier than working out a lifetime of personal problems.

"As I studied each sheriff," he wrote, "I discovered their paths of anguish."

The night shrinking, he tried to add another few paragraphs. The words came slowly, sometimes stopped at the gate by his own doubt. Writing was so hard. Would the other students laugh at him, the wilderness cop with the backwoods history? Was he really up to a project of this size? Did he have anything to say? And if he flunked, then what? A retreat back to the old self-paralysis of ten years ago?

He returned to the introduction, thinking about what tied together the ghosts he was pursuing. He wrote: "The history of mankind through the world has been filled with tragedy and violence."

A cop's view of the world, no doubt. Nothing about triumphs over ignorance, or scientific breakthroughs that freed generations from disease and early death. By professional background and personal experience, Bamonte took a glum view of things. His life, several years into middle age, had been soaked in hard times, much of it his own doing. As he tried to sketch the first words of his thesis, what came forth were the faces of victims. He loved losers, underdogs. From 1911 to the present, they changed very little; the old stories were not much different than the life he lived every day among the people of the Pend Oreille. The victims had a timeless, even generic quality. The faces had bruises and tears; they dripped blood and they hid themselves in shame. Bamonte had been to their homes, riverfront A-frames without electricity or phone lines. He had been a messenger, delivering news of a dead child found snagged to a log in the river. He had been called out of bed in the middle of the night by a shrieking voice over the phone, begging the sheriff to come save a life; and when he arrived at a cabin where wood stove smoke blended with the smell of pot and beer, the caller's face was puffy and red and she said it was too late—the abusive husband, the bully, was gone.

Early on in the research, Bamonte realized that he could not detach himself from this history he intended to write. He realized this while following the travails of a particular country doctor in old clippings of the Newport *Miner*—a weekly, the only newspaper in the county. When he came to a story about the doctor's untimely death, he grieved, feeling as if he had known the man himself.

Bamonte went to bed. In a few hours, the morning light would slip through the fortress of mountains around Metaline Falls, and it would be time to drive the forty miles south to Newport, headquarters of the sheriff's department. Bamonte pulled the covers up to his neck, snuggled with Betty, but did not sleep. Fresh ideas excited him. Insight into his character was an even more powerful stimulant. As

Bamonte saw it—though he certainly didn't mention this to Professor Carey—the master's degree was also a chance to save himself from his own worst instincts. By studying the private anguish of the ten men who preceded him, he hoped to find some hints on how to hold himself together; so the last chapter of the thesis would indeed be built upon the mistakes of the previous ten. History as shrink.

What troubled him most, in the final year of the 1980s, were his self-doubts. Though he was a handsome man, wiry, with long legs and blue eyes that lit his face, he did not swagger with the confidence of those who know they are good-looking. He walked as if on ice. Though he was a generous man, using his precious free time to help somebody fix a septic tank or fight a bureaucratic edict in a county where the federal government owned most of the land, he was always afraid that he was being used or set up. Though he was a smart man, able to juggle three thoughts at once, to make leaps of logic that impressed his prosecutors and his professors, he could not shake the recurring image he had of himself as a rube, the kid in hand-me-down clothes who flunked his senior year in high school.

HE WAS a tiny boy when his mother left him and moved to Hawaii with a musician and his father was sent to jail. He remembered the strange men who used to come to the house in Wallace, Idaho, when Louis Bamonte was off working in the mines. Tony was born in Wallace in 1942—in the same hospital where a miner's wife gave birth to Lana Turner. He lived his first years in a town with two dozen whorehouses, set in a valley where more silver was yanked from the ground than in any other place on earth. The skies were ever dark with factory smoke, and the streets were thick with coal dust. Only when the wind was blowing could the top of a six-hundred-foot smelter smokestack be seen. They called the Coeur d'Alene River drainage on the western side of the Bitterroots the Silver Valley, but its dominant color was a gray that covered faces and streets and houses and trees. In the afternoons, Lucille Bamonte baked cakes, and when Tony asked for bites, she shooed him away. The goodies were not for Tony and his brother and sister but for the men who came to visit their mother. A honey blonde with blue eyes, Lucille was considered by some men to be the prettiest woman in the panhandle of northern Idaho. In a valley where smelter toxins killed all the nearby forests and poisoned the river, and a haze of poison air hung over the drafty company shacks, a beauty such as Lucille Bamonte stood out like a rose in pavement. Deep inside the mine shafts, air vents often failed or supports crumbled. Because death was common, Silver Valley miners' jobs were sometimes more like combat than earning a living.

Tony saw strangers come through the small house in the dirty mining town, eat his mother's cakes, and then go off into a bedroom. When he was six, after the family moved sixty miles west to Spokane, his father came home early on Christmas Eve and caught his mother with a musician, a man who was not coarse or crude like the filthy miners. Tony was a skinny string of a boy—no more than forty pounds. Frightened by his father's rage, he scrambled under a bed and watched him savagely beat the man.

The police arrived and found the musician unconscious. One of the officers knelt down next to the bed, coaxed the scared little boy out from under it, and hugged him. Tony never forgot the two giants in blue with their guns and badges, angels in uniform. Both parents were taken to jail. His father was booked for felony assault; his mother was held on vagrancy charges, the catch-all crime of the Spokane Police Department. The three children spent Christmas morning with the two policemen.

Louis Bamonte had come to America from Italy and was alone in New York at an early age after both of his parents died. One of six children, he had spent most of his childhood homeless in the Bronx. Nicknamed "Bull," the dark-haired Bamonte could swing an axe or wield a mining pick with ferocity. He also read poetry aloud, practiced ballroom dancing, and insisted that his children go to Catholic mass. On Sundays, even when he lived in a tent near a logging camp, he put on a suit and read or composed verse. He was not a heavy drinker, like so many of the miners and timber beasts of the inland Northwest, but he had a temper. If the police had not come on Christmas Eve, Bull Bamonte would have killed the man he found with his wife.

Shortly after the Christmas fight, Lucille Bamonte fled to Hawaii with her lover. Tony did not see his mother for two years. He hated her for what she had done, breaking the family up, treating the children like they didn't matter, forcing his father to jail. For a while, he lived with his maternal grandfather, but then he died. With the three closest people in his life gone—his father in jail, his mother in the Pacific, his grandfather dead—the boy retreated into his inner self, trying to escape the closed and frightened world where adults beat each other up and were always leaving each other. Every time somebody turned to exit, he thought, could be the last.

Once out of jail, Bull Bamonte took the kids to a logging camp in the northern part of Pend Oreille County, one of the last truly wild areas in the American West. Red cedar, Douglas fir, tamarack, and ponderosa pine all grew to great heights in the Selkirk Mountains. The elevation was high enough to knock down the clouds and squeeze out sufficient rainfall, so the forest was more like that of the western Cascades than the drier pine woods of eastern Washington.

Tony slept on a straw mat on the floor of a tent. At night he listened to the labored breathing of his father as he coughed up the accumulated residue from years in the Silver Valley. But as long as the boy could hear his father's chest heaving in and out, he was happy —it meant that Bull was alive. Most mornings, he would not let his father go off to work without him; while he should have been in school Tony insisted on following Bull to the logging camps in the woods. The willowy kid became the shadow of Bull, the tree-cutting machine, a man who worked twelve and fourteen hours a day, logging and skinning small cedars in the mountains around Metaline Falls. Bull's dream was to save enough money to buy his own small mine, and then he hoped to strike it rich in this land where the rivers carried gold nuggets downstream, and the rock walls glistened with galena.

After several months in the tent, the family moved into a one-room cabin, two hundred square feet, with three windows. Tony slept on an old service cot with "United States Army" stamped on the side. There was no running water or electricity inside the cabin, but it sat beside a creek that was full of trout and attracted deer. Food was never any farther than the wild game outside the cabin door; his father killed a deer every six weeks or so. But Tony grew to hate the taste of venison. Even now, he cannot go near deer meat without thinking of the time spent inside the one-room cabin. In the depths of winter, they moved into an abandoned dance hall, the Red Rooster, a few miles north of Metaline Falls. The old beer hall, which had roared with timber workers and their women during Prohibition, had been silent for a number of years. The stench of alcohol remained, and the walls were pockmarked from the shrapnel of bar fights. But for a seven-year-old boy, it was a mansion, an indoor frontier. The Bamontes set up their home on the hardwood dance floor and cooked meals on the giant wood stove. One of Tony's jobs was to make sure the fire never went out.

When he was enrolled in first grade, the separation from his father so frightened him that he seldom made it through a full day without a crying tantrum: he was sure his father would be gone for good when he came home from school. Tony begged his father to let him skip school and follow him to work, and Bull relented, allowing the boy to tag along on days when the weather wasn't too harsh. Tony would sit on a stump and watch Bull split cedar logs into fence posts; he was never happier. But the relationship was mostly a one-way affair. Growing up, Tony was never told by the man he idolized that he loved him. More often, Bull expressed his feelings with a razor strap on Tony's bare ass. Still, the beatings left no ill feelings with Tony; he always thought he had it coming.

Two years after the Christmas Eve fight, Lucille Bamonte returned from Hawaii and attempted to gain custody of her children. Tony's first encounter with the law in Pend Oreille County came when a sheriff's deputy served a warrant on Bull Bamonte at the Red Rooster. Again, he looked up at a tall man in uniform with a badge and a pistol strapped to his leg, an intermediary between a man and a woman who had come to hate each other. For a long time, the two parents had scrapped over who would get the kids; once, the struggle was physical, the two parents literally tugging at Tony, each holding an arm. In the end, Bull Bamonte was given the kids, and Lucille went off with her latest husband—one of eight men she married in her lifetime.

After five years in the Red Rooster, the family moved out of the dance hall to Osburn, Idaho—another ravaged mining town in the Silver Valley, near Wallace. Although doctors had told Bull to keep out of the mines if he wanted to stay alive, he couldn't curb the silver bug. All he needed was one break, he kept telling Tony. But the smelter-fouled valley proved to be no luckier for the Bamontes this time than it had been seven years earlier, and so they moved back to Pend Oreille County to start anew. In the boom-and-bust nature of hard-rock mining, ventures fail and go bankrupt more often than they produce riches. But something is always popping up to keep the allure of a big hit alive. It is somewhat like fishing, in that a single nibble after a day-long skunking is enough to make the angler want to return. In the Pend Oreille, Bull became a partner in an old silver and gold mine, and he sunk every free dollar—the stake from years of peeling cedar poles and scraping silver in Idaho—into it. The family moved into another small cabin, right next to the mining portal into Mount Linton. They used the mine's dark, cold shaft as a refrigerator. Their latrine was an earthen ditch. At the same time, Bull ran a small sawmill, trying to make enough money to keep his family alive during the speculative months of the mine. Never had Tony felt so impoverished or seen his father work so hard.

The boy's clothes were hand-me-downs which he picked up from a local house of charity. Sometimes, he showed up at school in a sweater or pair of pants that another boy recognized. "Hey, that's the shirt my mom threw away!" a schoolboy shouted at Tony in seventh grade. The other kids laughed and pointed at the skinny son of the Italian miner. Occasionally, he answered the taunts with fists, but even after a brawling triumph he went home ashamed. He had no use for school anyway. In his view, the way to get anywhere in life was to work hard outdoors. It was a simple equation: the more cedar you split, or the more silver you blasted from beneath the skin of the earth, the better off you were. But Bull insisted that Tony stay in school; he did not want this life of bone-crunching servitude for his boy. As if to prove his point, the price of silver collapsed, and the machinery in the Bamonte mine broke down during a particularly harsh cold spell, just as Bull and his partners had reached a rich vein deep inside the core of the mountain.

Isolated from other kids throughout his school years, Tony developed the attitude of an outsider. The slang used by high-schoolers was not his language. As a teenager, he began working with his father, the shadow now helping the aging machine split logs or burrow into Mount Linton. After years of watching Bull from his perch on a stump, Tony knew the routine. The work kept him out of school, and he fell so far behind that the teachers flunked him his senior year. To every other humiliation of growing up was added this final slight: he stayed behind, the flunkee, while the other boys went off to join the army or go to college or take a union job at the mill.

When he finally graduated from the high school in Metaline Falls, Tony was ready to see the world outside of Pend Oreille County. His hands were dark, callused, and cut up; but he had all his fingers and all his toes, a rarity for anyone who had worked the woods. Only two jobs are considered more hazardous than logging: crop dusting and professional football. He took a year-long job in the mines, breaking rock ("beating grizzly," they called it), drilling with a diamond bit, driving diesel trucks underground, and then enlisted in the army.

Leaving home, he looked for some sign of love from Bull, hoping his father would at least drive him to the airport before the shadow left behind the world of straw mattresses and earthen latrines and home in the Red Rooster. But the old man, who had come to the Northwest in 1932, chasing water and opportunity, was exhausted, his body and spirit broken. He died a few years after Tony left the Pend Oreille, a victim of cellulitis, a cancer caused by exposure to mining dust. Tony scattered his ashes inside the mine that had helped to kill him, the tunnel into Mount Linton.

BAMONTE RETURNED to the Pend Oreille in 1975, picking up where his father left off, working in the woods, a father himself with his own son, trying to earn a living from the forest. During his fourteen-year absence, he had sealed off many of the memories of childhood; a tour in Vietnam, followed by eight years as a Spokane policeman, provided Bamonte with fresh horrors to replace the pain of his youth. He protected those images of the dance-hall home and schoolmates laughing at his hand-me-downs and the parade of men who came to sleep with his mother.

It wasn't until the late 1980s, when he started work on his master's thesis, that he began to replay some of the incidents witnessed by the little boy who was always afraid of being left alone. By then, he had a cushion: the visitor to the early years was a graduate student, deliberately detached; he tried to treat his own memories like history. As he drove through the river valleys or along deep-rutted roads in the Selkirks, he saw empty homesteads. The wind carried laughter, tears, and table talk from the abandoned sheds, their roofs caved in after years of heavy snow. Sometimes, he heard the voices of his own family. More often, they were strangers'.

Leafing through the old files of the sheriff's department, the student found a story about a shoot-out in 1929: Black Jack Rowden, holed up in a log home, had died in a spray of rifle fire. Bamonte recognized the location as a cabin where he had picked bullets from the wood as a kid, and that sprang open a cage of memories about playing and waiting for his father to return, his fears mounting with each minute closer to dusk.

Reading about another sheriff brought to mind the stern-faced man with glasses and a huge forehead who had served his father with court papers over child custody. The boy who had looked up at the lawman outside the Red Rooster, wondering if the sheriff was coming to take his father away as the other uniformed man had done in Spokane, was replaced now by a forty-six-year-old graduate student whose job included serving similar papers on divorced parents.

Back further, back in the Depression and the days of Sheriff Elmer Black, the police reports often spoke of immigrants and transients who slept in the woods near the road. They were usually dismissed with a pejorative swipe—the "unwashed itinerants," "Okies," or "failed sod-busters." Those who had jobs and property, and the sheriffs who protected them, were on one side. Those without were on the other. Tony wondered how his predecessors in law enforcement would have viewed his father, the Italian who grew up homeless in the Bronx, joined the Marines at age sixteen, kicked around the country during the 1920s, and finally landed in the forests of the inland Northwest in 1932.

Also in the archives was a case where a man had been shot over butter. The student knew all about hunger, but this was almost beyond belief. The deputies' logs spoke of faceless men who were said to be too hungry to obey the law—so desperate that they stole food from the farmers of the Pend Oreille.

Bamonte read further: George Conniff, the Newport night marshal, was killed after he came upon a pair of gunmen who were robbing the creamery. The victim was a lawman, like Bamonte. The killers were never found. Beyond that, the information was sketchy. Bamonte asked around town. Whatever outrage the killing had generated was long gone. A few old-timers remembered Marshal Conniff. Hell of a man, they said; shot by butter thieves. The killers got away with it. Afterwards, the Conniff family fell apart. Moved away from Newport, God knows where.

The student's chapter on Sheriff Black's tenure, which included the Conniff killing, was only one small section of a thesis that would run well over five hundred pages when completed. Initially, Bamonte did not plan to spend much time on the marshal's murder; he didn't really know what to make of it. At one time he was going to skip it, or mention it only in passing. But then he found the file on the case, buried in a tomb of county records. A half-century of inactivity had turned the papers yellow and thin. He could barely read some of the lettering, handwritten in pencil or typed. There were no leads, and Black's notations indicated a particular frustration with the case.

Maybe, Bamonte thought, Black was still around somewhere. He might make a good interview, providing answers on the Conniff case, firsthand information on Depression-era law enforcement, as well as some fresh insight into the times of Bull Bamonte. Checking the records, he discovered that Sheriff Black had served from 1934 to 1942. And then, the files showed, he was called back as an informal consultant in 1955. Two decades after the killing of Marshal Conniff, some new information had surfaced in the case, the files indicated.

Black had been the original investigator of the marshal's killing.

He was the plodding sheriff who initiated his probe by lugging around a pair of pawned pants and a greased door. He had gone twenty years without a decent idea of who had killed George Conniff. Then, in the summer of 1955, the investigation was reopened, and Black was summoned to help with what looked like a major breakthrough in a long-standing mystery. What he learned that year was that the Spokane Police Department had apparently solved the case back in 1935 but had kept the killer's identity under wraps. Shortly after Black heard the new information, he fell forty-five feet to his death from the bridge that spanned the Pend Oreille River east of Newport. A child found his body near shore, on the Idaho side of the river. He died of a skull fracture. There was no follow-up investigation of Elmer Black's death. The sheriff of neighboring Bonner County, in Idaho, theorized that the old lawman had become dizzy and lost his balance.

10.

The Sheriff

If Elmer Black could fall off a bridge that he had crossed hundreds of times, then the Pend Oreille River could flow uphill. What seemed obvious to Bamonte, reading about this fatal accident more than three decades after it occurred, was that gravity was not the sole culprit. Bamonte knew the interstate bridge like a barge pilot knew the side currents of the Mississippi. Just about every kid who grew up in northeastern Washington considered the span over the wide Pend Oreille part of his private playground. From the bridge, a boy could toss a twig that might end up in the Pacific Ocean, or watch ospreys snag trout and carry them back to their big stick nests atop pilings. The bridge's guard rails were standard federal building code—thirty-six inches high. At the very minimum, it would require a deliberate effort, or a very big slip, to get up and over the rail enough to fall. Bamonte wondered if Black's death was a suicide. If so, then the seventy-one-year-old retired sheriff left nothing for the instant archaeologists: no note, no signs of lingering despondency; he was not terminally ill. And what a way to go—a long dive into a concrete base, smashing his skull.

Bamonte suspected that somebody had pushed Black. His death, coming after he had learned dramatic new information about the 1935 killing of Marshal Conniff, was a hard coincidence to swallow. It cried out for further investigation. But there was none. The book on Black was closed a few days after his death in 1955.

To the student in Bamonte, this was a telling point: a sleepy sheriff's office had accepted one person's theory of a suspicious death. Dulled by bureaucratic inertia, no one had checked the guard rails for fingerprints or signs of struggle, or conducted tests to see if Black could have fallen at the angle that left his body below the bridge. If the sheriff of Bonner County thought Black had gotten dizzy and fallen, that was good enough for the sheriff on the Washington side of the river. Besides, everybody knew Elmer Black was slow in his way, sort of accident prone, and the death seemed to match his personality.

The sheriff in Bamonte wanted to start a new investigation—thirty-four years after Black's death—to see what was behind the fall. When he mentioned this to a few associates, word got around town that Bamonte was getting ready to go off on another one of his impossible expeditions. There was the usual round of snide remarks and rolled eyes: the stubborn son-of-a-buck was at it again. Elmer Black? And what about all the unsolved burglaries? The missing animals? The kids spraying rap slogans on the train underpass? The people of the Pend Oreille weren't paying their sheriff to chase ancient history.

THE INEPT HANDLING of Black's fall was typical of what Bamonte had run into ever since he came back to the Pend Oreille. As a boy, he knew little outside his father's harsh world: cut trees; dig inside the mines; keep the roof from leaking and venison on the table. Suffering was not questioned; pain was part of the landscape. As a man, he was not so passive. He had been exposed to the highest level of American intrigue in the dawning war in Vietnam. While serving as a military guard in 1962, he heard Henry Cabot Lodge, the United States ambassador to South Vietnam, tell President Ngo Dinh Diem that everything was fine one hour before Diem would fall in a coup supported by Washington. Later, as a helicopter door-gunner, Bamonte was ordered to fire at whatever human movement he saw on the ground below—children, women, and combatants alike. Once, his pilot chased a fleeing family carrying all their possessions in an old wooden cart. As the chopper lowered down atop them, the family members fell to their knees, crying for mercy; the pilot flew away laughing. Bamonte felt betrayed and confused by his country's mission in Vietnam. In 1966 he joined the police department in Spokane and saw the foolish crimes and the patterns of petty fraud that form the education of a cop. He stood on the outer edges of a good-ol'-boy system among Spokane police, where a case of whiskey at Christmas could keep an officer loyal to a duplicitous merchant. He had shunned the after-hours parties to attend night classes at college. After eight years of off-and-on study, the boy who flunked his senior year in high school ended up with a bachelor of arts degree in sociology from Whitworth College.

Back in the Pend Oreille in the 1970s, Bamonte did not expect to find his home frozen in time. Pend Oreille County, one of the poorest per capita in America, is still an area where much business is done by bartering. A family might trade two cords of wood and a case of canned huckleberries for a used television and a case of beer. A barterers' fair, held once a week along the banks of the river, is the principal shopping exchange for many. A few tourist dollars pass through the county during the summer, but the only steady source of money comes from timber and mining. Still, there are few sites in more gold-plated counties to match a dawn in the Selkirks, when the mountains shake the clouds from the hair of the forest.

Bamonte came back to the Pend Oreille to construct log homes and run a small mill that produced cedar shakes. After eight years riding a motorcycle for the Spokane Police Department, law enforcement was behind him—or so he thought. He built more than a dozen log homes, selecting and cutting the trees himself, skinning the wood and notching pieces together. A Bamonte log home was no wooden hovel but a grand house, usually three bedrooms or more, with skylights and brick fireplace and vaulted ceilings of clean-smelling cedar. His father could have lived his last years in regal comfort had he been around to experience the creations of his son.

Trying to keep a family alive on the speculative schemes of an elegant-log-home builder was a continuous fight. The work was long and it did not pay well. Most of the land in the county is owned by the federal government and administered by the Forest Service. Throughout the 1970s, as the service stepped up its program of selling trees from national forests to the highest bidder, great swaths of the Pend Oreille's pine, cedar, larch, and Douglas fir were mowed down by large timber companies. When all the trees in a given area were cut, and roads carved into the hillsides, the slash, or woody debris, left on the ground was burned. The idea, promoted by the timber industry, was to get rid of all the excess vegetation so that when the land was replanted, only a few stands of commercial trees would grow back, without competition from the random plantings of nature. In late summer, smoke from the government-sponsored fires drifted down the Pend Oreille valley and stung the eyes. The haze lingered for weeks, fouling what is usually some of the cleanest air in the country.

Bamonte was disgusted by the clear-cuts and slash-burning and bidding among buddies. The entire forest did not have to be leveled and burned in order to bring wood to mills, he told the rangers in the Kaniksu and Colville national forests. Why not leave every other tree standing, protecting the scenery and habitat for elk, bears, caribou, and the tiny creatures who work the floor of the forest? He was told clear-cuts and deliberate fires were government policy, and one little gyppo logger was not going to change things. Bamonte began showing up at the auctions, the lone critic, submitting his bids for small parcels; and when all the buying and selling was done, he would be left with nothing but salvage. For a price, he would be allowed to take whatever the big timber companies left on the ground, the unwanted scrub wood. The Forest Service was simply not set up to serve one-man operations. If Bamonte could lay waste to an entire mountainside, as the bigger companies, like Boise Cascade or Louisiana-Pacific, were doing, then the government might be able to accommodate him.

"A good logger doesn't want to clear-cut," Bamonte told the Forest Service land managers. "A good logger respects the forest." The industry men would look at each other, holding their smirks: who's the Boy Scout?

He wrote letters to federal bureaucrats in Washington, politicians, the newspapers. He made noise at every auction. He was a pain in the ass. He tried to get the United States attorney in his district to investigate possible collusion and antitrust violations. After a while, Bamonte's noisemaking began to pay off, and he started to get more than salvage. It looked as if he might be able to make a decent living. His crowning achievement during this brief spate of cooperation was a masterwork of log construction, a six-thousand-square-foot home, forty feet high, with an indoor swimming pool. He selected and peeled every one of the logs that went into the home. But the project nearly broke him, physically and financially. He slipped further behind; like his father, he found his only solution was to work harder, more furiously—to become a machine.

After three years of trying to make a go at it, worn down by the fights with the Forest Service and wresting logs from the Selkirks, Bamonte closed his timber operation. The woods had not brought him any riches, but he made his mark nonetheless: three top Forest Service officials were transferred out of the Pend Oreille, and the service ended noncompetitive bidding in the inland Northwest. In meadows shaded by aspen groves and lanky pines are Bamonte log homes, designed to hold their own against the ages. The builder, unable to afford any of his creations, moved into a rental unit.

Even though he could make more money if he went back on the Spokane police force, Bamonte decided to stay in the Pend Oreille. From his father he had inherited a tenacity to cling to the land, no matter how much heartbreak or backache might come from the attachment. He took a job with the county sheriff's department as a deputy, earning thirteen thousand dollars a year. In 1978, he ran for sheriff, a Democrat trying to unseat the Republican, William "Pete" Giles, who'd been the law in Pend Oreille County off and on since the early 1950s. Bamonte campaigned on a plan to bring some of the technology and skill of late-twentieth-century crime fighting to the wilderness of northeastern Washington. The department had no written policies on how to make an arrest, conduct an investigation, file an accident report, follow up on a crime, store stolen property. It was a black hole, run by a man his own deputies characterized as an incompetent antique. "To him, the three biggest crimes are cattle rustling, safecracking, and cohabitation," one of Giles's deputies said during the election.

Bamonte was a youthful thirty-six—nearly half Giles's age—and he promised to bring a fresh approach to the Pend Oreille. The voters approved; Bamonte whipped the Republican in the 1978 sheriff's race.

He inherited a department in chaos—one part Mayberry, one part backwoods dictatorship. Work-release prisoners were given keys to the jail and put in the same cells as fresh felons. There was no record system for case files, and several major investigations were stalled or fell apart completely because files were lost or could not be found. Most police departments hold auctions several times a year to sell excess or unclaimed property. Bamonte discovered that the last time the Pend Oreille County sheriff's office had offered such a sale was in 1914. He immediately announced plans for annual auctions. But during his first month in office, when Bamonte conducted an inventory of the property room—a search for all the guns, stereos, engines, tools, and money confiscated by officers during the last half-century —he discovered there was nothing to sell. The property room was empty. The spoils of police work in the Pend Oreille, some of the older deputies explained to their new sheriff, have always belonged to the officers themselves. The idea that a cop could skim off whatever excess he picked up from criminals was not unique to policemen in Newport. Bamonte had run into this attitude before, during his years in Spokane. The new sheriff laid down a new law: the property room belonged to the public.

Within a month of taking office, Bamonte drew up a set of written guidelines, covering everything from officers' ethics to investigative techniques. Still, change came slowly to the deputies of the Selkirks. Early on in Bamonte's first term, a woman's body was found inside a car; she had been shot. Homicides are rare in Pend Oreille County—a murder every two years or so. The undersheriff who was sent to investigate removed the body and towed the car away before thoroughly checking the crime scene. Bamonte demoted him. A dispatcher who spent her night shift catching up on her sleep was suspended. (During a civil service hearing on the suspension, she claimed her eyes were prone to "momentarily shutting" which gave the appearance of sleep.) Officers who would not go along with Bamonte's new policies were fired or threatened with demotion. They said Bamonte was tyrannical, shaking things up too fast, an upstart headed for trouble.

"If I get a deputy who is not honest or not doing the job, I get rid of him," Bamonte said at the time, explaining his policy to the Newport *Miner*, which was fed a steady diet of leaks by disgruntled officers. For a while, there was a different story about turmoil at the sheriff's office every week, with unflattering pictures of Bamonte, his eyes half-closed or looking away in a scowl, under headlines that labeled him "embattled." Even when he was vindicated in court or during public hearings, the stories castigated him. Thus, when Bamonte won an early triumph in a civil suit brought by a former deputy, the article in the *Miner* was headlined BAMONTE AVERTS CONTEMPT CHARGE, and the lead sentence ran, "A legal technicality foiled a temporary restraining order and possible contempt charge against Pend Oreille County Sheriff Anthony Bamonte Tuesday." Tony's wife, Betty, would clip the worst of the stories out before presenting her husband with the paper in the morning, but the Swiss cheese only told him it was going to be another bad day, full of whispers.

One undersheriff got his revenge by snapping a picture of a marijuana plant in Bamonte's office, then giving it to the *Miner*, which ran the photo on its front page. The implication was that the young sheriff was growing six-foot marijuana plants in his office. In a county where pot has been the major cash crop, grown in the pleats of land high in the roadless Selkirks, the charge was taken seriously by some, though Bamonte simply was using the pot plant as a training tool for his officers and for Forest Service employees who roamed the backwoods. The deputy who took the picture was fired.

And it was not just among sheriff's deputies that the old ways were challenged by Bamonte. To him a politician, even one who controlled his budget, was just another citizen. So when Bamonte caught a key county commissioner speeding one night, he issued a citation and also wrote him up for driving without a vehicle license. The commissioner was outraged. He got his revenge when it came time to approve Bamonte's staff budget. All money for the sheriff's office—twelve full-time employees—was held up. With no funds to operate, Bamonte declared his department broke and shut it down. All patrol cars were parked. For one week in late summer, there was no official law enforcement in northeast Washington. Stories about the dispute ran in newspapers all over the country. The commissioners blinked first, approving $2,000 for gas money, so that there was at least fuel for the patrol cars to respond to emergencies. They eventually passed a skeletal budget, about $350,000—far below what Bamonte said he needed to bring the sheriff's department out of the dark ages.

Sheriff Bamonte then committed an unpardonable offense: he went to bat for a convicted felon, a man who had spent seven years in the penitentiary after a jury in Pend Oreille found him guilty of shooting a sheriff's deputy (a nonfatal wound). Bamonte discovered evidence that the wrong man had been locked up, the victim of police zealotry and incompetence. It was his duty as sheriff to admit that a mistake had been made by his office and to try to get the man his freedom. His deputies could not believe what their sheriff was doing; even if he was right, he was taking the position of the Other Side. A cop simply did not break ranks with other cops. When the new evidence uncovered by Bamonte was brought to court, the man, Jackson C. Marshall, was freed. Bamonte was considered a traitor.

Near the end of Bamonte's first term, seven former employees ran against him. The *Miner* also campaigned to oust the young sheriff. His critics said he was too righteous for his own good, too hard on his deputies. By most indications, Bamonte *was* difficult to work for during his first term: he lacked diplomacy and tact; he was stubborn; at times he seemed wired with the pulse of a two-year-old on a sugar high. But he got results. FBI statistics showed a drop in all major crime categories in the second half of his first term. When a day worker from a hay ranch was stomped in the Usk Saloon, and nine witnesses watched him bleed to death on the sidewalk outside the tavern, the prevailing attitude in the timber village north of Newport was to let it die. Just a bar fight and a dead stranger—Who cares? Bamonte leaned on each of the nine witnesses until he found one who said he was sober enough to remember what happened. Manslaughter charges were filed and a conviction obtained.

Bamonte won the 1982 primary election by seventy-six votes, from nineteen hundred cast. Two months later, he beat the former deputy who had tried to frame him with the pot plant. He was in for another four years.

His targets were more select in the 1980s.

Each human life was sacred, he told his deputies, no matter how awful a piece of scum someone might be. The law did not make distinctions for character, or uniform, or smell. This philosophy guided Bamonte when a convict was killed while fighting a forest fire in Pend Oreille County in 1986. Every summer, the state of Washington would take work-release inmates out into the woods to build trails or fight fires. A man named Cash Hopkins, who was finishing up a sentence for burglary, was working a burn in the Selkirks when a flaming tree came falling down on him. Hopkins was crushed by the hot pine. In announcing the death, the Forest Service said it was a simple accident: if Hopkins had run, he would not have been crushed. Bamonte investigated further and discovered that the fire had been started by the Forest Service—a slash burn to help the timber industry. Examining the government's manual for prescription burns, Bamonte found that the Forest Service had violated its own policies. They weren't supposed to start fires during high winds, or times of extreme temperature, or on steep slopes, or after a prolonged dry period, when the woods were tinder. And after starting the fire, the service initially let it burn unattended, and flames had jumped the boundary of the controlled burn. What's more, Bamonte produced two Forest Service rangers who said they'd been told by their superiors to keep quiet about the fire.

"If a civilian had started this fire I would have initiated charges of reckless burning against him, and because of the death, he could have been charged with manslaughter," Bamonte said. The sheriff could not charge the federal government, but he tried to interest the United States attorney's office in the case. After all, the Forest Service itself had initiated prosecution of campers or loggers whose negligence had led to fires. Was there a double standard: one for individuals, another for bureaucracies? The Spokane office of the Justice Department turned Bamonte down. Who is this guy? Trying to sue the government? Sticking up for a dead convict? Doesn't he have better things to do?

Thwarted at the local level, Bamonte sent his investigative report to the office of Edwin Meese. To Bamonte, it was very clear: the government was morally and legally accountable for the death of Cash Hopkins. The United States attorney had betrayed the public trust by not investigating the fire that killed the convict. "Justice was not served," the sheriff from the wilderness county in northeast Washington wrote to the highest law-enforcement officer in the land. He was surprised when Ronald Reagan's attorney general did not respond.

Most nights, Bamonte could not leave the problems of his county inside the sheriff's office. He brought them home, kicked them around at the dinner table, ran them through his head while lying awake, and then started the next day with the stale conflict as his first thought. All the criticism, the ridicule by the newspaper and the contempt from the older deputies, had started to wear him down. More and more, he would lapse into self-doubt, the little boy who used to sleep in the tent next to his father, scared of being abandoned. He wanted most what he could not control: the affections of his wife, the esteem of the community he served. Betty wanted to see less of the sheriff and more of the man, but he could not rest while things were unsettled. She urged him to laugh more, to relax, to unclutter himself. There was, after all, plenty to laugh about. The Rainbow Family, for example—seven thousand aging hippies, led by a man named Laughing Heart, who one year had chosen a wide, flowered meadow in the Selkirks as the site of their annual gathering. For five days, they ran naked through the fields, camped in tepees and lean-tos, a carnival of herbal confections and pubic hair. One of Bamonte's deputies donned a green mask and a cape—he called himself "the Green Ranger"—and galloped through the meadow on a black horse.

A year later, an encounter with the chairman of the school board, who'd been accused of neglecting his horse, turned into a kung fu–type showdown in Metaline Falls. The man returned the sheriff's accusation with a claim that Bamonte's dog had bitten his girlfriend on the hand. He then challenged Bamonte to a fight, telling him to leave his guns inside his house and meet him in the middle of the street. Citizens gathered to witness the duel between public officials. When Bamonte showed up, the challenger—an expert in the Korean martial art of Tang Soo Do—was in the midst of a choreographed tune-up, slicing the air with his hands and feet.

"Come on, hit me!" the chairman shouted at the sheriff. "Give me a reason!"

Bamonte stood and watched his neighbor for a few minutes; then his patience wore out. He grabbed the man by the head and squeezed. "You can't stand around and watch that kind of stuff all day," the sheriff said.

BAMONTE EASILY WON a third term as sheriff in 1986, beating a former deputy. By then, he had learned that his energies and the rhythms of the county, while they often seemed incompatible, actually had much in common. Many people in the Pend Oreille expected to fail, expected things not to turn out, expected bad times, incompetence, broken hearts. Most homeowners seemed to cut twice as much wood as they would ever need for the winter, afraid to trust even the certainty of the following spring. Bamonte was just as prone as his neighbors to feel run over by the world. His troubles at home were mounting. In darker moods, which were becoming more frequent, he felt like a failure as a human being. Always there was the shadow of Bull, whom he idolized, and his mother, whom he despised. The traits of his parents came out in flashes of anger, fits of stubbornness, days of feeling unloved.

He took refuge in the master's project. But in studying the private notes and public travails of former sheriffs, Bamonte began to think of himself as an heir to the problems those men had left at their gravesides. And so rather than lessening his load, the master's project added weight. In seeking help from the past, he picked up new responsibility. History was not a shrink, as he had hoped it would be, but a ghost.

In early 1989, Bamonte was asking questions that had not been asked for decades. Nobody seemed to care what Black had found out about the shooting of Marshal Conniff, or whether this new information had any connection with Black's fall from the bridge. Although Bamonte's queries produced nothing new on Black's death, he would not let up. He recorded each setback, a cop's way of internalizing frustration.

Alone with the past, Bamonte wrote:

"Murder is a great tragedy, but to have no one care is greater still."

11.

Metaline Falls

AT NIGHT in the muffled refuge of Metaline Falls, Bamonte sat up with the old police files, looking for what Elmer Black had seen. Outside, snowdrifts piled up three feet and more, curling over shrubs and woodsheds, blanketing the industrial dust that covered the town. The cement factory groused through an evening shift. There was very little truck traffic through the village this time of year; the sounds that drifted up to Bamonte's third-floor study came with the wind— an occasional barking dog, branches clawing against an icy window, a distant whine from the factory. Bamonte had written a brief history of the mining town, which once aspired to become the "Pittsburgh of the West" but now struggled to stay out of the register of ghost towns, its population 305 and sinking. Metaline Falls had come to life suddenly, born in the spontaneous rush to a freshly revealed mother lode, and now seemed to be aching through its final years. Young people left town as soon as they got out of high school, fleeing with the familiar lament of many small western towns, that there was no work, no future. The factory was laying off, cutting back purchases, letting things go to hell. A few routines—the Thursday-night cribbage game at the Western Star Tavern, fresh blackberry pies at the Hangout Cafe—held the community together.

Bamonte knew all the swindling and whoring stories from the glory days of mining, when gold nuggets were scraped out of Sullivan Creek and the town mogul hired a team of prostitutes to recycle back to him the wages he paid his miners. On this winter night, as ice formed at the edges of the Pend Oreille River, Bamonte was looking for other voices and other stories. Elmer Black had died just after hearing from Charley Sonnabend, the retired Spokane detective who had conducted the initial investigation of the Conniff killing. Now, Bamonte found something about Sonnabend on a typewritten report, the paper faded to the color of beaver teeth. During an earlier sweep of county records, Bamonte had passed over this report; tonight, it revealed itself as if the type were throbbing neon. Not long after the Conniff case went dormant in 1935, Sonnabend left police work and returned to his first love, carpentry. He framed houses throughout Spokane, built with pine beams, sheathed in cedar. In the mid-1950s, Sonnabend—who carried nearly 300 pounds on a six-foot frame—had a massive heart attack. Lying on his back in a hospital room, Sonnabend thought he was going to die. He summoned to his bedside the United States marshal in Spokane, Darrell Holmes, a former Pend Oreille County sheriff. Sonnabend told the marshal he did not want to die without first revealing something that had happened during his last years as detective. The federal marshal called Pend Oreille authorities, who sent the retired Elmer Black and a prosecutor down to Spokane to hear the deathbed tale of Charley Sonnabend.

On a late-winter day in 1955, near dusk, Sonnabend told the story he had kept to himself for twenty years. The carpenter talked for two hours. A summary of his revelations was contained in the memo that Bamonte found in the files. The top of the page read:

STATEMENT OF CHARLES SONNABEND

March 3, 1955
Time: 4:00 p.m.
Subject: Murder of George Conniff, Newport Marshal

When Bamonte read the next paragraphs, even with their misspelled names, spelling inconsistencies, and grammatical roadblocks, his heart raced. Here is what he saw:

Mr. Sonnobend gave this statement as to what he knew of the Conniff Murder. During that time which was back in the fall of 1935 there was a lot of creamery robbing going on. Mixed up in this was a fellow who was sent to the Federal Pen for interstate motor vehicle theft and after three weeks of questioning this suspect Acie Logan, he broke and admitted his part of the creamery robberys. He also put the finger on one of the City Detective's as Clyde Roston who owned a ranch a short distance from Spokane. According to Logan there were several men connected to this ring of robbers but the stolen butter that was taken in these robberys was taken to the Roston Ranch and later disposed of through the Mothers Ketchen located on River side Street in Spokane. Mr. Sonnobend does not recollect just what the mans name was who was operating the cafe at the time. Logan also admitted to breaking into a box car and robbing it of shoes which was taken to the Roston ranch for later disposal. Logan also admitted robbing a wholesale house in Spokane of Ciggeretts, Cigars and Tobbaco which was disposed of through Mothers Ketchen.

The night of the Conniff Murder the Spokane Police constructed a blockade at the north city limits and it was conducted by two rookie officers who told Sgt. Mangrin of the Spokane Police Department that they stopped a car which was boiling and hot and appeared as though it had been driven very hard and driving this car was Detective Roston. He and another person who we at this time don't know.

Roston was a very close friend of Acie Logan. Logan was the only man in the gang who could go direct to the Roston range. The two Officers at the blockade are not known at this time. Sgt. Mangrin retired from the police department in 1939. Mangrin knows all about this Murder and the affiliations of Roston and Logan. Roston is supposedly the ring leader.

Bamonte sat upright, rubbed his eyes. He stood and paced the length of the room, talking to himself. Here was a possible answer —and a half-dozen questions—about a killing that had gone unsolved for fifty-four years. It all seemed so antique: a gang peddling black-market butter and stolen shoes, run out of a place called "Mothers Ketchen," masterminded by a Spokane police detective. Who was this "Sgt. Mangrin"? And who was this "Roston"? The last name was vaguely familiar, a snippet of sound graffiti from the Stone Fortress.

Bamonte felt an affinity with Marshal Conniff, like himself a log-cabin builder, a father, struggling to stay alive in the Pend Oreille. He thought of the marshal facedown in a puddle of blood in an alley next to the Newport Creamery. The building was still around, used now by the Fraternal Order of Eagles. Could it be he was killed by a police detective? Nobody would believe such a thing.

The Sonnabend memo contained a few more telling details. The carpenter told of taking two guns off Logan and his partners when he arrested them in the World Hotel. One of the guns in Logan's possession had been previously signed out of the Spokane police property room by Detective Roston. The whereabouts of the pistols was addressed in the last line of the 1955 Pend Oreille sheriff's memo: "The guns mention we are unable to find any trace of them any where."

Bamonte wondered why Roston had never been arrested. "Go after him!" he said to himself. By Sonnabend's account, they had a strong case against the detective: a confession from Logan implicating Roston as his partner; a gun that was traced to the city detective; and the roadblock—two officers who stopped a car driven by Roston about one hour after the killing. A fistful of leads; and yet Bamonte could find no evidence that this Roston had ever been questioned, let alone brought to trial. The files indicated that Logan had gone off to jail on his interstate-theft plea bargain—stealing shoes from a boxcar. Roston had gone . . . where? Was this behind Elmer Black's forty-five foot drop from the interstate bridge? Somebody ought to know. But everyone who had been at the meeting on March 3, 1955, was now dead—Charley Sonnabend, Elmer Black, Darrell Holmes, and the Pend Oreille prosecutor, Roy Jones. If Bamonte could have five minutes with any one of those men, he would have asked a single question: Why didn't you go after Clyde Roston?

*　　*　　*

WHEN TONY WENT to tell Betty the news of his discovery, she was asleep. He woke her, talking fast.

"Honey, you're not going to believe this. Remember I told you about Elmer Black? I found something else—a memo—and it looks like there's this other guy, Roston, a detective, a real asshole from what it sounds like, and he—"

"Go to sleep."

"No, there's more. The guy—the guy got away with it. Black probably found out about it. Then he fell off the bridge—or somebody pushed him. I don't know."

Betty was in no mood to talk about ancient crimes. There were more immediate concerns in Metaline Falls—their marriage, for example. Couldn't he sense the gulf between them? Tony was obsessed with work. He didn't know when to stop. He never took vacations. He always had been a good provider, but she needed a man who was a full emotional participant. Cops developed calluses, protection from the failures of the heart. This graduate project, which Betty had encouraged, was taking up too many of his extra hours. And now that it was coming alive, it was crowding out the living partner in his life. In the middle of the night, snow rounding out the hard features of the dying town, when Tony wanted to talk about Charley Sonnabend's deathbed story of 1955, Betty wanted no part of it. Not now. She was worried about their eighteen-year-old son. He had the strong body of Bull Bamonte—he won the school weight-lifting title, breaking the record for his division—and the soft face of Betty. But more and more, what he seemed to have inherited from his father was the emotional fragility.

A CITIZEN was on the line: somebody had poisoned his horse—he was sure of it—and he wondered what the goddamn sheriff was going to do about it. (The sheriff would send a deputy as soon as he could free one up.) Snow was piling up on the few roads that were passable during winter, which meant more accidents. A county commissioner was on another line, demanding a meeting to go over Bamonte's latest budget requests. Another citizen called about poachers, two men shooting deer out of season. (Call Fish and Game.)

Bamonte took his tie off. He usually walked around the office, even during winter, with his shirt sleeves rolled up and the collar open. His office always seemed to be closing in on him—a room stuffed with unzipped files and oddball artifacts. Two pictures were on prominent display inside the sheriff's office: one was of Chief Joseph, the leader of the Nez Percé, who was said to have died of a broken heart on the Colville Reservation, just west of the Selkirks; the other was a portrait of Geronimo, the Apache leader. Bamonte liked them because they were underdogs who held on to their dignity in the face of failure and retreat.

A call came in from the local Democratic party. Would Bamonte be attending the fund-raiser in Spokane? A lifetime Democrat in a forest of conspiracy-divining Republicans (a local state legislator introduced a bill in Olympia, the state capital, to outlaw teenage sex, and fluoride in the water supply was still considered evidence of a communist plot to take over the inland Northwest, even as the Cold War came to an end), Bamonte wasn't sure how much he wanted to do with partisan politics after the debacle of Michael Dukakis.

A call came in from out of state—a scholar doing research, he said—asking about the Nazis. Somebody was always asking about the Nazis. Bamonte put his feet on the desk and told the short version. He was building a log home in 1975 around Metaline Falls when he met a small, introspective young man from Arizona, Robert J. Mathews, who had just moved to the Pend Oreille from Arizona. Mathews hated the federal government, hated big cities, hated what America had become. He used to lecture his parents about the dangers of the Federal Reserve Board and castigate them for watching television. Bamonte didn't know much about Mathews when he met him, but he knew a lot about the piece of land he was building on; it was the site of the shoot-out between Black Jack Rowden and a posse half a century earlier.

Mathews took a job at the cement factory and mostly kept to himself. One day a letter appeared in the Newport *Miner*, signed by Mathews. In part it said, "Our people have degenerated into some of the most cowardly, sheepish degenerates that have ever littered the face of the earth." To prove that he wasn't a coward, Mathews founded the Order, a group of about thirty men, most of them excons or semiliterate drifters, who set out to start a revolution. Following a six-point plan hatched by Mathews, they robbed banks, blew up public buildings, sent hate mail to Jews and blacks, shot and killed a Denver talk-show host, and plotted the assassination of numerous public figures, including former secretary of state Henry Kissinger and Fred Silverman, the onetime programming chief of NBC. The Order collapsed after Mathews was killed and most of his followers were convicted of federal racketeering and conspiracy charges. Like Black Jack Rowden, Mathews had died in a shootout with dozens of lawmen.

Yes, Bamonte told the caller, he knew Robert Mathews fairly well. The neo-Nazi's mother, who still lived in Metaline Falls, had given Bamonte the last letter she ever received from her son, a note in which he was already casting himself for posterity as a martyr. Bamonte said Mathews was one of those urban rejects looking for the good life in the Pend Oreille, who came in search of the simple rhythms of nature but strayed to the darker impulses of isolation.

"We used to talk about pileated woodpeckers," Bamonte said. "Know what a pileated woodpecker is? Lives in tree snags. A beautiful bird. Mathews would spend hours watching 'em. You never think a guy could like animals so much and still have such a grudge against people."

AT DUSK, Bamonte slipped out of the office. The sky was pink, the air cold, the Selkirks holding the last blush of alpenglow. The rodeo stands just across the street from the sheriff's office were stuffed with snow, and its overhang seemed to be sagging.

Back in Metaline Falls, the main road was clear, snow-plowed by a volunteer. Bamonte wanted to talk to Betty, to apologize for his moods and fits. He also wanted to reach out to their boy. Nobody was home.

He went to the study, intending to have a quick peek at the graduate project. He removed his shoulder pistol, loosened his collar. The room was cold.

As he fanned through another stack of documents, a single page jumped out at him; it was written on yellowed paper with the same wobbly type as the 1955 summary. A Pend Oreille officer's report, it summarized another visit with Sonnabend, in November 1957. In the two years since his first recounting of the 1935 shooting, Sonnabend had clung to life. Back in the hospital, he thought he was down to his last days, and wanted again to tell something about the Conniff case. The doctors had sent him home—perhaps for the final time. There, the big carpenter added a considerable footnote to his earlier revelation.

The summary was written by Sheriff William Giles, the man Bamonte had defeated in 1978. It read:

Pend Oreille County Sheriff
Officer Report

Officer: William M. Giles
Date: 11/19/57

Received a call from Darrell Holmes, United States Marshal of the Eastern Washington District and he reports that retired Detective Charles F. Sonnabend had some more information regarding the MURDER OF GEORGE CONNIFF.

I arrived at the Sonnabend home located at 3218 Rosamond Street Spokane, Washington at about 1:00 P.M. and met Mr. Sonnabend and he stated that he had been ill and in the hospital and was due to go back 11/20/57 for an operation.

Mr. Sonnabend stated that while he was in the hospital he remembered that he had given his nephew a 32 Savage Automatic which was given him at the Spokane Police Dept after the arrest of Acie Logan and Warden Spinks for the burglaries and the theft of an Automobile from Montana.

Mr. Sonnabend stated that Acie Logan was with Clyde Roston when they went through the police blockade on North Division on the night Conniff was killed. He stated that he had arrested Logan a short time after in a Hotel room in Spokane on a charge of Theft of a car, and upon searching the room he found the gun that was claimed by Logan. The gun a 32 Savage Automatic srl # 40946 was intered on the property cards as Logans gun and that he himself had signed and took possession of the gun after Logan was sent to McNeils Island to serve time.

Sonnabend stated that he had attempted to question Logan regarding the murder but was refused the permission by his superior officers. He had made an attempt at the Penitentiary and was told after going over there that he would have to have at least advance notice and special permission to interrogate Logan. This he never got.

Had a good long visit with Mr. Sonnabend and he expressed very much his desire to cooperate and help solve this crime. He still thinks that Sgt. Mangrin who he believes is tending bar some where around Hungry Horse, Montana, has complete knowledge of the identity of the Murderer.

What impressed Bamonte was the tenacity of Charley Sonnabend. At least *somebody* was outraged that a cop killer had escaped justice. He pictured the 270-pound carpenter propped up in bed, one day before going into the hospital for an operation that could likely end his life, trying to pass on the key to solving an old murder—a living will of sorts. He had carried the story around with him for more than two decades, but what had come of it since? Who had carried it for the last thirty-two years? In Bamonte's mind, the last official words from Sonnabend raised more questions than they answered:

• The gun. Earlier, Sonnabend had said one of the pistols taken from Logan had been signed out by Detective Roston. Now Sonnabend was saying that he had taken possession of a gun and later gave it to his nephew. Was this the murder weapon? Was Sonnabend himself covering for Roston by holding on to the pistol that may have been used to shoot Conniff?

• The roadblock. Could there be a police report, or better yet, one of the original officers, somewhere, with details of what happened the night of the roadblock? If Roston had indeed been stopped at the North Division Street roadblock, with an overheated car and a passenger next to him, one hour after the shooting—the time it would take to drive from Newport to Spokane—that could be a damning piece of evidence against the detective.

• The follow-up interview. Why was Sonnabend prevented from interviewing Logan at the McNeil Island Penitentiary? Logan had already confessed Roston's role, or so Sonnabend said; but Sonnabend apparently needed something more. To Bamonte, it made no sense that the Spokane Police Department would deny permission for one of its veteran detectives to pursue a killing. But this raised the larger question of what had come of Sonnabend's case. If Logan had indeed told the whole story of the butter racket and the shooting, why hadn't Roston been arrested? And what had happened between Sonnabend's initial summoning, in 1955, and this second one, in 1957? Did the new investigation die with Elmer Black? Down went Black and up went the old Blue Wall.

Bamonte shivered from the cold. He wiped away a thin layer of frost inside his window and looked outside. The streets were dead. He opened the refrigerator and stared; he had not eaten anything since lunch, but he wasn't hungry.

He hated being alone. His worst fears grew quickly, all out of proportion, without the leveling effect of a trusted companion. What if Betty left him? The thought took him back to the Christmas when his mother and father were hauled off to jail.

He stretched out on the couch and fell asleep. When he awoke, sometime in the predawn, he felt chilled. He walked to the sink and washed his face.

"Betty . . . ?"

No answer. He looked in the bedroom, not expecting to find anything. The clock blinked—and Betty was asleep.

Bamonte was drawn back into the study, lured by another stack of forgotten police reports and by the voices waiting to tell their stories. Just a quick peek. Within minutes, he was out of the family doubts and back in the winter of late 1957. The temperatures were plunging to thirty-five below zero around Newport. When the Conniff case was presented to Sheriff Giles by Sonnabend, he had worked only a single homicide: a drunken seventeen-year-old, attempting to start a fire under his car as a way to heat the vehicle up, got into an argument with his uncle and pulled a knife on the older man. The uncle shot him; a jury later ruled it was justifiable homicide.

With Sonnabend's narrative, Giles had a more difficult task. From what Bamonte could tell from the records, Giles, who had jurisdiction over the Conniff killing, decided not to reopen the case unless he could find some compelling piece of physical evidence to back what Sonnabend had said. The deposit of clues from the dying Spokane cop apparently was not enough.

"What more do you want?!" Bamonte said, slapping the papers with the back of his hand.

Also in the stack, Bamonte found two letters. One was from Giles, the other from the FBI. The first note, dated a day after the 1957 Sonnabend meeting, was a request to J. Edgar Hoover that the FBI director examine the .32 pistol which Sonnabend had retrieved from Logan and given to his nephew. He also sent along a packet of spent bullets—slugs taken from the groin, armpit, and rib cage of Marshal Conniff. A few weeks later, one of Hoover's assistants returned the bullets and pistol with a short note:

"None of these .32 bullets could have been fired from the gun submitted."

12.

A Family Visit

ON SATURDAY MORNING, in the basement classroom in Colville, Bamonte told the other students what he had found. The class met once a week in the pine country east of the Columbia River. The sheriff was always dragging stories in from the Pend Oreille and trying to wedge them into the discussion. When the study group was first assembled, nearly two years earlier, some of the students expected ignorance and hayseed homilies from Bamonte. And at times he even played along, doing his cowboy-sheriff role to live up to the stereotype. Once when the class was gathered for a dinner party at Professor Carey's house, Bamonte arrived late, on his motorcycle, dusted and breathless.

"Where you been, Tony?" Carey asked him.

"A murder. How's the food?"

"What kind of murder?"

"Guy hacked up another guy after he caught him screwing his wife."

And of course that ended all discussion, for the time being, of grade points and career goals.

But Bamonte was a serious student, incapable of looking out at the flat surface of the Columbia River near Colville, backed up by dams, without thinking of the Indian tribes that used to gather at long-buried waterfalls to trade salmon with Hudson's Bay Company scouts. On this Saturday, as he discussed his research project, he sounded like a scientist who has just emerged from years in the lab with a breathless discovery.

"I can't believe they sat on this!" he said. "It's a damn shame!"

After he told the class about Detective Sonnabend's revelations, there were dozens of questions:

What happened to Sonnabend?

He died, free of the story he had carried for the last third of his life, but frustrated because nobody had ever been brought to trial for the killing of George Conniff.

Didn't the sheriff's office at the time try to do anything?

Yes, they sent a gun to the FBI in 1957. But after it was returned the case went dormant again.

What about Detective Roston and this Sergeant Mangrin mentioned by Sonnabend—were they ever found, or questioned?

As near as anyone could tell, both men were dead, their secrets buried with them. The files indicated that Sheriff Giles, in the mid-1950s, could find no trace of either man.

So they got away with it?

Bamonte held his response for a minute.

"That appears to be the case."

A FEW DAYS LATER, Professor Carey was chatting with Carol Bonino, editor of *Signum*, the quarterly publication of Gonzaga University. Looking for stories, she asked Carey if he had any interesting students or anecdotes to share.

The teacher thought of Bamonte. "There's this one middle-aged guy in the MOL class in Colville," Carey said. "A sheriff. . . ."

On page two of the spring 1989 edition of *Signum*, a small story appeared, under the headline SHERIFF BAMONTE BRINGS RUGGED WEST ALIVE WITH MOL THESIS. The piece told about Bamonte's thesis—filled with "short biographies on previous Pend Oreille

County sheriffs, but also macabre, tragic, and sometimes heroic true stories about enforcing the law in this corner of Washington."

The Conniff case was mentioned only in passing, somewhat inaccurately, and not by name, as "a story that goes back to 1935, when a marshal in Newport was shot and killed, with no suspects. Two policemen from a nearby community were implicated in the shooting when, in a deathbed confession, an acquaintance of one policeman revealed his friend's involvement in the incident."

The story ended with a quote from Bamonte, his answer to a question about why he was doing the project. "I wanted to leave something behind," the sheriff said.

Carol Bonino told her husband, Rick, a reporter and columnist at the *Spokesman-Review*, that Bamonte might make a good story. The tip was passed on, and eventually the story was assigned to a feature writer, Jim Camden. He was fascinated by the sheriff-scholar from the wilderness county. The paper's morgue had plenty of clips on how Bamonte was always getting in trouble with the local powers, or digging up an obscure fact to counter what everybody had already concluded, or nipping at the boot heels of some federal bureaucracy. But meeting him was another thing entirely. He was lean, edgy, with a whispery voice, talking about history and theory with a .38 strapped to his chest, unsure of himself or his intellect, sometimes killing his words in mid-sentence, jumping in and out of his seat, offering coffee or interrupting to show a picture of Bull Bamonte or taking a call from an enraged citizen. He never put anything on hold, and so his days were chaotic and overcrowded. Around the office, some of the clerical staff thought the master's degree would help the sheriff sharpen his organizational skills. But here he was going off in three new directions.

Spokane's morning paper, which circulated all over eastern Washington, northern Idaho, western Montana, and southern British Columbia, ran a story about Bamonte's master's thesis on page one of the February 11, 1989 edition, under the headline SHERIFF WROTE THE BOOK ON CRIME IN HIS COUNTY. Like Bonino's piece, the story told of the hyperactive cop and his unusual master's thesis. "I love to write," the sheriff was quoted as saying. "This gave me a chance to get some professional help." The article recounted each of the major chapters in the developing thesis, the sheriffs and the crimes of their time. Midway into the piece, the reporter mentioned, in a single paragraph, the killing of the Newport marshal, although he reported incorrectly that he'd been gunned down in the late 1920s, and that two police officers might have been involved.

"The murderers were never caught," the story said, "but years later, the deathbed confession of a Spokane policeman revealed that he and a fellow officer were partners in a robbery scheme that led to the murder."

GEORGE EDWIN CONNIFF, JR., was stoking the wood stove inside his home in north Spokane when his wife summoned him to the breakfast table and pointed at the front page of the newspaper. "Take a look at this," Jane Conniff told her husband.

He closed the door to the stove and walked to the table. Tall, smooth-faced, and skinny at age seventy-three, the only son of the slain Newport marshal had gone nearly fifty-four years without the slightest hint of who had put four bullets into his father in 1935. When the shooting happened, he was twenty years old and had just returned to the Pend Oreille. Father and son had worked throughout the hot summer of 1935, laboring under smoky skies to build a new cabin to replace the home destroyed by fire. They had become close in a way that had never before been possible. For the next half-century George Jr. worked in sawmills and fruit orchards, fought against the Japanese on a destroyer in the Philippines, fished on commercial boats, and eventually settled on a career as an electrician.

"Is that your father they're talking about here?" Jane Conniff asked her husband.

George took his glasses off and sat down. He read and reread the single paragraph about the marshal, then looked out the window at the frozen ground.

"I'll . . . be . . . damned."

The date given in the paper was wrong, but the circumstances seemed right. No other Newport marshal had been gunned down by robbers. What stunned George junior was the line about a deathbed confession implicating a Spokane policeman; he had never heard such a thing.

He called Bamonte. The sheriff was startled to hear a voice to go with a family name.

"George . . . Conniff—"

"Junior. I'm his son."

"My God!"

Bamonte invited George and his family to come to his office and take a look at what he'd found. No longer would it be just Tony Bamonte talking to himself and the yellowed police reports in the middle of the night.

THE PEND OREILLE was under heavy snow when George and his two sisters, Mary and Olive, drove up to see the sheriff in early March. Even in late winter, when most landscapes looked ragged and tired, the Pend Oreille held its beauty: the larch, pine, and fir forests marching up the Selkirks, trickles of clear water pushing through stream channels frozen at the edges. George was the baby of the family; Mary Pearce was seventy-five and Olive Pearce was seventy-seven. Driving north along the Newport Highway, they were children again, a family growing up on a sixty-acre stump ranch in a meadow with views of Hoodoo Mountain. George remembered the Kalispel tribal elder who'd invited him in to see his tepee and feel the bearskin floor. The boy caught fish with his hands and swung from rope swings in the trees and dove into river pools. He thought of what 1935 was like in the Pend Oreille, cutting firewood for a dollar a day, and then eating that dollar at night to restock the calories burned up with the axe.

Olive saw the exhausted face of her father, who never seemed to rest, working by day to build the cabin, dragging himself through the night shift to protect the merchants of Newport. The fire that burned their home on the stump ranch had come at the worst time; for a while, they thought they might join those other Americans who took to the road in boxcars. This road, paved and fast, had been its own trail of tears, a route for dust-bowl refugees and forest fire mercenaries and platoons of Civilian Conservation Corps workers. The drifters emptied into the Pend Oreille near Sandpoint, thirty miles east of Newport, where three railroad lines converged. Many of them ended up in the transient camp along the Pend Oreille River. In the absence of leads, all three children suspected that a drifter had killed their father, somebody whose empty stomach drove him to kill.

As the Conniffs entered Newport, and took the left-hand turn off the highway toward the sheriff's office, George remembered his father's dying hours. After spending the night in agony on an operating table in Newport, he was transferred to the ambulance that would carry the bleeding marshal to a hospital in Spokane. As he was lowered into the car, the marshal winced and spoke his last words:

"Make it snappy, boys."

BAMONTE GREETED the Conniff family like lost relatives. Their grief was still evident, but they were gratified to have a partner after fifty-four years of unanswered questions.

The sheriff started talking nonstop, bringing up Sonnabend and Elmer Black, pawned pants and police cover-ups. "There's so much to tell you," he said. He went off on another verbal gallop, then pulled the reins back. "On second thought, I'll let you see for yourself. Some of this stuff you won't believe."

He brought out a large box holding the old typewritten police reports, a few pictures, letters to and from the FBI, and two summaries of the 1955 and 1957 interviews with Sonnabend. The sheriff left them alone for a while, in the room with the written words.

Olive, broad-shouldered, stern-faced, bespectacled, became very angry, near tears at one point. "Why?" She lashed out. "Why didn't they tell us any of this?"

She had worked in the Pend Oreille sheriff's office in the 1940s and the early 1950s and knew every deputy from her father's time. One of the county's lawmen, Sheriff Holmes, was a neighbor of the

Conniffs at the very time he had heard Sonnabend's deathbed story; yet he never said a word about the new information to any member of the victim's family. What was there to protect? Had any of the Conniffs been told of the evidence linking a Spokane detective to the killing, they would have hounded the police for some resolution, Olive said. Alma, the marshal's widow, died in late 1955, several months after Sonnabend summoned the authorities to his bedside. Though she had been assured that things had been thoroughly investigated until all leads were exhausted, Alma Conniff went to her grave frustrated by the great mystery of her husband's murder.

When Bamonte returned to the room, he found George and Mary subdued. But Olive was red with outrage. "How could they keep this from us?" she asked.

Bamonte was gentle, the velvet-voiced cop accustomed to explaining random accidents that take children from mothers and spouses from lovers. He could have been explaining why a deer sometimes shatters the front window of a pickup truck, for he was no longer surprised by his conclusion.

"You wonder why nobody told you about any of this? So did I. It's a big question without an obvious answer. I'll tell you what I think: the people who were supposed to protect the public seem to have been the very ones responsible for the murder—"

"Dad was killed by a Spokane policeman," Olive interrupted.

"But they're dead, aren't they?" George asked. "Everyone who had something to do with it is gone. So why would they continue to cover up?"

"You don't understand. These are cops. They're sworn to uphold the law, but a cop's first loyalty is to his own kind."

"So is this it?" Olive asked. "Can't you do anything more?"

"Do you want me to?"

The Conniffs looked at each other, a silent survey.

"We do," Olive said.

"You're damn right we do," George said. "We want to know what really happened."

"I can't promise you anything," Bamonte said. "But if you give me some time, I'll go after this. I'll open it up. I'm the sheriff here. This murder happened in my county. I don't see why we can't kick over a few rocks."

The Conniffs were encouraged, but only moderately so. It was not the first time a Pend Oreille County sheriff had made such a statement.

13.

Men With Badges

WITH AN ENLARGED HEART, a stump leg, and narrowed arteries, Dan Mangan's body was a wreck that he dragged around the house and parked, for most of his waking hours, in front of a television set. The frame of the old man, held together by bolts below one knee and powered by a battery pack for the heart, was the least of his baggage. A few years shy of his ninetieth birthday, Mangan lived with his youngest daughter, Rosemary Miller, in a well-kept rambler in Spokane. He told the doctors that all he needed to stay alive were R and R and cigars, but the joke was feeble, a tired line he should have left behind when he sold his tavern in Hungry Horse. He needed much more than Canadian whiskey and stogies, and his daughter, who had grown up hating him, gave it to him. But it was care at a cost. Rose would let him stay in her home, drink his beer and an occasional blast of bourbon, carouse with his seventy-six-year-old girl-friend once a week. But he had to abide by her house rules, the most important of which was that he listen when she talked. In the early evenings, they would each crack open a beer and Rose would start in on him.

In her living room were pictures of her mother, Dan Mangan's ex-wife, the former Joan Helen Sinclair. The photos were haunting, for they showed Helen at her best, barely a hundred pounds, lithe and striking—before the bruises, welts, and scars of his fist reshaped her face, before the poverty and pain gave her a set of eyes that stared out at the world with trepidation, as if peering from behind a fence. During the mean years of the Depression, the family of six lived in a four-bedroom house in east Spokane, not far from the shanties of Hillyard. Mangan's police salary was more than enough to pay the eight-dollar-a-month mortgage, but he still missed payments, and went days without bringing home a scrap of food. He spent his earnings at Albert Commellini's, buying rounds of bootleg liquor and romancing women he had met through Clyde Ralstin. For Rosemary's First Communion at Saint Ann's, she wore undergarments sewn together from muslin sacks discarded by the Sperry Flour Mill. The mill's logo showed through the dress, so that Rose's First Communion picture looked like an advertisement for Sperry Flour.

When Mangan finally consented to a divorce, after the police found Helen half-dead on the floor of her house, battered and bleeding, in 1946, he took with him the life insurance money from a son who'd been killed in the war. Helen moved the family to the white pine country of Idaho, and she went to work as a clerk in the Potlatch Mill. She lived, as best she could, for her children, and maintained a faith in God, as interpreted by the Irish Catholic ministry of the inland Northwest. She loved to sketch and paint and write poetry; but as she aged, she lost her talents, one by one—robbed by Alzheimer's disease. In her last years, living with Rose, she could barely remember her name. She died in 1985.

Now, four years later, Helen's former husband sat in the den where she had spent her final days, his big, knobby hands clasped around a beer bottle, surrounded by her pencil sketches of Jesus. And then the oversized Irishman, who was once so mighty he pulled runaway houses from a river in Montana during a flood, and later rented them out, would get another dose of his toxic past. He preferred talking about Hungry Horse, where he had set up a bar on a pair of two-by-sixes planked over sawhorses in the boomtown that sprouted around the federal dam on the Flathead River. For forty years he held court at the Dam Town Tavern. He could outlift, outdrink, outbrag, outfuck, and—he used to think—outlive anything.

133

But Rose did not take him into her house to hear old boys' stories. He would reminisce about the time his picture was displayed on the front page after he captured a particularly dangerous felon—Alfred the Hunchback, a killer of two women, the papers said—and she would reply with a more painful truth: he was one of the crookedest cops west of Chicago.

For most of her life, Rose hated her father. It was only during the last years, when he was crippled, that she occasionally felt sorry for him. At Rose's house, the old wife-beater, womanizer, animal killer, and deal maker was like a dependent child. Once a month, she took him down to the Police Guild for the regular gathering of retired Spokane cops. He ordered his R and R and sniffed around, looking for familiar faces, muttering to himself. He didn't know a soul. Occasionally, when Rose would introduce her father, somebody would say, "Mangan? Sergeant Mangan? I thought he was dead!"

"No such luck," she would reply.

After a few drinks, Mangan's small eyes would cloud up behind the thick, wire-rim glasses and he'd say something about wanting to talk to a detective.

"What for?" Rose would ask.

"Got something I need to talk about."

"Tell me."

"Can't. It's something a detective needs to hear. Something I gotta do."

"Then you want me to call a detective?"

"No, no. You . . . I'll do it on my own time."

"What the hell is it?"

"Something I got to do."

Rose, the old man's conscience, would shake her head; she was finally starting to chip away at the black heart of her father. Or maybe he was just trying to get her to ease up on him.

IF BAMONTE was going to reopen an old murder case, he would need more than a hunch developed through his master's degree project and a sheaf of police reports burnished with age. There was no statute of limitations on homicide, so he had adequate legal justification. The murder was committed in his county—no jurisdictional problem. But his resources, in the vast Pend Oreille, were stretched. And there were his critics to contend with, the citizen-taxpayers, who howled any time the sheriff assumed the role of whim chaser and provocateur of the status quo. In the history of Pend Oreille County, seven killings remained unsolved. Why go after this one? A fresh investigation, using the information from Sonnabend's 1950s tale, could tarnish the names of people long dead, smudge institutions, and break a few links in the fraternal chain that held policemen together. But if the victim's family, the aging children of Marshal Conniff, were clamoring for justice, that could help his cause.

After meeting with the Conniffs, Bamonte asked each of them to write him a note about his or her feelings and offer suggestions on whether he should proceed.

On the way back to Spokane, the Newport marshal's three children decided that the distant possibility of achieving justice was worth the pain of reviving bad memories. A week later, Bamonte received two letters from the family.

"Always, after the death of our Father, there was the question of who would have done such a thing to us," George wrote. "Was the man someone we knew? Was he from somewhere else? At first, you believe there will be answers, then you only hope. As the years pass, you face the reality that there will never be the finality of knowing the answers to the questions that are always there."

Bamonte set the letter down; this aging voice of outrage was more than enough motivation to reopen the case. George Conniff wanted finality. If nothing else, Bamonte would try to help the Conniffs spend their last years free of doubt. And the sheriff was haunted by something Olive had said, when she wondered why her neighbor, Sheriff Holmes, a longtime friend, never told her what he knew. The implied thought was: cops treat each other like family, sharing vital secrets, and everyone else gets the filtered facts and official shrug. Whether the Conniffs would come to trust him or not, Bamonte heard the last cry of the slain marshal.

"You are the voice of the dead," he told his deputies whenever they investigated a murder. And sometimes, in reaction, his subordinates would look at each other, then throw their eyes to the sky. Right—voice of the dead. I hear one coming in now on the radio.

"There is a lot of emotion," George Conniff wrote, and continued:

You're forced to think about a very hard time in your life and your own wounds, after fifty-four years, can still hurt. Despite that pain, it is better to know than not to know.

People who had close personal ties to the family heard the confession and yet chose not to tell us. The questions now for us are: Why weren't we told in 1957 when the confession took place? Could anyone involved with the crime or coverup still be alive?

There are no feelings of hate or revenge but there is the thought that somehow honesty and truth do prevail. Our Father stood tall and died for these very things.

Olive wrote the other letter, a shorter one than her brother's. What came through was her faith in the power of conscience:

My first reaction after hearing this information was of shock. The facts had been known for so many years and the family was never given any knowledge of the findings. I had always felt there would be a death bed confession some time. It would seem this information was not to be made public. One of those with knowledge of the confession was considered to be a personal friend and could have contacted the family.

For a time, after the tragedy, our thoughts were not so much along the lines of who had done this to us as about our mother. Nothing could change what had happened. We tried to avoid the subject but later realized she really needed and wanted to talk about it. Mother was a brave lady and loved our Dad very much. He was one of the best. She never found real happiness again.

Not long after Dad's murder, we learned the investigation had come to a dead end.

We very much appreciate the fact that this information has been revealed to us. Had it not been for Sheriff Bamonte, we may never have known. Sheriff Bamonte has been very helpful. Needless to say, even after fifty-four years, the tragedy is very real.

DURING THE LAST DAYS of winter, a chinook blew up from the south, warm and feisty, melting the snow that covered the Pend Oreille Valley. The white of winter storms always brought out the dark by-product of the cement factory in Metaline Falls, a heavy soot that splayed against the ground like spots on a dalmatian. With the wind, the ugly snow swooshed away, leaving metallic-colored pools of slush in the streets of the hamlet. The factory sirens still called in three shifts a day to process limestone and shale into cement dust. But there was much talk in Metaline Falls that the plant, which had been the lifeblood of the community for eighty years, might close. A French conglomerate, the LeFarge Corporation, was negotiating to buy the factory from the German manufacturing firm, Heidelberger Zement, that had owned it since 1977. At one point, the plant had turned out half a million tons of dry cement a year, material that was used in the Grand Coulee Dam on the Columbia River and the Hungry Horse Dam on the Flathead River in Montana. But now the European owners were not showing any signs that they wanted to return the plant to its glory years. They were letting things go into disrepair, laying off workers, ignoring sales requests. Some plant workers said the prospective buyers had no intention of actually producing anything or trying to keep the town alive. The speculation around the village built at the confluence of the Pend Oreille River and Sullivan Creek was that LeFarge, in keeping with the corporate climate of the 1980s, wanted to purchase the plant from Heidelberger and then kill it—for the sole reason of knocking out an international competitor.

In late afternoon, Bamonte arrived at his home in Metaline Falls, a three-story brick building erected in 1928. Across the street, one way, was the high school, Bamonte's alma mater, where the kids used to tease him about his clothes. The school was a grand brick design by the architect Kirkland Cutter that rose in 1914, when Metaline Falls was young and cocky. Cutter had created the Davenport Hotel and the Spokane Club, two celebrated historical fixtures in eastern Washington; but his work in Metaline Falls seemed destined to fall with the ages. The factory also was within steps of Bamonte's door, its ashen towers rising from behind a wire fence. Bamonte had tried to keep up the appearance of his red brick building, sanding and varnishing the deep-colored wood trim, making cabinets and alcoves, laying carpet, replacing old plumbing with new. But it was a losing struggle. The place was cavernous; paint peeled from the high ceilings of rooms that he never had time to attend; the faucets in a neglected extra bathroom were rusted. Like Metaline Falls itself, Bamonte's home resisted change, wearing the same face it had worn for more than fifty years, the only difference being the accumulated layers of gray from the factory.

He called out for Betty, then realized she was not yet home from the cement plant, where she worked as clerk. His son was also gone. Most days, Tony didn't know whether to hit or hug the boy. A year earlier, Tony was at the sheriff's department's annual picnic when a call came over the radio at headquarters that somebody had been spotted in Bamonte's car, brandishing a gun. Sheriff's vehicles raced to the scene, the deputies fearing that their boss was in mortal danger. They found his teenage son with a BB gun, playing with a friend. The prank was still a sore spot. Through the fall and into the winter, the boy and his father seldom spoke other than to exchange basic information. Bamonte was repeating the habits of his father, the silence and the distance. In turn, his son was developing Tony's dark doubts, picking up his father's debilitating insecurity.

Tony and Betty had been fighting over the usual things—money problems, his long hours, his moods. A trip west to Seattle, six hours in the car each way, had only heightened the rancor. He felt awful about the scrapes, but instead of talking about it, he worked harder, longer, going deeper into the past, spending more time with the people from 1935 who had suddenly become such a big part of his life.

With nightfall, temperatures dropped in the mountain valley, and the slush turned to black ice. Bamonte went to his study and put a piece of sheriff's department stationery in the typewriter. He addressed a letter to Terry Mangan, Spokane's chief of police (who was not related to the old man who lived with his daughter in the Spokane rambler). Mangan had come to Spokane from Bellingham, in northwest Washington, promising to make the Spokane Police Department one of the best mid-sized units in the country—a formidable task. In the early 1980s, when parts of Spokane were under siege by a serial rapist, the leading detective on the case advised women, if they were attacked, to "lie back and enjoy it."

With Elmer Black and Charley Sonnabend both dead, Bamonte felt it only logical that his formal investigation begin in the Spokane Police Department—his old haunt, the palace of secrets. In typing the first words of his letter, Bamonte left the realm of academia and upgraded the Conniff project to official business.

He made copies of the police summaries of the Sonnabend interviews and included these in his letter, for reference. He also enclosed the Conniffs' notes. He wrote:

> Dear Terry:
> Will you please review the enclosures? There appears to be strong probable cause to believe the marshal of Newport, who was murdered in 1935, may have been killed by a Spokane police officer.
>
> It appears that at least one other Spokane policeman knew about Roston's involvement and covered for him.
>
> On March 3, 1955, Detective Sonnabend from the Spokane Police Department came forward with knowledge of a confession from one of his accomplices. It appears that he knew of this information for over 15 years, but did not attempt to push it until his health started to deteriorate. This was never followed up, and in fact, he was refused permission to work on this case.
>
> When I first was hired by the Spokane Police Department, I remember hearing about Roston, his ranch and crooked ways.

This was in 1966. I also remember some of the graft during my earlier years.

This case has the markings of politics and cover-up. During this entire time, none of this knowledge was ever shared with the Conniff family. It is also very interesting that Sheriff Black, the sheriff at the time of the Conniff murder, became dizzy and fell 45 feet to his death from the interstate bridge in 1955, just 3 months after Detective Sonnabend was attempting to bring light to this murder.

It may be possible for some of the suspects to still be alive. Could there be an old man out there somewhere with a dirty conscience?

Let me know what you think and if any of your old records still exist.

Sincerely,
Anthony Bamonte, Sheriff
Pend Oreille County

A week went by, and Bamonte heard nothing from Spokane; then another week. This was unusual: it was police courtesy to respond promptly when another agency asked for help. Bamonte called the department and asked for the chief. He was given an assistant, who told him that the chief had not been happy to receive the letter from the sheriff in the wilderness county. For one thing, there were several implicit allegations in his letter—of cover-up and corruption that continued, through institutional memory, to the present day. The chief was offended at the very thought. Sure, cops from the old days were dirty—untrained, uneducated, driven by anemic salaries. But Terry Mangan, only the second chief ever to attend college, a former priest, had a master's degree. To become a Spokane policeman today required passing a civil service test and two months at the police academy, which included sessions on constitutional rights. Just what was Bamonte getting at with this suggestion that there could be "an old man out there somewhere with a dirty conscience"?

* * *

IN THE ARCHIVES of the Spokane Police Department there was plenty of information about Bamonte. He was hired by the department not long after he returned from Vietnam, where he'd served on forty-two combat missions. The war disgusted him. When he came home, he initially retreated to the woods around Metaline Falls, a half-world away from the hot breath of the tropics. As always, there was very little work in elemental Pend Oreille. The land was rich in beauty and little else: tamarack trees with needles that turned gold before they died, low clouds filtering through the Selkirks at first light, the smell of alfalfa after a cutting. In 1966, after he took a civil service exam and passed fourth from the top out of ninety applicants, Bamonte began an eight-year stint with the department. He wore the same badge and whispered in the same halls as Sonnabend, Mangan, Ralstin. When he started in patrol, a sapling-framed cop chasing burglars and drunks in the railroad district of Hillyard, only one name from the circle that shared a Depression-era secret was still on the payroll. Bill Parsons, a rookie in 1935, was chief of police in 1966.

Like Parsons, Bamonte learned about police work by throwing his body against the usual adversaries. Rookie-year scuffles left him with a broken nose, a dislocated jaw, and a succession of shiners. The first time he fired his gun, in pursuit of a burglar, he hit a window, two cars, a phone booth, and a house. The burglar was never touched.

The older cops showed him the way they treated the alcoholics who lived near the railroad tracks downtown. They would find one with a bottle in his back pocket, then whack his ass with the billy club. The glass would shatter; the wino would howl. Another trick was to lead a drunk up to a police call box, then open the metal door in his face, drawing blood and knocking him to the ground.

Vagrancy was still the all-purpose crime it had been in the 1930s. "If a guy looks at you wrong, arrest him for vagrancy," Bamonte was told again and again during his first year on the job. Free meals were available at certain restaurants, though Mother's Kitchen was no longer a popular hangout. A bottle or two could be had at Christmas.

From an old county coroner named Doc Jones, now dead, Bamonte was introduced to another departmental tradition—stealing from the dead. He arrived one day, alone, at the house of a man who had passed away. Doc Jones came a few minutes later, made a routine inspection of the body, looked around at the man's possessions, then at Bamonte: "I'll take half, you take half." The dead man had no close relatives. The two civil servants could lift a couple of items, and who would ever know? Bamonte balked. Back at the station, he told a colleague, saying he wanted to turn in the coroner. Doc Jones? He's harmless. Besides, the rookie didn't want to get anybody in trouble, did he? Make waves?

Another routine, dating back to the days of Hacker Cox, was the elevator assault. Between the first floor and jail, the boys at the Spokane Police Department would bloody a suspect's face, poke a kidney, or bruise a knee. It was great fun, and nobody ever bothered them. When Bamonte asked if this could lead to trouble, he was told cops were immune; it would always come down to their word against the suspect's. Any time an officer used excessive force, be it gun, club, or fist, the rule of thumb among Spokane police was to minimize it later in the police report—don't even bring it up unless there were witnesses or bullet wounds. A magic pencil, a little creative writing, could go a long way.

After work, Bamonte shied away from the patrolmen's boys' club. Instead, he took night classes at Whitworth College and socialized with a few friends, mostly younger cops. He bucked some of the more rigid rules. The department insisted that everyone wear crew-neck T-shirts, and he wore V-necked, which drew him a reprimand. He liked to play practical jokes, but he had no tolerance for cutting corners in the field.

When in 1966, he fell for a striking, electric-eyed waitress at Sambo's Restaurant named Betty, his approach was in character. Not yet twenty-one, Betty was waiting in her car for somebody to buy her beer after getting off work one night. From behind her came police lights and a siren. She steeled herself for an interrogation, but Officer Bamonte, who had noticed her in the restaurant, had only a single question: how about a date next week?

Three months later, they were married. He brought her flowers in the afternoons and inspired her with his ambition; he said he wanted to be a detective, the best cop in the world. In his weaker moments, he let her in on shards of what he had seen in Vietnam—the old men shot in the head, the strafing of children—and he shared the doubts and fears of his youth.

Bull Bamonte died the same year Tony was married. The son seemed lost without his father. At the funeral, he threw himself onto the casket, sobbing without restraint, trying to squeeze some last bit of life from the outdoor warrior who had brought him up in dance halls and one-room cabins and canvas tents. For months after the funeral, Tony would retreat to a room, close the door, and not say anything. His father left him with a set of Great Books, the classics, and Tony took to the collected wisdom from the ages as if he were harboring a lost twin.

Five years into the job, Bamonte was working as a motorcycle cop, dressed head to toe in black leather. On a bright Saturday in October 1971, he was patrolling downtown Spokane when a call came over the radio—a gunman had just robbed the credit office of a department store. A few seconds later came another call—a woman had been shot and killed in the robbery. Bamonte raced up to the store, jumped off his bike, and sprinted inside.

"That's him!" a customer shouted, pointing to a man in the stairway who was fleeing with a wastebasket. "He shot the lady upstairs!"

Bamonte raised his pistol and ordered the man to stop. When the suspect drew his revolver in response, Bamonte fired a single shot, which hit the man dead-center between his eyes, shattering a pair of sunglasses. Bamonte's partner, Ron Graves, rushed in behind him. He saw the man lying on the floor, a bullet in his forehead, a wastebasket by his side, and shouted: "Jesus Christ, Tony! You shot the fucking janitor!"

If so, the janitor was sweeping up more than dirt; $8,300 in cash was found in the basket. The injured man, brain-damaged, lived to stand trial and plead guilty. A prosecutor's inquiry found that Bamonte was justified in the shooting—a life-threatening situation because the suspect had raised his gun. After the shooting, the department switched over to hollow-point bullets, which shatter on impact, usually assuring a kill.

Having fired his weapon at somebody gave Bamonte a certain status inside police headquarters. The old-timers, who had shunned the younger cop, began to share some of their own stories of the days of instant justice, when an officer had more freedom to enforce the law, when might made right and no lawyer or prosecutor or journalist could say otherwise. It was then that Bamonte first heard the name of Detective Clyde Ralstin. Although Ralstin was long gone from the force, he was still a legend to some at the Stone Fortress—a man to be admired, the biggest and toughest cop from the old days, a maverick detective who worked by his own code and left under his own terms.

A few traces from the Ralstin years—the protective internal code, the petty corruptions, the grab bag of the property room, the handouts of booze and small change—remained. Bamonte was a hard-nose, and when he continued to resist the temptations of the fraternity, he was an outsider once again. When he left the force in 1974, some of the older men in uniform said "Good riddance."

IN LATE MARCH, nearly four weeks after Bamonte wrote his letter to the Spokane police chief, he got a response. The official reaction was negative and curt: "We can find no employment records of any of these people, and most of the principles [sic] involved in this are dead anyhow."

14.

A Stirring

AT HOME in his daughter's rambler, Dan Mangan sometimes would open the photo album, looking for back-door relief from the pain that accompanied the last days of his life. For an hour or more at a time, he left his bent and broken body and returned to those days when his back was straight and his fist was unchipped and he walked through the Stone Fortress with a proprietary swagger. He looked at pictures from the newspaper, half-dissolved clips showing Mangan inside a new police car in 1938, or the front-page photo of him after he captured Alfred the Hunchback. He pulled out pictures from hunting trips—smiling drunks, Spokane's Irish Mafia on holiday. He stared at the young man in uniform, his high forehead, resolute gaze, and then he would start to cry. On more than one occasion, he fell asleep with his face still wet with tears.

In the final week of March, a second story about Bamonte's master's degree appeared in Spokane's morning newspaper. This piece told how the project had gone from academic curiosity to a renewed investigation. The headline read: FAMILY FINALLY LEARNS DETAILS OF '35 MURDER. The story centered on the Conniffs, and their surprise at hearing about police involvement in the killing of their father.

It detailed Sonnabend's attempt to unburden himself, the memos Bamonte had found from 1955 and 1957, and the search for a Sergeant Mangrin and a Clyde Roston. But the story said the new investigation, only a few weeks old, was already running into dead ends. "It apparently will go nowhere because all those involved are dead," the story said. "Investigators say they can't locate personnel records confirming when or if the detective suspected of involvement in the Conniff murder worked for the Spokane police department."

The day the article appeared, Rosemary Miller received a call at home from an old acquaintance, a widow of a Spokane policeman. "Rose, did you see that name in the paper today, a Sergeant Mangrin?"

"I don't remember much about it," Rosemary said. "Why?"

"That's your dad they're talking about," she said. " 'Mangrin'— they mean Mangan. That's your dad."

Rose hung up and went to see her father, who was asleep. When he awoke, she gave him the paper. He read through the story, slowly, then again. The color drained from his face, and his eyes went off in the distance. He said nothing for several minutes.

When he spoke, his voice was like a gavel on a judge's bench. "Hell, I know all about that," he said.

"You *what?*" Her face flushed, Rose moved closer to her father. She was angry, close to losing her temper.

The old man did not back off. "I said I know all about that."

"Look at me!" Rose demanded. "What exactly do you know?"

"I know who did it."

"God damn you!" Rose could barely control herself. She always knew her father was a collection of mildewed secrets, but this was a new low. "You mean to tell me you've known about this killing for fifty-four years and you never told anybody?"

"Well . . . yes. That's what I wanted to talk to a detective about."

"I'm calling the police. We're going to march right down there and you're going to tell them everything you—"

"No. . . . I . . . we've got to be careful."

"Careful! This poor family . . ." She picked up the paper, checked the name. "The Conniffs. They've gone their entire life without knowing who killed their father. Think of the pain you've caused them."

"I didn't mean . . . It just . . ."

"It just what?"

"It just never came up."

"You owe this Conniff family the truth. I'm calling the police chief, and the sheriff from Pend Oreille County."

"No!"

Mangan rose, defiant, and walked away. He slammed the door behind him and did not say a word to his daughter for the rest of the evening.

The next morning, when he came forth from his room, the bluster was gone, and he was a tired old man again with a stump leg and a worn heart.

"Call them," he said.

THE RECKONING came a few days later, in early April, on an afternoon when the air was warm with the promise of new life and all the gravel-flecked snow had disappeared from the streets. Rose drove her father to the Police Guild Building, not far from the Stone Fortress, which was now an office and retail building. The Spokane Police Department had moved across the river, to the courthouse and jail complex beneath a Gothic tower. Mangan and Rose were soon joined by Lieutenant Gary Johnson, of the Spokane police internal affairs office. When Bamonte arrived, he put a twenty-dollar bill on the table and invited everyone to have a drink. Mangan ordered a shot of R and R, his usual medication, and sat back. He wore his prosthesis for the occasion, but it itched.

At first, Mangan seemed suspicious of Bamonte. Nobody had ever questioned him about the events of September 1935. What exactly was Bamonte after? Why now? What was he going to do with the information? Was there a risk of self-incrimination?

Mangan's defensiveness raised a question in Bamonte's mind: just who, after all these years, was he trying to protect? But even if

Mangan's motives were murky, the sheriff was happy, after having been told by an assistant Spokane police chief that everybody from the old era was dead, to have found a single witness. When the rejection letter came back, Bamonte promised the Conniffs that he would not let up. He said he would scratch and kick and harangue and stumble on, trying to find a nugget of living memory in the dirt that had been piled over the crime. Then Mangan appeared, and it validated his optimism.

"Sometimes, it pays to not know any better," he said to the Conniffs.

He and Mangan talked about police work, the grunt's task of banging heads. Mangan took Bamonte back to 1932, his first year on the force, when Spokane was on a roll, and silver from the Idaho mines had helped to pump up the banks and build the big mansions on the South Hill. In the valley, bootleggers ran nearly a hundred operations, slaking the thirst of miners, loggers, and itinerant fruit pickers. A patrolman's arsenal included tear gas and sawed-off shotguns—and not for the war against the bootleggers. There was no such war during Prohibition, as far as Mangan knew. The heavy weaponry was for labor strife, used against Marxist woodworkers and the various rabble-rousing free-speechers who were always trying to organize timber beasts and miners.

Mangan was slow to talk, answering Bamonte's questions with little elaboration. When he was asked if he knew about corruption, he replied matter-of-factly, "Hell, yes. There was graft and corruption all around. Everybody was dirty."

"Everybody? Who? How 'bout a few names, Dan?"

Mangan sipped his R and R, quiet again.

Bamonte thought he might be embarrassed—or afraid—of letting his daughter hear the truth. "Let's go into the other room, where we can talk privately," Bamonte said.

The internal affairs officer, the sheriff, and Mangan went behind a closed door. Bamonte picked up where he'd left off.

Mangan remained reticent; each sentence had to be dragged from him. "I got envelopes," he said.

"What kind of envelopes?"

"Envelopes with money inside. Ten-dollar bills. They came in the mail, or somebody would drop 'em off."

"What were they for?"

"For looking the other way."

"Who else got 'em?"

"Everybody I knew. That's the way we did things."

"What about Charley Sonnabend. Was he dirty?"

"Sonnabend?" Mangan rubbed his chin. "Big guy. Detective, I think. . . ."

"That's right."

"Sonnabend was a pretty nice guy. He was honest."

Bamonte brought up some of the names from Sonnabend's report. Acie Logan, the tattooed con from Mississippi.

"I remember Logan," Mangan said. "He was always at Mother's Kitchen."

"Mother's?"

"On Riverside. A diner. Logan was there with Ralstin"—

That was the first time Bamonte had heard the name spoken since his days at the Spokane Police Department. It was "Ralstin" not "Roston" as the old summary had indicated.

—"and I knew Ralstin pretty good," Mangan said.

"How good?"

"We chippied a little bit. I knew his wife, before they got divorced." Mangan allowed himself a half-smile, remembering the women from the Mother's Kitchen circle, cheating on Helen, a night with Ralstin's wife.

Bamonte steered him back to the detective.

"Ralstin was into something," Mangan said. "He was involved in the creamery burglaries and he was peddling."

"How did you know that?"

"It was common knowledge."

"Was he involved in the Newport Creamery burglary?"

Mangan fell into silence again. If he was thinking of the days when a ten-dollar bill was all it took to own a policeman and butter was sold on the black market as a moonlighting scheme, he did not let on.

"What do you remember about the Conniff killing?" Bamonte asked.

"I think Ralstin . . ." He did not finish his sentence; it was as if the story, buried for so long, was incapable of coming forth.

"Hacker came out and said he had a package that Ralstin gave him that he wanted to get rid of . . ." Mangan said quickly, then trailed off, leaving his sentence on the table like a hot wire dropped in a driveway after a storm.

"Hacker?" Bamonte and Johnson were confused. Mangan explained about William Harrison Cox, his partner during the 1930s, and the nickname that paid tribute to Cox's skills inside an elevator. He had died years ago.

"Hacker brought out the package and set it on the seat. It was shaped like a pistol. We took it to the Post Street Bridge and dropped it off the bridge."

Was Mangan talking about the missing murder weapon? Bamonte followed up with a series of questions on the pistol, but Mangan's responses were muted, confused. He had temporarily lost his memory—or regained his loyalty.

Bamonte stood, motioning the retired cop to get up with him. "C'mon, Dan. Let's go for a ride."

"A ride? Whereabouts?"

"To the river."

Paraded through the Police Guild, accompanied by two active lawmen, Mangan looked a bit sheepish in front of his daughter and the handful of old-timers who gathered for drinks in the early evening. They whispered as Mangan walked by, and the word "snitch" passed a few lips.

THE MIST from Spokane Falls rose nearly a hundred feet, dampening the cement rails of the Post Street Bridge. Snowmelt pouring into the river had swollen the city's most prominent landmark; the water crashed through its basalt gorge with much noise and froth. For years, the river was an open sewer, carrying the industrial and human waste of the metropolis built on either side of its banks and toxic shavings from the mining operations of Idaho. In 1935, the year that Officer Dan Mangan stood above the falls with another officer, the river was ranked as the foulest waterway in Washington. The city no longer dumped its garbage into the Spokane, but the river covered more than a century of secrets and bad habits. Now Mangan was there with Bamonte to talk about a single disposed piece.

"Why did they choose you and Cox to get rid of the gun?" Bamonte asked him.

"Well . . ." Mangan looked east, in the direction of the old brewery home of the Hotel de Gink, and then he looked west, where the river tumbled further down into the valley where dust bowl migrants had taken up refuge. "The captain—Hinton, was his name—the captain called me into the station at the time and gave us this package."

"The gun?"

"It was shaped like a gun. Weighed about what a gun would weigh. Felt like a gun. And Hacker and me . . . we drove up here. . . . He said the gun was from Ralstin. That Ralstin was in trouble. Hacker brought out the package and set it on the seat. . . ."

"Why would this Captain Hinton call you in?"

"The captain was very good friends with Ralstin. Hinton was about three or four years older than Clyde."

Bamonte wondered if Hinton was alive. Mangan told him he'd died more than twenty years ago.

The sheriff was struck by how many people inside the Stone Fortress—not just patrolmen but detectives and high-ranking officers—knew something about the killing.

"Hacker said, 'Ralstin wanted us to get rid of it,' " Mangan said.

"So who threw it in the river?"

"Hacker did. He just dropped it."

"Where? Show me."

Mangan took a half-step toward the rail and looked down. The water was deep and muddy and ragged-topped, collecting itself against a sheer rock face after coming through the falls. Mangan motioned toward the shore, next to the rock face, an unlikely place to bury a weapon. Most people, Bamonte thought, would throw it into the middle of the falls.

"There." Mangan lifted a bony finger, squinted. "Right over there."

"Did he throw it or drop it?"

"He dropped it."

Mangan seemed very tired, struggling for breath. He needed to sit down somewhere. Bamonte had one more question. Then he would be done with him, and Mangan could go back to the Police Guild and his R and R, or back home with Rose and his scrapbook.

"Did you know what that gun was used for?" Bamonte asked. "Did you know what you were doing?"

Mangan's mouth zippered into a line. He held his jaw tight. Bamonte did not try to rush him.

"I knew about that murder. . . ." Mangan said. "And I thought this might have been the murder weapon. But . . ."

"And you never told anybody?"

"No."

"Why?"

"Nobody ever asked me about it."

A FEW DAYS LATER, another story ran in the *Spokesman-Review*, the second piece by Bill Morlin, the paper's crime reporter, and the most thorough account yet written on the case. Morlin interviewed Mangan, Bamonte, the present Spokane police chief, and members of the Conniff family, and described an investigation that was now considered the oldest active homicide case in the United States. The headline, on page one, read: 1935 SLAYING PROBE RE-OPENED. The story, picked up by the Associated Press, ran in papers around the world. In the article, Bamonte was quoted as saying, "Now, the cover-up is over."

Within a week, letters and tips started to trickle in to Bamonte's office in Newport. Among them was a note from a retired New York City police officer—a letter that sent a chill down Bamonte's spine.

A Stirring

"You're starting to sound like the Serpico of the West," the former cop wrote, referring to the New York detective who blew the whistle on corruption among his fellow officers. He concluded with some advice for Bamonte:

"You never badmouth a brother."

15.

The Net

IN THE LOFT of Snake River high country set aside for displaced bands of the Nez Percé Indian tribe, a local police chief read the story in the Spokane paper and then picked up the phone. Keith Hendrick, the top lawman in the reservation town of Lapwai, Idaho, dialed the number of the Pend Oreille sheriff. Then he hung up before anyone could answer, opting to cage his doubts for the time being. Those newspaper guys would print anything to sell a paper; now here was this libel about a Spokane detective from the 1930s labeled as the likely culprit in a half-century-old murder case. The story, without naming Clyde Ralstin, gave enough details to lead Hendrick to believe they were talking about a man he used to know very well—a man who was like a father to him. But the Clyde Ralstin he once knew wasn't a dirty cop, and he certainly was not the type of person who could ever kill somebody over a few pounds of butter, putting a final bullet in him as he lay mortally wounded. When he left town, more than a decade ago, he was one of the most revered figures on the reservation, a white man who married a young native woman and spent his days trying to uphold the law.

Several hundred miles east of Spokane, in a Rocky Mountain hamlet, a woman who told Sheriff Bamonte she was afraid to give her name said she knew a fellow—a former Spokane police detective—who once tried to rape her. He was tall, arrogant in a crude way, and rough, matching the description in the paper. She remembered his face, the pointy nose, the motor charge of his voice, and his threat after assaulting her: there wasn't a thing she could do, because the law couldn't touch him.

Nearly two thousand miles to the north, in the mummified Alaskan gold-rush town of Skagway, the name Acie Logan, carried by the wire service story, stirred memories. Could this Acie Logan, this Mississippi con who was supposed to have had a hand in the 1935 shooting, be the same stretch-necked southerner who showed up in the frontier oasis of Skagway just after the war and stayed on for several decades? Mrs. Joseph Shelby, whose husband was an engineer on the railroad that carried timber, food, and minerals over Barstow Pass, remembered Logan as somewhat of a rounder who set up a homestead on a bar stool in one of Skagway's darkened watering holes. But he was a damn good fireman on the railroad. Nobody ever asked him about his past, even when a son from a distant marriage arrived one day and Acie walked around town boasting about what a great daddy he was.

In northern California, a retired policeman read the story and also dialed the Pend Oreille sheriff's office. He told Bamonte he knew a man who fit the suspect's description, a violent old cuss, always showing off his guns. What's more, he used to brag about his misdeeds.

In a trailer park on the eastern fringe of Spokane, Bill Parsons realized during the first week of April that he would not be able to die in peace—not with Dan Mangan telling the world about what had been the best-kept secret of the Spokane Police Department. Now that the institutional safe was open, all the valuables would eventually spill out. Parsons, the former chief, holding to life with the help of his oxygen bottle and shelfful of pills, was so mad he nearly fell out of his breakfast chair. Not only was Mangan blabbing; he didn't even get it right.

Bamonte used to say he was just stupid enough to believe in luck and smart enough not to trust it. Casting his net across a gulf of time, the sheriff was finding out that the world was full of people with something to report or something to hide. The trick was separating the swollen consciences from the bad memories.

* * *

WITHIN THE WALLS of the Spokane Police Department, discretion still had its place. In a second request, Bamonte had asked for the personnel files on Clyde Ralstin, Dan Mangan, Ed Hinton, Charles Sonnabend, and others. The records were kept underground, in a former missile silo. Weeks later—and only after he castigated the department in the press for its lack of cooperation—information came back to him on all of the men but one: Clyde Ralstin. Spokane police had no record of any such man ever working at the Stone Fortress; the name drew a blank.

Bamonte was livid. "I'm a cop, trying to solve a murder in my county—what the hell's going on!" he thundered.

A month earlier, they had told him not to bother pursuing the case because nobody was alive from that era. Then Dan Mangan appeared, holding the rusted secrets from September 1935. Now, as Bamonte tried to follow a paper trail, he ran into another wall. He produced newspaper clips in which a Detective Clyde Ralstin was mentioned for some deed or another in the line of duty. In addition, he found a picture of the phantom, from an archival yearbook, showing Clyde in the uniform of a Spokane police detective, the big nose sloping out from beneath a cap with a badge atop its brim. Please look again, Bamonte asked the department.

AT HOME in Metaline Falls, the alders were starting to leaf out on the south face of Mount Linton. The ravines in the lower elevations of the Selkirks were full of snowmelt, water coursing down the mountain pleats and filling the Pend Oreille. Tony and Betty talked very little, their lives becoming more detached, their thoughts held close and contained. Over twenty-three years, they had lived through a miscarriage, hospitalized bouts of hepatitis, death threats from liquor-pumped cons, weeks without money, and winter nights so black and cold it was as if all life had been sucked out of the valley. What did they have now? Suspicion and pride, walls and fences.

They exchanged information about work. Betty was worried for her job, wondering what the true intentions of the potential buyers of the cement plant might be. Work was continuing to slow, orders dropping off, the plant deteriorating. The air-raid siren called just two shifts to work, the seven a.m. and three p.m. rotations, but it was starting to sound like a dirge. Rumors blew in with the spring wind—harsh half-truths about closing the factory and ending the pension obligations to men crippled and diseased in service to cement—and then blew out on a breeze of gray dust.

Tony noticed other ominous signs in the valley: the resort and cafe that always drew a respectable clientele along the river's banks in summer was for sale. Tourism was supposed to be the future for the Pend Oreille; if the resort had no confidence in the coming years, what should everyone else think?

Bamonte wanted just to sit down with Betty and tell her everything: the discoveries from the Stone Fortress, his fears that their marriage—like the town—was dying. But that would involve exposure, showing wounds. What he knew from his father was that emotional concealment equaled strength. He also knew that his father was wrong. But changing a life habit—where do you start?

He went into his study for another session with the men and women from 1935—just a peek, he told himself, a quick escape. He opened the new batch of information from the civil service archives in the missile silo. Sonnabend had been a model officer, just as everyone said, a big, sturdy cop with a commendable record. Dan Mangan was another story. His personnel file was full of citations and warnings—supervisory descriptions of a far different man than the gimpy old tavern owner who had led him to the bridge a few weeks ago. One letter in particular caught Bamonte's eye. It was dated May 14, 1946, and addressed to the Spokane police chief.

Chief:

At 5:07 a.m. we had a call that a man was beating his wife at 2508 E. Pacific. This is the home of Sgt. Mangan.

We sent the South Side car and also Sgt. Moulton. In a few minutes after the first call, the second call came, so the Emergency Dr. and I went to the above address.

Sgt. Mangan had taken his car and left before the car and Moulton arrived.

I talked a few words to Mrs. Mangan for she was in poor condition to talk. She said Dan came home a few minutes before and she asked him who he had been laying up with and he choked her and beat her head against the wall, and that he was drunk.

Pat Mangan the girl called the station and she was a witness to the trouble.

Sgt. Moulton and I looked for Sgt. Mangan for about (1) one hour but could not find him. I think maybe he left for Loon Lake.

Casualtie has been made.

Capt. Cox

Bamonte recognized the reporting officer: Hacker Cox, identified by Mangan as his longtime partner.

The narrative on Mangan in his personnel file ended a month after he bashed his wife's head into the wall. The note from June 3, 1946, was addressed to the Police Pension Board.

Gentlemen:

I respectfully request that I be retired by reason of physical disability incurred in the line of duty and through no fault or neglect on my part, on certificate of disability from the Pension Board Physician, and Dr. Harvey, his Associate and from the City Physician.

In accordance with the provisions of Remington's Revised Statutes of Washington, I request that this retirement be deferred until October 3, 1946, on which date I will have had six months sick leave.

I was appointed to the Spokane Police Department Jan. 21, 1930 and have served continuously to the present date and now hold the rank of Sergeant at the salary of $226 a month.

Yours respectfully,
D.A. Mangan
Police Sergeant

Wasn't that just like the police department, Bamonte thought. Sometimes, he was truly ashamed to be a cop. He loved the discoveries, the adrenaline that comes with a chase, the resolutions, the authority. But he also knew too many people who became cops for the wrong reason, seeing the badge as a license to bully. Mangan's file was full of the kind of crimes that would land most men in jail. He took payments from bootleggers, burglarized stores, and nearly killed his wife. His reward, after such a distinguished career, was a disability pension and six months of sick-leave pay to get him started. Then he was off to Hungry Horse, where he lived off the thirst of dam builders.

A basic question about Mangan remained unanswered. What was it that made him now give up the story of tossing the piece in the river? Was he still trying to protect someone—himself, perhaps? A conscience as shriveled as Mangan's was not so easily self-started.

The sheriff dialed Rosemary Miller; he needed another session with Mangan. Something more. Shake and scratch and kick and dig. You never know. Wasn't there something Mangan might still want to talk about—a small detail, a minor fact?

But Rose had bad news: her father had just suffered another stroke—not a big one, but significant. He was in the hospital, in no shape to talk.

A FEW DAYS LATER, Bamonte tangled with the other Mangan, Spokane's chief of police, who was mad over an article in the Newport *Miner*. The weekly newspaper of the Pend Oreille had elevated Bamonte-bashing to the journalistic equivalent of aerobics. But in late April, with their sheriff receiving attention in newspapers around the world, the *Miner* ran a rare complimentary article about Bamonte, a long piece on the state of the Conniff investigation. When asked why he was spending county time on the case—at fifteen dollars an hour, was the sheriff *really* giving the taxpayers their due?—he explained that because there was no statute of limitations on murder, he was bound by law to investigate all new evidence.

"My major concern is to solve this and to put it to rest for the sake of the family," Bamonte told the paper. "I have never seen a victim of an unsolved tragedy with peace of mind and the Conniff family is no exception. I owe it to our community and the Conniff family to extend our best efforts."

One of the main problems, he said, was the Spokane Police Department; they were not fully cooperating. Bamonte said he had tried to lay out the importance of the case to the chief, but the man never bothered to respond directly.

After the *Miner* story appeared, Chief Mangan fired off a letter to the paper, saying his department had cooperated as best it could with the sheriff. He said he had assigned Lieutenant Gary Johnson, head of the department's internal affairs unit, to assist Bamonte, but that the resources of the Spokane Police Department were badly stretched. "Perhaps it is time to remind Sheriff Bamonte that his case is exactly that—a Pend Oreille County case. We certainly could 'lay out the importance' of our current Spokane Police caseload, which includes recent unsolved murders, rapes etc." Pend Oreille County, he wrote, had no murders in 1987, the most recent year for which full crime statistics were available, while Spokane had sixteen.

Bamonte felt humiliated and hurt when he read the letter. If he was to solve this case, he would have to do it with the largest neighboring police department as an obstruction. Chief Mangan's tone sounded patronizing. Why all the nastiness and sarcasm?

Bamonte penned him a private note. "It is interesting that you can take the time to write your negative, misleading and uninformed letter to the newspaper; however, you have been above responding to me personally," he wrote. "I will not trouble you about this case again and I am truly sorry about your apathy. This appears to be just another slap in the face to the Conniff family from the Spokane Police Department."

BY MID-APRIL, the sheriff had yet to receive anything from Spokane police on their former detective Clyde Ralstin. The Conniff investigation, after a burst of fresh information in March and early April, was stalled again. Bamonte added up his case: he had a police report, from an interview with long-dead Charley Sonnabend, in which Ralstin was named as Conniff's killer. He had the troubling death of Sheriff Elmer Black, falling from a bridge shortly after he tried to reopen the investigation in 1955. He had a near-dead witness, Dan Mangan, who said he and his partner had disposed of a gun a few days after the killing on the instructions of a Spokane police captain, in order to protect Detective Ralstin. It all added up to an intriguing tale. But where was the physical evidence to back the story? The gun? Fingerprints? Blood samples? Or a living suspect—Logan, Ralstin? The case was built on sand.

But the net was still out there; Bamonte was still trolling. In the third week of April, he snagged another voice from 1935.

He received a call from a woman who thought she could help solve the case. She had read about the Pend Oreille sheriff in the newspaper and had wanted to call earlier, but her husband said she shouldn't get involved. She might even be vulnerable to prosecution, as an accomplice. Morally, she felt dirty, and wanted to wash herself of this secret.

"I know who killed that man Conniff," the woman told the sheriff over the phone. Her voice was distant, like a scratchy record, yet showed some feistiness and strength. "And I can help you prove it."

"When can I meet you?" Bamonte asked, ready to camp on her lawn if necessary.

"You can't use my name in the paper. Because my husband, he doesn't want me to get involved too deep and get my name in the paper. He said it doesn't look good at my age. He said that a lot of people would say, 'She's just an old bag trying to get her name in the paper.' "

Bamonte promised not to release her name without her permission. At her suggestion they agreed, for the time being, to call Pearl Keogh "Ms. X."

16.

The Nurse

PEARL KEOGH was tiny, overwhelmed by her overcoat, with eyes the color of a muddied sky. She drove herself to Sak's Restaurant, amidst the sprawl of ranch-house suburbia east of Spokane known as the Valley, and then she looked around for the man whose picture had been in the paper. When she found Tony Bamonte she said, "You're quite a handsome young guy."

They sat in a booth during the lunch hour, the elfin eighty-five-year-old woman and the cop, as the burger train went back and forth. Pearl ordered coffee and kept her coat on. She was a nurse, she explained, and her life had a symmetry that bolstered her belief in divine justice. Sin was like excess weight: the more you put on, the harder it was to lose. But the same thing went for virtue. When she was a girl, going to school with Flathead Indians on the floor of a grand valley shadowed by the Mission Mountains, the Sisters of Providence took care of her. And when she was older, in her sixties and seventies, she nursed some of those same nuns through their dying days.

Try as she might, Pearl believed that she had not lived a perfect life. Her sense of adventure, her mischievousness, and her pride sometimes led her to do things she later regretted. She loved to flirt. Though married, she sometimes went to Mother's Kitchen during the bottomed-out days of the Depression, because the men said flattering things, and the cops radiated action. They had pride and a paycheck—two legs at a time when many people couldn't walk. It was better at Mother's than going home to empty cupboards and a husband thrown out of work—Hoovered, as they called it. Also, bootleg gin and whiskey were plentiful at the diner, which meant there was always a party of sorts. Pearl didn't drink, but she confessed to finding some people more interesting after a few shots of hooch. Cops and whiskey and the nurse: after midnight, it was seldom dull at Mother's Kitchen. She told Bamonte that some of the boys used to call her " 'sweetie,' 'honey,' and all that crap."

The sheriff turned on his tape recorder. He asked his first questions in a commanding voice, well above his usual soft tones. Pearl told him he didn't have to talk so loud; her hearing was fine. And he shouldn't make the mistake of assuming she was some weak old lady. Just a few summers back, she had wrestled a king salmon half her size into the bow of a boat riding the swells of the Pacific off the Washington coast.

Over the phone, she had mentioned that she used to hang out at Mother's during the 1930s because her sister, Ruth, worked as a cook and manager there. When Pearl's late-night shift at Sacred Heart Hospital was over, she usually walked down the hill to Mother's. Bamonte brought up their earlier conversation as a starting point.

"You were telling me about the wrappings from the Newport Creamery on this—"

"Yes." Pearl jumped right in, hastening back to 1935 and the nights spent with Virgil Burch, Clyde Ralstin, Dan Mangan, and a three-hundred-pound cop named Tiny Stafford. She described Ralstin as the power at Mother's: "sneaky-eyed . . . he would never look right at you when he talked to you, and I always feel if you're gonna talk to somebody at least give 'em an eye once in a while, you know." Burch, Ralstin's buddy, the owner of Mother's was blue-eyed, light-haired, a womanizer who could flatter and scorn with the same sentence. She remembered Mangan as "Danny"—a garrulous sort, always talking up his latest scam. Every cop at Mother's seemed to have something going on the side.

"They would complain," she said. "They didn't want to arrest any-body, because there was no money to feed them. They had no money. The county was broke."

As she talked, plates full of food, picked-over sandwiches, half-eaten salads, and soups gone cold passed by on their way to the garbage. Pearl narrowed her big eyes. "Tony, money was tight."

Mother's Kitchen was an oasis of hot food and fast talk, and it never closed, Pearl said. But she had not contacted Bamonte to talk about her social life a half-century ago.

"When my sister was cooking there and managing the restaurant for Zada and Virgil, she was very suspicious because he brought butter in without wrappers on it, and she asked and wondered why the wrappers were missing, and he said, well, he just thought it was better to bring the butter in and save her from unwrapping them. Well, she said that was good enough. So then she emptied some garbage one day and she found these wrappers, two or three of them that hadn't been destroyed. And she looked at them, and then she jumped Virgil about it. Virgil says, 'Oh,' he says, 'I bought some butter from them. . . .'

"See, after this man was murdered and this talk was going on and around and around about everybody knew who did it and they wouldn't say nothing about it, she took the wrappers to the sheriff. . . . Well, he said he would try to look into it and see what was wrong, and she said, 'I think it merits an investigation, because there's been too much butter, cream, cottage cheese, and whatever dairy products that they use there has been brought in.' And she says, 'I've been suspicious for a long time but I can't do it on my own.' Well, he says, 'We'll take care of it.' That was it. So, anyway, she got real upset about the whole thing and she left, she said, 'I can't work under these conditions.' "

"She quit because of that?"

"Yes." Pearl looked straight ahead at Bamonte, unblinking. A life-time in the outdoors had hardened and cracked her skin. Her hair, which she used to wear in long black curls, was bristly and gray, cut short. The eyes alone carried the intensity of her youth.

"And Virgil says, 'Well, to hell with ya! I don't care. We can get lots of cooks.' "

That was not the end of it, Pearl explained. She kept an on-and-off friendship with Burch. He was attractive, and she found him more charming than she usually cared to admit. A few years after the Conniff killing, Pearl and her husband moved into a house in Spokane that Burch had lived in during the mid-1930s. She remembered the year, 1940, because she had just taken in her brother's baby, born to a sick mother.

"We lived in this little house on Jackson Street and it had been Virgil's before he married Zada. And the funny part of it was, I was cleaning out a cupboard and I found a bunch of Newport wrappers."

"You found them yourself?"

"It was Virgil's bachelor shack, see, that's where he stayed before he married Zada, and here I was cleaning all these shelves out and I pulled out these whole bunch of wrappers, Newport butter wrappers."

Her memory seemed good, and to Bamonte's relief, she only answered questions if she seemed to know what she was talking about. Thus, when he asked her about a broad cover-up, and whether she ever saw the Spokane police chief in Mother's, Pearl answered, "Oh, dear, dear, dear man—it's awfully hard to remember."

He asked Pearl for a precise description of the butter wrappers from the creamery.

"Well, they were little thin papers that wrapped around the butter, then they were put into cartons to ship. But they didn't have any cardboard cartons . . . just thin paper. But it said 'Newport Creamery,' and something else . . . maybe the address, could be, I don't know. But I do know it said 'Newport Creamery,' and they were just white papers with black writing on them. As near as I can remember it was black. And that's all I know about that."

And what had Pearl done with the wrappers?

"I threw 'em out."

She and her sister had already been to Ralph Buckley, the Spokane County sheriff, in 1935 when Ruth found the Newport wrappers.

Though Buckley promised to investigate, nothing that she knows of was ever done. Neither of the sisters was ever contacted by a detective.

The butter wrappers were circumstantial, Bamonte thought, a small bit of evidence. It could be explained. But it was something new; the smallest detail can sometimes break open a case.

Pearl kept talking, steaming toward "what I came to tell ya about. . . ."

A year or so after she found the wrappers, Pearl moved from Spokane to Portland. In the early 1940s, there was more work than men on either side of the Columbia River. Two dams—one completed near Hood River, the other under construction at Grand Coulee—held the promise of nearly unlimited electricity, for pennies. This spurred heavy industry, shipbuilding near Portland and aluminum smelting up and down the river. Virgil Burch and his wife had also moved to the Portland area, after selling Mother's Kitchen. They lived across the bridge over the Columbia in the Washington town of Vancouver. One night, Pearl had them over to dinner.

"I'd cook a big dinner and maybe they'd have a beer or something . . . and then he'd get to talking about his old days in Spokane and that bragging, see."

She remembered virtually every word of the conversation with Burch from that night; nearly fifty years later, it continued to bother her. As a Roman Catholic, Pearl believed she could live her entire life as a moral and honest person but still be condemned to everlasting hell if a singular stain—a mortal sin—were not first removed from her soul. She seemed now to be in a great hurry to free herself of the mark from long ago. The same time as the dinner with Burch, she explained, there had been a robbery in Pearl's neighborhood in Portland, which prompted a particular conversation.

"I said, 'I can't understand it.' I said, 'I thought the robbing days were over.' And this was when Virgil chimed in."

A few beers under his belt, Clyde Ralstin's best friend could not resist telling about an achievement of his own, in Newport, about seven years earlier—the creamery heist, Pearl recalled. Burch said he had worked as a plumber at the creamery. He told this by way of detailing the craft of a thief.

"They had this all planned out, see. And he left this latch where he could raise this door up. Well, when they raised this door up, it made a noise. It alerted the watchman. And that's what he said."

Bamonte was astonished. "The watchman being Marshal Conniff?"

"Yes. That's who he was."

Bamonte jumped up, rubbed his hands. He wanted to hug Pearl. She raised a finger, a wait-for-the-good-part ellipsis.

"Then Virgil said, he said, 'Well, I'll just get the hell out of here.' That's exactly the words he said. But Ralstin went clear around and I guess this Conniff probably had a gun. I don't know, but apparently, the way Virgil thought, this night cop pulled his gun, and Virgil got scared, and Ralstin . . . just blowed his brains out. That's the way the story came to me."

Here, for the first time, was a living witness—not firsthand, but a witness nonetheless. She was old and shrunken, but she spoke well. Any chance Bamonte had of getting this story in court would depend on the specifics. He pressed her for the fine print.

"When Virgil told you this story, did he actually see Ralstin shoot the marshal?"

Pearl held her answer, then shook her head. "I don't know if he actually seen it, but he was standing beside him when he did it."

"He was standing beside him?"

"He said they were both . . . He said he thought that Conniff was raising the gun and he said he let him have it 'cause Conniff would have recognized Virgil."

"Because he had been in the creamery for two or three days?"

"Working there, yeah. Virgil."

"So he was right beside—?"

"Yeah. He said they both turned the corner at the same time, because they were gonna go in that door, and when they raised the door, it creaked. And Conniff came around another corner, and he said, uh . . . somebody said, somebody either hollered 'Halt' or 'Stop,' and he said when they saw that, there was a little bit of light coming from the yard light or something like that, and he said that they thought that this guy pulled a gun and he said Ralstin said, 'He's not going to shoot me. I'll get him first.' "

"Ralstin said that to Virgil?"

"Yeah. Said that to Virgil. And Virgil repeated it. Said 'It was us or him.' Virgil didn't give a hoot then, you know. It was all over."

Burch also told Pearl about the roadblock, just outside of Spokane, which had gone up shortly after the shooting. Bamonte had heard of the roadblock from the police summaries of interviews with Charley Sonnabend. Without prompting from Bamonte, Pearl had just brought up a key detail that was quite similar to the Sonnabend account. As Burch explained to Pearl, the killers knew that the police would be looking for three suspects, so they had to hide at least one man.

"Virgil said, 'By God, I sure thought I was gonna get it.' He says, 'I thought my day had come.' And he was under a tarp in the back of this car and they had that loaded with butter."

"What kind of car was it?"

"It was an old REO Flying Cloud. You know what they are? A real old one. They didn't make it more after the thirties, I don't think."

"A four-door?"

"I believe it was a four-door."

"Okay now, who was in the car with him? That was the night Conniff was killed?"

"Yes."

"He used to talk about that?"

"Yes."

"Who was with him when he was in the car?"

"Well, I think that this Logan and Ralstin, the way he talked."

Bamonte was pumped, riding the surge that comes with discovery. He repeated some of his earlier questions; he wanted to hear Pearl answer them again.

"Who did he say did the actual shooting?"

"He said that Clyde did it. He said, oh, he said Clyde did it. You know."

Bamonte returned to the roadblock.

"Well, he said, he said that they went—that he was in the car when they were stopped. But he said it was either Logan or Ralstin that knew one of the guys that stopped him. And that's why they went by so easy. But the one guy wanted to search them. And the one guy wouldn't do it. He said. . . . 'You're clean.' "

"Did he ever mention who the policemen were who stopped him?"

"No. He said one of them was Ralstin's buddy. That's all he said."

"That's all? They let him go? And this was right after the murder?"

"Yeah. The same night. . . . Do you know who those guys were that stopped him?" Pearl asked.

"No. I'm trying to find that out."

At Mother's Kitchen in the first days after the killing, Virgil Burch was "an absolute wreck," Pearl recalled. When she asked him what was wrong, he snapped at her. "I'm sick," he said. But he grew stronger every day. Soon it was a joke, banter between him and Ralstin. What seemed particularly odd to Pearl was how open they were about it. "Who'd you kill today, Detective?" Everybody at Mother's shared in the laugh.

One cop in particular came to mind. "Did you know Jimmy Manning?" Pearl asked Bamonte.

"No, I didn't."

"Well, I used to walk his beat with him when I would get off work at midnight . . . I was young and full of life and knew him quite well. And I knew he was married, see. . . . I'd walk with him maybe five or six blocks and I'd say, 'Jimmy, I gotta go now, I gotta go.' And I was married, see."

"You were both married?"

"But I was just being a smart aleck, see. But he thought he had something going. . . ."

And she was off with Jimmy Manning for five minutes—dancing at a beer hall, pulling his shirt out of his pants when she was mad at him, daring him to arrest her. Pearl could not talk about Manning without feeling the blend of guilt and pleasure that is the moral imprint of Catholicism. Bamonte had not asked Pearl for any details of her nights with him, but she wanted this story out.

The sheriff tried to steer her back to his case. "Now, Manning—

the same guy who was trying to hustle you—he was telling you all this stuff. What all did he tell you about the murder?"

"He knew about that gun being thrown over the—the, . . . whatchacallem."

"So he thought it was Ralstin that killed the marshal."

"Yes. He knew all about it. Every policeman in town knew about it."

"What did he tell you about it?"

"He said . . . he just said . . . 'Virgil and Ralstin is in this business of stealing and robbing and making a living like that.' He said, 'I'm not gonna do nothing about it.' "

Tiny Stafford, the three-hundred-pound patrolman, was another regular at Mother's. He claimed he was going to do something about Ralstin, Pearl recalled. "He said, 'There's gonna be some investigations about this. There's gonna be somebody that's not going to be around here very long—you know, talk like that. He was gonna see that this was done. But he never did anything either."

"Was he on the take? Was he honest?"

"I heard he used to go to these sporting houses downtown. . . . He'd go in there and demand money from them . . . and take it— you know, for hush money."

"Okay now—after they shot Conniff, did they steal the dairy products and then take off, or had they already had some—"

"They had it loaded."

"They already had it loaded?"

"Yes. And they were trying to go back for more. They didn't have it all. They only had butter. They had butter but they didn't have cream. Virgil said, 'That's the only thing that didn't make my day.' Because, he says, 'We lost our cream.' "

In recounting the crime over dinner in Portland, Burch laughed throughout, Pearl said—crowing about how "we pulled it off, we got away with it." One of the few things that still surprised Bamonte, a cop for twenty-three years, was a killer's lack of remorse. In the Conniff case, the women alone—Pearl, Ruth, and later Mangan's daughter, Rose—carried the weight of conscience from September 1935.

"They made light of it," Pearl said. "To think that a life had been taken. Somebody ought to just bang them one."

Bamonte had this trio—Ralstin, Burch, Logan—pictured. He had known people like them in high school in Metaline Falls. He had known them in Vietnam. He had known them on the Spokane police force. He had a simple, old-fashioned word for Ralstin—"bully." As he listened to Pearl, his stomach tightened and his fist balled; he wanted to tangle with them.

"Do you have a picture of Virgil?"

"I could have gotten a picture of him."

"Where?"

"From Helen. But she's dead now. You see, they went to Missoula and he got into a mess over there and she divorced him."

"Is Virgil dead now?"

"Oh yeah. He's been dead quite a while."

"And Logan's dead?"

"Is he?" She wasn't sure what had become of Logan.

Ralstin, of course, was the one Bamonte really wanted. The last time Pearl had seen him was about 1937, two years after the killing. He came into Mother's Kitchen and said goodbye. He was off to South America, he said, with a new bride, Dorothy, one of the waitresses. They were going to make a killing in the frontier of South America, where a man could still carve out his personal fiefdom with nothing but a rifle and strong will.

"He came into the restaurant and said, 'I'm not a policeman anymore.' He said, 'There's gonna be some of those SOBs over there pay for this,' only he used the full word—I won't say it."

Bamonte asked Pearl if there was anything else she wanted to bring up. She said no, she had covered most everything she could remember from those days. The sheriff closed his notebook, turned off his tape recorder, and thanked her.

"It's not you who should be thanking me but me who should be thanking you."

"Why's that, Pearl?"

For fifty-four years she had tried to tell the story to somebody, but nobody had ever listened with enough interest to want to do anything about it. So Pearl and her sister had kept the story to themselves; they were never able to find a comfortable place to lodge the secret.

"What year were you born, Pearl?"

"1905."

"1905?"

"You want to see my driver's license?"

"No."

Pearl put on her scarf, buttoned the top of her coat, and disappeared out the door and back to wherever she had come from, somewhere in the folds of time. She seemed to walk with a lightness of foot, as if a plaster cast had just been removed from her leg. Bamonte was jubilant; he felt more powerful than at almost any other time as sheriff. The lift came from bringing history alive, of being able to change things after they were already set and gone.

Before she left, Pearl gave the sheriff a picture of herself when she was twenty-nine—a dark-eyed beauty in a white dress, cut short and daring, with wavy, shoulder-length hair and a coy half-smile. The woman in the snapshot was full of possibilities; her eyes said as much. She had lived an entire life since Mother's Kitchen, of course, but it did not seem that way to Bamonte. He had just spent the lunch hour with the Pearl Keogh of 1935.

17.

Home

THE RAINS CAME and sluiced away what little snow was still stuck in the shadowed draws of the Selkirks. Driving home, Bamonte had seldom seen the river so enraged, or the landscape so weepy. The Pend Oreille was inflated with runoff and mud, and it careened through the canyon below Metaline Falls, tearing out the graveled sides of the riverbank with it. Even the little carpets of civilization on either side of the river seemed to be slipping, pulled toward the river. The golf course, which should have been spruced up by now, looked seedy and overgrown; it had sprouted a For Sale sign since the sheriff last noticed. Plywood billboards, their sandwich layers peeled open by moisture, advertised firewood—cut, dried, and delivered for forty-nine dollars a cord. As Bamonte crossed the bridge into town, he saw a bright poster outside a tavern: Welcome, Canadians. And on Main Street, two of the town's three cafes were also on the block.

Whatever confidence people in the valley had maintained about keeping Metaline Falls alive was gone with the sale of the cement factory. As expected, the LeFarge Corporation had purchased the plant from Heidelberger Zement. It might as well have bought a corpse. The new owners gave notice that layoffs would soon begin; and the factory—once the cornerstone of the town's big dreams—

went into a "shutdown mode," as the managers called it. The worst suspicions of the cynics were borne out: the purchase appeared to be a ploy by an international company to buy and bury a potential competitor.

Already, Pend Oreille County was one of the most depressed areas in the West, with one in four people out of work. When mining went bust in the late 1970s, and then timber prices crashed with the recession of the early 1980s, the Pend Oreille took a gut punch and never recovered. The railroad, with its lone spur from Metaline Falls to the outside world, was abandoned. A big paper mill opened in the late 1980s, providing two hundred jobs; but other than that, there was no real stable source of income for the people of the Pend Oreille.

All around, Bamonte saw omens in things he never used to notice. Gray frosting from the cement factory, made thick and viscous by the rains, oozed down street gutters. The plant would likely close within a year, and then crumble and wither over time; but its legacy, a dusting similar to the leaden rain that fell over eastern Washington after Mount Saint Helens blew up in 1980, could remain in the hair of Metaline Falls for decades. The airborne effluent never used to bother Bamonte, but it looked ugly now.

The revelations from Pearl Keogh had sent Bamonte's spirits soaring—and then he fell into despair. How to prove what Pearl and Dan Mangan had told him? The net was still out there, but the returns were diminishing.

In the Pend Oreille, the sheriff's obsession with an ancient murder case brought the cranks to the front again. "Doesn't Pend Oreille County have other crimes its sheriff could be tending to?" one man wrote to the *Spokesman-Review*. "Is he really earning his $30,000 a year?" wrote another. "Or is he wasting tax dollars?" "Bamonte is making a fool of Pend Oreille County," a third letter writer asserted.

There were always people in the county taking potshots at him; being a target came with the turf. During low moments, Bamonte took the complaints personally. He was incapable of enjoying personal triumphs, because he sensed disaster in the shadows. A gift of good fortune, a glimmer of happiness—these were to be distrusted. Better to force your own breaks.

From his father, he had learned to cast a cold eye on luck. Unlike a load of silver or a pile of fresh-cut cedar, luck was not something that could be brought forth by sheer force, and therefore it was unreliable. He thought of Bull Bamonte often on these days when the sky lost its color and the forest held the clouds close to the ground. He would look in the direction of Mount Linton, the mine shaft where he had scattered his father's ashes, and recall the awful slog in a freezing rain to his graveyard. Lost in thought, he had stepped off the faint trail and stumbled into a tangle of wet brush. When darkness came and fresh snow covered the way back, he was still traipsing around with his father's ashes, trying to find the cursed mine shaft that had been the old man's final earthly passion. At last, he put the powdered remains to rest. But he had never made peace. He couldn't let him go. As Tony tried to make his way down the mountain to Metaline Falls, he was confused and wet and angry. Why hadn't his father said something before he died—a hint of love, a confession of affection? Why had his mother been such a flirt and a cheat, acting like a whore, driving Bull to a tortured life in one-room cabins and abandoned dance halls? After his father's death, Bamonte never reconciled with his mother, though that is apparently what she wanted. In her son's eyes, what she had done was unforgivable: sleeping with other men, breaking up the family. She had chippied, he said, and the consequences were still being felt. Late in her life, she had wanted to be a grandmother to the boy born to Betty, but Tony wouldn't let her in the house for long. They would talk for twenty minutes and then he would start to feel the old revulsion. She married seven times after divorcing Bull, and died without her son's forgiveness.

At home on the third floor of his brick building, as Bamonte tried to talk with Betty, he sounded like his father and felt like his mother. Betty wanted to take a vacation with Tony, a few days, maybe even a week, somewhere far removed from the Pend Oreille. In his nearly twelve years as sheriff, he had taken off only five days. Seven-day work weeks were his norm. "We need some time together," she told him.

"I don't have any time. There's too much going on."

"Is there something new with the Conniff case?"

"I'll tell you later."

"I have to read about it in the newspaper?"

"Nothing. There's a few leads."

"I feel like you're shutting me out, Tony."

"I'm not trying to. I'm just . . . busy. Worried about everything. The shit's starting to pile on. I don't know where to go with the case anymore."

"You came home late last night."

"You knew about that. Every Thursday . . ."

"What's special about Thursday?"

Bamonte had not been sleeping well; he looked gaunt and frayed. He came to bed late and never seemed to close his eyes. He was replaying 1935—over and over and over. And he was troubled by a pull toward a waitress he had met in Spokane. Their coming together had the force of gravity, inevitable. The woman had children of her own, including a boy who was sick with a life-threatening disease. Tony liked her because her voice was soft and she listened to all the old complaints without acting like she had heard them before. She was a friend, that's all, he told himself. But the friends grew closer, and didn't speak about what was happening. Before long, he was going out of his way to see her.

BAMONTE WENT DOWNSTAIRS to the first floor and put some wood in the lava-rock fireplace. The place seemed oversized and damp, wearing its years. Then he retreated to a cozier place—eight by twelve inches above a typewriter keyboard, wherein lived the story of Pend Oreille County's sheriffs, the world he had re-created from scratch. The master's thesis was all but finished, more than five hundred pages. Sitting in a pile next to him, this progeny looked bulky and commanding. It was a wonderful monument, making the sheriff feel a bit of immortality; his words would outlast him. All that remained was the chapter in the middle: the life and death of Marshal George Conniff.

The prosecutor of Pend Oreille County, Tom Metzger, also awaited the completion of Bamonte's findings. The press had asked Metzger what he would do if Bamonte turned up a suspect. Metzger, in his mid-thirties, affable and relaxed in the pace of the Pend Oreille, answered that he would do what the law demanded: if the sheriff produced enough evidence and a living suspect, he would consider filing charges. After Metzger's first statements, the sheriff told his prosecutor he not only hoped to crack the Conniff case but held out hopes of finding the killer and bringing him to justice in the Pend Oreille.

"Tony's doing a hell of a job," Metzger said. "Hell of a job. This case would seem impossible to resolve. But he's the most tenacious person I know."

And then, in private, the prosecutor had to chuckle. Only Bamonte, the obstinate son of a buck who had gone after the Forest Service, the Justice Department, and the neo-Nazis, among his many longshot crusades, could expect—in all earnestness—to solve a 1935 murder case. He wanted to tell the sheriff to drop it.

"If you take the legally admissible evidence, there is virtually nothing at this point," Metzger said. "Tony may well resolve this to the satisfaction of the Conniff family, but beyond that, I don't know."

What had started with police reports—of Sonnabend recounting Acie Logan's confession—blossomed with Dan Mangan's story of dumping the gun. Pearl Keogh had placed Newport Creamery wrappers in Mother's Kitchen just after the robbery. From Virgil Burch, she had heard an account of the actual shooting, and her description of the roadblock mirrored the Sonnabend-Logan version. Burch may have trimmed the story to his favor, but the details matched Logan's confession from 1935. Logan, Mangan, and now Pearl Keogh all had named Clyde Ralstin as the shooter. For his graduate thesis, Bamonte was prepared to believe as much. He saw Clyde as a brute with a badge, the worst kind of cop. Again, Bamonte's fist would ball up when he thought about him, because Ralstin was the embodiment of all the big, arrogant lawmen he'd known in his quarter-century as a cop—those people who smashed wine bottles in the rear pockets of homeless men and kicked around handcuffed suspects in the elevator.

He wanted to face *him*—not some old man but Clyde, the king of Mother's Kitchen, the strutting detective who bragged that nobody could touch him.

The emergence of Pearl Keogh had given the case a new direction. Just after talking to Pearl, Bamonte set out to find any trace of Logan, Burch, or Ralstin. Maybe one of them would rat out the other. Spokane County had no death certificate for any of the three members of the creamery-robbing gang. Logan's paper trail disappeared after he was released in 1938 from the federal penitentiary on McNeil Island. Ralstin, as far as the archives division of the Spokane Police Department was concerned, was a complete phantom. It had no record of his serving as policeman, even though there were dozens of stories in Spokane newspapers of the 1930s that mentioned Detective Ralstin.

The old papers also revealed a sketchy narrative of Burch's troubles in the months after Logan went to prison and Ralstin was demoted to patrol. In January 1936, a story in the Spokane *Chronicle* told of Burch's arrest on a charge of trying to influence a government witness. The FBI said that Burch had contacted Eddie Langenbach, who was going to testify about the creamery robberies, and offered him five hundred dollars not to talk. Langenbach was part of the loose network used by Clyde and Virgil to fence the stolen dairy products. Arrested a few weeks earlier, he pled guilty to interstate theft charges, and then fingered Burch and Ralstin. The detective was never arrested; Burch was left to take the fall for the creamery gang. At the trial, Langenbach lost his memory on the witness stand, and Burch was found not guilty.

Bamonte tried an electronic search. A computer check of all the western states still showed no record of Ralstin or Logan, but something came up on Burch—a report of his death. He had been living in Missoula, not far from the old hideout he used to share with Clyde, and close to the place where he'd been arrested for cattle rustling in the 1920s. In 1970, he was helping an old friend build a house not far from Missoula. Burch knew where his best buddy could buy a shower stall—cheap—from a wholesale connection in Seattle. He said they should go to Seattle together, an eight-hour drive, and bring the stall home in Virgil's pickup. The friend declined, so Virgil went alone. Shortly after he arrived in Seattle, he suffered a massive heart attack that killed him. He was sixty-eight years old. The friend he died trying to help was Clyde Ralstin. But there was no trace of what became of Clyde.

After learning about Burch, Bamonte started to interview cops from the 1930s, hoping one of the old boys might know something more than Mangan had told him. A surprising number of them were still alive, living on police pensions in overstuffed homes in and around Spokane. Some of the men, in their eighties, still listened to the police radio all day, reading Louis L'Amour stories with one ear tuned to the static and cackle of calls over the two-way. Bamonte went through his list, one man at time. He was chiseling away at the cement seal of the Cop Code, using guilt as a tool. There were two retired police chiefs he wanted to see: Clyde Phelps, living somewhere on the Olympic Peninsula, and Bill Parsons, said to be housed in a mobile-home park north of Spokane. But first, he built from the ground up, shaking recollections from retired patrolmen, the lifetime grunts. Some of the men were amused by the sheriff who never slept; did he *really* think he was going to get the Spokane Police Department to admit they had covered up a murder, and a cop killing at that? Most of the retired patrolmen remembered Ralstin as a tough and boastful giant; to a man, they recalled that he left town under some sort of scandal. But that was as far as it went.

Memory was selective, and if a lie could lodge itself long enough to become a fact, faulty. Conscience was more accurate. What the Conniff investigation had proved to Bamonte thus far was that most people could not outlive their pasts. The worst deeds of a lifetime could be buried or blurred to the point of being unrecognizable; but more often than not, they came back—the revenge of truth.

In his darkened room on a damp night in Metaline Falls, Bamonte heard the voices of killers trying to rationalize their deed, and he also heard the hauntings from his own past. What could possibly make Clyde Ralstin think he could kill a man and then live an entire life without facing justice? Bamonte asked himself the same question, in a slightly different form: could he repeat the sins of his mother, and follow the same pattern of neglect as Bull Bamonte had done, without his own life falling apart? The query answered itself in the project he was staring at; the past, this place he had taken refuge in, was a manacle.

EARLY MORNING, Bamonte was still at his desk. The room was cold, and he shivered. His home, a building that used to be one of the more elegant creations in Metaline Falls, seemed damp and crumbling. Until this spring, Bamonte never thought twice about the town's hoary slogan, passed on by the company managers who ran the hamlet: that one day Metaline Falls would be all bustle and gloss, a brawny city in the valley of the Pend Oreille. Now he was thinking of getting out, trying to sell the building; there was no future in a grit-coated brick stack across the way from a fast-dying cement factory, no future in Metaline Falls. If he could get twenty thousand dollars for the place, he would consider himself lucky.

Bamonte was due at work in an hour. Except for editing polish, the thesis was now done. His writing legs were wobbly; for every sentence that had made it onto the paper, three went to the dump. He wondered if Professor Carey, and his fellow graduate students, would laugh at his finished project. He was sure they were sketching out bigger themes, while he kicked around something that belonged in the fruit cellar, wrapped in cobwebs. He had tried so hard to stay with the class, doing extra papers, asking about books that were not required. Still, he believed there was a good chance the professor would flunk him. He decided to close out the chapter on Marshal Conniff with some questions left unanswered. After all, the idea behind the project was not to solve long-dormant crimes but to produce a history of law enforcement in Pend Oreille County. The student ended his story of George Conniff with a discussion of the gun, a reflection, subconscious or otherwise, of the hole in the sheriff's case. What Bamonte the investigator really needed was physical evidence—something solid to place on the table. Bamonte the student reached his own conclusions.

Initially, Bamonte thought the murder weapon might be tied conclusively to Ralstin, because one of the pistols taken from Logan had been signed out by Clyde. Later, when the case was reopened briefly in 1957, that pistol—still in Sonnabend's possession—was sent to the FBI to see if it matched the bullets that had been pulled from the body of Marshal Conniff. There was no match.

By Bamonte's deduction, the gun used to kill the Newport marshal was the one that Mangan threw in the river in 1935, not the one taken from Logan by Sonnabend. The timing and circumstances, and Mangan's precision, all pointed in that direction. In the half-century since the marshal was gunned down, the Spokane River's course had been adjusted several times, not by a wide margin, but the upstream dam-builders had pinched the flow enough to alter the main channel. Mangan had pointed to the froth at the base of the waterfall, against a sheer rock wall, as the burial site for the gun. After his initial interview with Mangan, Bamonte had raised the idea of looking for the gun. Perhaps, at the low-water point of the year, the river could be searched. Spokane police were skeptical, to the point of ridicule. Another blast of angry letters from Pend Oreille taxpayers hit the newspapers. The police chief said, diplomatically, that it is always appropriate for law enforcement to investigate new leads, but his men were stretched. An old case like the Conniff murder would have to be weighed against the more pressing crimes of the day.

The head of Spokane's internal investigations unit, Lieutenant Gary Johnson, also had his doubts about finding any physical evidence. Johnson was with the sheriff at the Police Guild when Mangan told him about throwing the gun in the river. He believed there had been a cover-up; he did not doubt that someone, long ago, in his own department had killed Marshal Conniff, and that the crime had been concealed, the secret kept, from generation to generation. But to Johnson, more worried about internal police concerns of the late twentieth century—officers who might be taking drug money to look away, or a shift supervisor who couldn't work with female cops—the question of justice in a 1935 killing seemed too distant. It was like a hobby. When Bamonte raised the question of searching for the gun, Johnson echoed his chief's words: the Conniff case was not a priority for the department.

Besides, he told the sheriff, he did not think the gun would still be lying around at the bottom of the river. "Fifty-four years is a lot of time," he said.

The message—from the citizens of the Pend Oreille, from Spokane police, from the prosecutor, from friends—grew to a chorus: give it up.

In his thesis, Bamonte said the marshal's murder was never vigorously investigated because the killer was a cop; there are no better protectors of their own kind than those sworn to uphold the law. He had no institutional remedy for this, a dilemma that was not unique to Spokane.

Most importantly, the Conniff case showed that conscience is a power that answers to its own rules. The burden of conscience had been passed on, like a baton in the night, from the original culprits to their sons and daughters and friends, a counterforce to the cover-up. Thus, by Bamonte's reckoning, in this epic struggle between criminals protecting their own and the weight of conscience, the truth eventually had forced its way out. Even so, the institution of the Spokane Police Department continued to cover up, following its instinct for survival.

So, Bamonte concluded in the final words he wrote on the Conniff chapter, the river held the last and most important clue. And, of course, it was impossible to pull back the layers of water that ran over the burial site. A river could not be stopped, no more than a person could outrun his past, or an institution reform itself from within.

"Do you want some coffee or something?" Betty asked her husband, peeking into the study, startling him somewhat. She was fresh, her hair done nicely, dressed for work.

"Please." She went back upstairs, and the student penned the last line of the Conniff section.

"There was no gun," he wrote. "The Spokane River holds the final and irretrievable piece of evidence."

18.

Men Without Badges

On the phone line, Keith Hendrick, police chief of Lapwai, Idaho, said, "Sheriff Bamonte, please."

"Can I tell him what this is regarding?"

"That murder case of his . . . the one from the Depression."

This was hard for Hendrick—giving up an old friend, a man he had known for nearly half his life, a father figure. He still was not sure he had the nerve to follow through with it, so he got right to the point.

"Sheriff, the man you're looking for is still alive."

"Excuse me?"

"You're looking for Clyde Ralstin, that right?"

"Yes, sir, I am," Bamonte answered. "Don't know if he's dead or run off or what the hell, but I'm—"

"You know where Saint Ignatius is?"

"Montana, somewhere."

"Montana, north of Missoula. Clyde's home."

"Home?"

"Yes. He's not dead. Or he wasn't dead the last time I checked."

"My God! Are you sure?"

Hendrick sketched out Ralstin, lean as a strip of jerky, a workhorse who used to cut ten cords of firewood every year, handy with a half-

183

dozen guns, a friend who valued loyalty over all else, at times mean enough to stop a train with his glare, but always on the Right Side.

"He have any trouble with the law?"

Hendrick fell silent.

"Hello?"

"I'm still here." He wanted to laugh. "Sheriff, up until a few years ago, he was the law."

"That's what they said about him in Spokane, that he took the law into his own hands and—"

"No, I mean legally. He hired me as sheriff in 1969. He was our judge, our stability, the person who kept everything in line. He decided who went to jail and who didn't, who was guilty and who was innocent."

"We talking about the same Clyde Ralstin?"

The ages matched. Clyde Willis Ralstin, born September 13, 1899, was just a few months away from his ninetieth birthday.

Hendrick had been to Clyde's eightieth birthday party, in Saint Ignatius—and what a bash it was, on a night when the first frost killed the last wildflowers in the high basins of the Mission Mountains, and a mob of stars pressed through the borderless sky of Montana. Most of the town turned out to fete Clyde; a better citizen, an easier neighbor there never was. All evening long, men came up to shake Clyde's hand or slap his back, and pretty girls gave him kisses, to which he always responded with a touch of charm. He talked about shooting bears, killing deer, felling trees, grub staking in the early days, framing houses later on, chasing wildcat oil jobs in South America—all these grand adventures, from the Roaring Twenties through the tortured years of the Depression, the boom time of World War II, when the Northwest came of age with the big dams and the bomb-building plant on the Columbia River, into the fifties and sixties, the years when he brought his brand of law enforcement to the Nez Percé Indian Reservation. Clyde was at the party with his young wife, a Flathead Indian who called him Dad, and his boy, barely a teenager, just learning how to shoot and cut wood in the mold of his old man.

"His boy?" Bamonte was incredulous. "You telling me Clyde Ralstin had a kid, at his age?"

"And a nice kid, too. Clyde used to brag about it, you know, being able to father a child at an age when most people have grown grandchildren."

When the boy was twelve, he and Clyde were deep in the woods of the Jocko Valley of Montana, cutting firewood. Clyde's chain saw slipped and ripped a deep gash in his arm. Most men would have bled to death, far from the nearest hospital, immobilized by shock. But Clyde wrapped a cloth around the wound, tying a tourniquet, and then directed his son into the pickup. Under his father's guidance, the twelve-year-old drove at top speed nearly forty-five miles into Missoula.

"Clyde has the strength of three men, in just about every way," Hendrick said.

And now that he was talking about the man he used to idolize, he was starting to feel better about turning him in. If the sheriff knew the real truth of Clyde Ralstin, maybe this business with the Newport marshal would prove to be a frame-up, or some awful mistake. "I remember seeing him, not too long before he left Lapwai to go to Montana, tearing a roof off this house. He was near eighty years old, and he was running the length of this thing, tearing it apart."

Hendrick told Bamonte how he had come to know Clyde, more than twenty-five years earlier. Ralstin was born near Spaulding, a hardscrabble village on the Clearwater River, just a few miles from Lapwai. For centuries, the dry mountain country of eastern Oregon, central Idaho, and southeastern Washington belonged to the Nez Percé. The tribe called themselves Nimipu, or "the Real People." They spent their summers hunting elk and picking berries in the Blue Mountains, just west of where the Snake River cut Hells Canyon, the deepest trench in North America. In the fall and early winter, the Nez Percé caught chinook salmon and steelhead in the spawning waters of the Snake and its tributaries, the Clearwater, the Salmon, the Grande Ronde, the Imnaha. The tribe held on to its land long after other natives were driven out of their homes, in part because

Idaho was the last state to be discovered by Europeans and settled by Americans. To this day, much of the state east of the Snake in the Clearwater mountain range, and south in the Sawtooths, headwaters of the Salmon (the River of No Return), is roadless—without stump farms or dams or any hint of the sloppy attachment to the land that is the trademark of much of the American West.

The Nez Percé have not fared as well as their former homeland. Refusing an order by the American government to leave their homes in the Blue Mountains, which had been promised them by an executive order, they took up arms against the cavalry in one of the last Indian fights, in 1877. An epic retreat—down Hells Canyon, through the untracked mountains of central Idaho, across Yellowstone Park, and up through Montana on the way to Canada—ended just short of the border, in defeat. Chief Joseph, who led the defiant march, was taken away in shackles, relocated to Oklahoma, and then placed on the Colville Reservation of eastern Washington with a small band of his followers. Other members of the tribe were forced to live on a cutout of scrubland east of the Snake River—the Nez Percé Reservation.

Five years before Chief Joseph died, Clyde Ralstin was born on his father's homestead in Nez Percé country. The Ralstins didn't have a pindrop of Indian blood in them. But with passage of the Allotment Act in 1887, whites were able to buy up tribal land from individual natives, most of whom sold their allotments, at bargain-basement prices, out of desperation. Today about 80 percent of the Nez Percé Reservation is owned by or leased to non-Indians.

There were five children who grew up in the hillside ranch of the Ralstins; Clyde was the oldest. He never cared for school, but he took to the land as if he had sprung from a petroglyph; he became a flawless shooter, chasing deer, elk, antelope, sheep, mountain goats, pheasant, and other creatures of the Snake River country, which ran from the Seven Devils Mountains in the south to the Clearwaters in the north. As a seventeen-year-old boy who wanted a piece of World War I, he tried to enlist in the Marines but was turned down. In 1928, he parlayed his best qualifications—his fists and his utility with guns—into a steady job with the Spokane Police Department.

Years later, when Ralstin returned to his home in the land of the Nez Percé, where his brother Chub raised Appaloosa horses, he advertised himself as a man of the world. Not only had he completed nearly a decade with the Spokane police, first as motorcycle cop, then as patrolman and detective, but he was a patriot, he said—an important man in two places where the American war machine was being put together in the early 1940s. After returning from South America and an assortment of jobs on oil rigs and in construction, he had landed in San Diego and climbed his way up to a supervisor's position for a company, Consolidated Vultee Aircraft Corporation, that built bombers. During the last years of World War II, he was back in Washington, at Hanford, where plutonium for the world's first atomic bomb was manufactured in the desert along the banks of the Columbia River. Ralstin told Hendrick he was still sworn to secrecy about some of what he had seen and done at Hanford. His job was plant security supervisor for General Electric, a big subcontractor at the nuclear facility. What went on inside the five-hundred-square-mile government camp was one of the best-kept secrets of the war, and Ralstin took a great deal of pride in helping to keep the lid on it. When a commercial airplane crashed inside the nuclear reservation, Ralstin helped to put out the fire and made sure the report of the accident never went public. Though nearly a hundred thousand men worked and lived in the instant city at Hanford, they were essentially phantoms. So loyal was Ralstin to the secrecy of his mission that when one of the workers under him was arrested on a charge of stealing a truck outside of town, Clyde refused, in court, to say what the man did for a living or even if he knew him. The case was dismissed.

Lewis and Clark had put the Nez Percé population at six thousand in 1805—one of the largest tribes in the West, and the most populous of the Sahaptin-speaking peoples of the Northwest. In the early 1950s, when Ralstin moved back to Lapwai, the Census Bureau counted 608 full-blooded Nez Percé in Idaho. The reservation land was bleak; the wind blew through homesteads constructed a half-century earlier and long since deserted and left to rot. It seemed as if the land, dry and harsh, had been scraped bare by a marauding force of nature. The big chinooks that used to swim more than seven hundred miles inland from the Pacific, following a migratory route up the Columbia to spawning waters in the Salmon, Snake, and Clearwater rivers, had disappeared—centuries-old runs killed by the hydroelectric dams constructed in a single generation's time. Most of the Indians had no jobs; those who could find work cut timber, or fought fires for the Forest Service, or picked wild rice around Saint Maries. Staggered by alcohol, deprived of most of the land on their own reservation, they quarreled among themselves, committed acts of thievery and domestic abuse.

For Clyde Ralstin, veteran lawman, keeper of the peace in depression-torn Spokane, and protector of America's nuclear secrets along the Columbia, it was a perfect situation. The tribe needed law and order; he arrived in Lapwai with a resumé and a mastery of guns to back it up. The little reservation town had a long tradition of subjugating its culture and destiny to non-Indians. Henry Spaulding and his wife had established a Christian mission there in 1836—the first place in Idaho where whites lived on a more or less permanent basis. Ralstin had family throughout the Nez Percé country. His brother Chub had achieved a degree of local celebrity when he sold one of his prize Appaloosa ponies to John Wayne. If the citizens of Lapwai had checked Clyde's personnel file in Spokane, they would have found nothing about the affairs he ran out of Mother's Kitchen, or the reprimands and disciplinary actions taken against him, or the time he nearly killed his son-in-law, or the report of the woman who said Clyde tried to rape her, or the suspicions of Detective Sonnabend. For that matter, they would have discovered nothing at all—his file had disappeared, with Clyde, when he left the force in 1937.

"He tried to look after our little town," Chief Hendrick said. "Tried to look after the best interests of everybody. He was a real wise man in that way."

Until Hendrick was hired in the late 1960s, Ralstin was the law in Lapwai, first as enforcer, later as judge. He held court at night— "after all the suspects had a chance to sober up," Hendrick said— and his sentences were usually stiff. Nine out of ten people who came before him were Indians who had run afoul of the law because of alcohol. A drunk could expect to spend ten days in jail. When the town had some crisis—political, financial, or other—Ralstin was always the first citizen to rally the resources. Hunting season was sacred to him. While in Lapwai, he still saw Virgil Burch; the old buddies kept a hideaway on the Idaho-Montana border, where they stashed good whiskey, antique rifles, and stories that never left the walls of the cabin. A particularly valuable gun, a .30 carbine with a bayonet, was stolen in a burglary; later, in the 1980s, it turned up in Clyde and Virgil's hunting cabin. But this story did not come out until Virgil was dead and Clyde had given up his official duties.

Ralstin hired Hendrick, giving him the badge in the way that sheriffs used to do in the days when western towns were built in a hurry. But even after Ralstin retired from active law enforcement, when his job was pounding a gavel and sentencing small-time lawbreakers to short-term residency in the Lapwai hoosegow, he kept a hand in the physical end of the law. Clyde liked to beat people up. "He'd see somebody assaulting somebody else, and he'd jump in," Hendrick said. "No matter how old he got, he enjoyed using his fists."

Ralstin left for Saint Ignatius, the land of his wife's people, in 1970. Most of the town of Lapwai was sorry to see him go. When he arrived in Saint Ignatius, about 180 miles northwest of Lapwai, he built himself a house that was said to be worth $100,000 at a time when homes that sold for a fifth of that price were considered lavish by the standards of the Mission Valley. In his eighties he took up another career, working around Saint Ignatius as a carpenter for hire. He constructed kitchens, bedrooms, garages, shelves. His ears grew floppy and oversized, like those of Lyndon Johnson; his hair thinned; his nose seemed to become even more pointed as the rest of his face shrunk; and his eyes receded behind layers of weather-buffed skin. He hunched over a bit, but he never put on an ounce of fat.

What Bamonte knew of Clyde Ralstin began in the late 1920s and ended in 1937, when he left Spokane. Now, after hearing about the second half of Clyde's life from Hendrick, Bamonte formed another picture of the man, more ambiguous. The Clyde Ralstin of Lapwai, Idaho, didn't seem to be the bootlegger, the career breaker, the womanizer, the boaster and tyrant, the corrupt and cynical police detective described by Pearl Keogh and Dan Mangan and Charley Sonnabend. Here was a First Citizen. From what Hendrick told him, the sheriff had little doubt that Ralstin would cooperate with him.

"I suspect he'll sit down and tell you anything he knows about this," Hendrick told the sheriff.

"Why hasn't he contacted me by now?"

"Don't know. But I'll tell you something else—he's a law-and-order man, Clyde. First and foremost he's a cop. That's what he stands for—the law."

"I can't tell you how much I appreciate you calling with this," Bamonte told him.

Hendrick said he nearly didn't call. For several nights, he had been unable to sleep, debating between keeping quiet and helping a fellow cop. He tried to let it go, to forget about it. What particularly bothered him, he said, was reading about the Conniff family and their years in the dark. It wasn't right.

"One last thing, Sheriff. If you don't mind, I'd rather you didn't tell anyone where this came from."

"Why's that?"

"Clyde's just like a father to me in many ways, like I said."

THE NEWS that Clyde Ralstin was still alive made Bamonte swell. He felt like doing back flips. It was the goddamnedest, butt-luckiest kind of break. A few days after he closed the book, as a student, on the Conniff case, the story had risen from the dead. Again. Clyde Ralstin seemed to have rolled away a tombstone and crawled out from the grave. Bamonte couldn't help feeling like the power behind the resurrection. But he also felt a deadweight of responsibility, not only for stirring up all the old stories, remaking the image of a man who, by all recent accounts, was a fine human being, but because Bamonte alone now carried the load of history from those who had shared something of Ralstin's past. Charley Sonnabend had unburdened himself; Dan Mangan was free of the anvil he'd dragged around for half a century; so was Pearl Keogh. Chief Hendrick had just shed his share of the guilt. Burch was dead. Logan had disappeared. The pressure was on Bamonte, as the carrier of the story—and, of course, on Clyde Ralstin. What remained was for the two of them to have it out. If the facts warranted it, he planned to arrest the man, to bring him back to Pend Oreille County to stand trial for the night of September 14, 1935.

The sheriff wanted to call Betty. His good fortune, the breakthrough call from Chief Hendrick, was her good fortune, and she deserved to share it. He wanted her to be the first to know. He couldn't reach her by phone; she was somewhere between work and home. Then he started driving toward Spokane, thinking of his new friend. When he saw Linda and told her, she was overjoyed. She kissed him. They went to dinner, then back to her place, where they talked into the night. For a while it was wonderful—a new person, someone who made him feel better about the pressure. Toward midnight, amid the sweat and the thrill, he saw images of his mother in the Idaho mining town, showing a stranger her bedroom. He feared that he was becoming the part of her that he hated most.

SAINT IGNATIUS, in western Montana, was inside the Flathead Indian Reservation, so Bamonte's first official contact was with the Bureau of Indian Affairs. They had nothing on Clyde Willis Ralstin, or a Mrs. Ralstin, or any children, in their files and computers. Next, he cabled the sheriff's office for Lake County, which includes Saint Ignatius. All they had was some basic information from a car registration, listing Ralstin as six feet tall, weighing 175 pounds, with green eyes. Bamonte wondered if he had shrunk.

The undersheriff in Lake County, Mike Walrod, gave Bamonte a description of the old man that matched, in character outline, what Hendrick had said: Clyde Ralstin was a hell of a man, a Rotary pinup, loved by those who knew and worked with him. Had a bit of a temper. Known as somebody you shouldn't tangle with. Loved guns. Yes, he was still alive. The undersheriff couldn't imagine that he might be mixed up with some fossilized murder case involving police corruption.

Bamonte said he wanted to come see Clyde, talk about the case.

He asked Walrod for help, and to keep quiet. It was an old investigator's tool, to question somebody before he has a chance to build a
shed of lies. But it probably was too late for a surprise interview, the
sheriff's deputy told Bamonte. He suspected that Clyde had been
following the stories in the Spokane newspaper and knew everything
that had been reported in the press, including Mangan's account of
dumping the gun in the river on behalf of Ralstin.

No matter. If Ralstin was starting to feel the rippled pressure from
the years, the voices and secrets from the Depression, the screams
of Marshal Conniff as he lay dying in the alley behind the Newport
Creamery, it was long overdue.

Bill Morlin, the reporter from the *Spokesman-Review* who had
written several stories about the case, heard Bamonte was on his way
to Montana to interview a suspect in the oldest active homicide investigation in the country. Bamonte knew Morlin well, liked him,
and trusted that he wouldn't print anything that would jeopardize
the case. Closing in on Ralstin, Bamonte decided to send another
wave over the mountains to Montana. Without naming Ralstin, Bamonte made a public appeal, through Morlin's next story in the
Spokesman-Review, to those human qualities that had worked best
for him in the Conniff case. He continued to believe that conscience
was the best weapon.

"For the benefit of the suspect's soul and conscience, and for his
children and the Conniff children, I am hopeful he will come forward
and talk about his knowledge," Bamonte said.

19.

In Big Sky Country

A FEW DAYS BEFORE his forty-seventh birthday, on a warm morning in mid-spring, Bamonte drove east, crossing the Coeur d'Alene
Mountains into the old silver mining country of his father, cresting
the Bitterroot Range near the Idaho-Montana border, and then following the Clark Fork into a broad valley north of Missoula. He
approached the Flathead Indian Reservation just as the sun left his
rearview mirror. All his life he had lived with cloud-humbling mountains, waterfalls that bounced from the heavens, and forests of great
size and age; but the Mission Valley was something else. When the
glaciers shrank and disappeared from all but the highest nooks of
western Montana, they left behind a lake, the largest natural body
of fresh water in the American West, that covers the northern part
of this breach between the Rockies and Bitterroots. Aquamarine,
Flathead Lake holds the color and character of the big sky overhead.
Even at its present size of two hundred square miles, the lake is a
puddle compared with what it once was. The old lake bed is level
like a prairie, yet forested with clusters of pine, cedar, and fir. Cottonwoods shade the trout streams; black bears and grizzlies clamber
over a vast habitat; elk and pronghorn stuff themselves in grassy
meadows; and hundreds of buffalo roam throughout the nineteen

thousand acres of the National Bison Range, bordering the Jocko and Flathead rivers.

If there is a more isolated big valley in the lower forty-eight states, it has yet to be found. The Rocky Mountains reveal themselves here as the scaffolding of creation, all exposed geology and millennial tiers of construction, one uplifted layer sitting atop another. As Bamonte drove the downslope of State Highway 200, passing through the towns of Thompson Falls, Plains, Paradise, Perma, Dixon, Ravalli, and entering Saint Ignatius, he was struck by the curtain of earth to the east, a subrange of the Rockies known as the Mission Range. The mountain wall was green and forested at the base, burnt-red and rusted in the middle, and eagle-capped along the summits with snow from the last seven months. To the north is Glacier National Park; south of that is the Bob Marshall Wilderness. The Continental Divide follows a winding pattern through this part of the Rockies, the eastern side falling off abruptly to the treeless plains, where Blackfoot Indians still live on a windswept reservation, the west side draining into the Pacific and the land of people who spoke the Salish dialect and fished for salmon.

When Jesuit missionaries first entered the area in the 1840s, members of the Pend Oreille tribe told them their land was called Sineleman, meaning "Place of Encirclement," where tribes from throughout the inland Northwest gathered to trade and barter. Surrounded by humpbacks of granite and basalt that rise nearly two vertical miles, the valley is protected from the worst storms that gather over Montana for much of the cold season.

The most prominent human landmark in Saint Ignatius is the mission, established in 1854 and named for Saint Ignatius Loyola, the founder of the Jesuit order. The first version of the church was built of whipsawed lumber and held together by wooden pins. Forty years later, the priests finished their arched masterpiece, built, with Indian labor, of stone and a million red bricks the color of sunset. Brother Joseph Carignano spent most of his adult life on his back inside the church, painting fifty-eight murals on the ceilings and walls, finishing the last picture around 1920. The church draws tourists to Saint

Ignatius, a town of 877 people, which might not otherwise attract outside visitors. Well-traveled Catholic clerics says their outpost in western Montana is one of the five most beautiful churches in the world, a house of worship made all the more stunning by its setting, alone against the mountains, an inspirational chip off the granite block of the Mission Range. The priests intended Saint Ignatius to be a spiritual fortress; just as the mountains protected the valley, the church was supposed to be a shelter from the harsher impulses of humanity. In the spirit of that design, Brother Carignano's murals depict scenes of great optimism instead of the usual Gothic gloom or graphic illustrations of the consequence of sin.

Pearl Keogh grew up in Saint Ignatius, raised in a mission school for Indians and whites, which the Sisters of Providence ran. When Bamonte told her that he had traced Clyde Ralstin to her girlhood home, Pearl detected the hand of God scripting a final and fitting act to both of their lives. She wanted to travel to Saint Ignatius by herself and confront Ralstin with September 1935. But Bamonte advised her against that; he promised to tell Pearl everything upon his return.

In Saint Ignatius, which the locals call Mission, there is a clear dividing line between the white and Indian sections of town. Members of the Flathead (or Salish), Pend d'Oreille (upper Kalispel), and Kootenai live near the church. Ralstin managed an apartment complex in the poor part of town, leasing the units out to Indians. He was not well liked by his tenants, who feared his flash temper. To be a few days late on a rent payment was enough to prompt an eviction threat from Ralstin. A few small businesses operate in the summer, selling dolls made of bear's hair, and moccasins with traditional beadwork. The whites live in what some residents jokingly call the silk stocking district, in wood-framed houses, well kept, some with metal roofs to speed the melting of heavy snows. The general store in this neighborhood sells vials of scented cover for hunters—"guaranteed 100 percent elk urine." At the local hangout, the Malt Shop, everybody knows everybody else's business and stool assignment. Although the original Flathead Reservation comprised 1.2 million acres, it has long since been opened up to homesteading, allotment sales, and leasing to non-Indians. The Confederated Salish and Kootenai Tribes of the Flathead Reservation now own less than half of the land promised them by the Hell Gate Treaty of 1855.

Bamonte found Clyde Ralstin's house in the white part of town at 365 First Avenue, a small, single-story home with a green tin roof and white siding. Next to the front door was a wooden sign inscribed "The Ralstins." Though the grass was still brown, newly unveiled from winter snow cover, the yard was neat and the hedges trimmed, reflecting the pride and the routine of its owner. The fruit trees in this neighborhood had yet to flower; their skeletal claws clacked against each other in the wind. Firewood was cut and stacked nearby. Bamonte drove by the house but did not stop his car.

When he checked in with the Lake County sheriff's department —a common courtesy when a cop from one jurisdiction is investigating someone in another county—a deputy told him that within an hour of his arrival, Ralstin knew he was in town. Clyde had friends. Bamonte smiled and pulled up a seat. Scenting and circling was part of the ritual of the hunt. He had traced Ralstin from a bootlegger's hangout in Spokane to a valley that seemed to be at the end of the earth.

RALSTIN SHARED the little white house on First Avenue with his wife, Marie. They socialized mainly with non-Indians, retired people who talked about hunting, fishing, the weather, and fixing things up. On occasion, the Ralstins would go to dinner at the Indian cultural center, on the other side of town; in Saint Ignatius, there was consent that the food was far better at the tribal center than anywhere else in the valley.

When the first news story came out of Spokane, Clyde had suspected Bamonte would eventually catch up with him. And with each new article, he cursed the sheriff from Pend Oreille County. Bamonte became a distant nag, lingering out of view. Of late, Ralstin's breathing was erratic, and sometimes he would wake up coughing and pained. He told friends he had not slept well since the graduate student's project came to light in February. In that regard, he and Bamonte were alike.

When Marie and Clyde sat at breakfast, Ralstin would offer a prayer, repeated every morning since the Conniff story broke. "Lord, get this off my back," said Clyde, his head bowed. "Please, Lord, make this go away." But the circle only closed tighter; the pressure increased with each new piece of information trickling into Montana from Spokane.

"Dad," his wife had asked him a few days before Bamonte arrived in Saint Ignatius, "what's this all about?"

"It's hogwash," he replied. And in angrier moments, he called it "bullshit," professing bewilderment that his life had taken such a strange turn. He told Marie that Bamonte must have thought he was dead; otherwise, he never would have stirred up so much trouble.

There was very little mystery to the Clyde Ralstin of 1989. He had come to Montana from Lapwai, riding into town on his reputation as a law-and-order man with fifty years of experience. He remodeled and managed his apartment complex, built a house outside Saint Ignatius, sold it, then moved into the little frame home on First. Most days, Clyde went for a long, slow walk, using his hand-carved willow cane for balance. To his neighbors, he was the sweetest octogenarian this side of the Divide. He respected his fellow citizens and he feared God. He was ever helpful. He was a fine storyteller. He had suffered from a peptic ulcer, and gout, and had a type of heart disease typical for a man his age; but overall, he was considered, by friends and by his doctor, to be a strong, well-preserved man. One thing he could *not* be, his neighbors were convinced, was a killer. To think that Clyde Willis Ralstin, the very embodiment of the self-reliant westerner, the pains and changes of the twentieth century etched in his face, this former judge, a longtime lawman, head of security at Hanford, kind and gentle neighbor, had once been a bootlegger of butter, and had fired four shots into the body of a small-town marshal—including a final, killing blast when Conniff was down—was a preposterous notion. As Clyde walked through town, offering advice on fixing a truck or finishing a chore, he was accorded

respect, the kind people want in their late years, the simple acknowledgment of a life well lived.

The Lake County sheriff's deputy told Bamonte that he had stirred
up a nest of trouble in the Ralstin home with his investigation of the
1935 killing.

"Imagine people will be mad at Clyde," said Bamonte.

"More likely mad at you."

"Me?"

"For bringing it up."

At the Lily of the Valley flower shop, Clyde was known as a ro-
mantic, one of the best customers. About once a week, he'd come
into the shop in the afternoon and buy a bouquet for Marie. The
ladies who sold him his flowers did not care what was in his past. A
person had a right to be forgiven and to move on with his life. "Even
if he did kill that marshal," said one of the store's owners, "it's so
long ago, who cares? Are they gonna hound the man to his grave? I
mean, that's not fair."

In the Tepee Tavern, where a schooner of Coors costs less than a
dollar, Clyde was a hero. Among regulars at the Tepee, some hoped
it was true that Ralstin had killed Conniff. "If he did it, and got away
with it, more power to him," said one patron. "There's something to
be said for a man who can pull it off, then live the rest of his life as
a righteous man."

A few doors away from the Ralstin house lived Olive Wehr, a
columnist for the weekly Mission Valley *News*. Olive was the same
age as Clyde, a few months shy of her ninetieth birthday, and she
spent her days in a big house full of books and western antiques, with
a large garden outside and a fenced-in quarter-acre of grass. She had
written four books; one of them, *God's Forgotten Garden*, a volume
of poetry about runaway girls, won a Mark Twain Award for Literary
Excellence in 1947. Olive Wehr still banged out her column, "The
Saint Ignatius Grapevine," every week in the local paper. What got
her back up was when somebody dared to call her contribution a
gossip column. Gossip was a form of torture, cruel and whispered.
Olive dealt in facts, writing about grandchildren who came to town
for a visit, comings and goings of her fellow townsfolk, who was sick

and who was well. There was a line that she would not cross. She had yet to write a thing about her neighbor, because she did not consider the rumors coming out of Spokane to be worth repeating in print. Nor had she talked about the killing with Clyde. "You don't ask about certain things," she said later. "Everybody has a past. We are a very close-knit and very protective community. In a small town, that's the only way you can get along."

She was outraged that Bamonte and his allegations had followed Clyde to Saint Ignatius in the last years of his life. "How would anybody feel if they'd lived their whole life only to have something like this thrown at them near the end?" she said. "I know Clyde Ralstin as a friend and a neighbor, not the person this sheriff says he is."

She had first met Clyde when he moved into 365 First Avenue; it seemed so long ago she could not remember exactly when the Ralstins had come to town. Olive hired him to build a sun room, expanding a porch and covering it. A superb carpenter, reliable, steady, and meticulous, Clyde was a magician with circular saw and hammer. And he was charming, chatty; he certainly never made a pass at Mrs. Wehr or went into a gallop of foul language. "He's a gentleman in every sense of the word," she said. "He stands for the right things."

After work, Clyde and Olive would sip lemonade and watch the golden light on the western flank of the Mission Range. He talked about the adventures of his life—the days in South America, the war period at Hanford, the years as a judge at the Nez Percé Reservation. "Once in a while he'd bring up something about his being a detective," she said. "But there was nothing shameful, nothing scandalous. He told me he was quite a good policeman, is what I remember."

As veterans discuss the war that scarred them for life, Olive and Clyde would sometimes talk about the Great Depression and what it did to them. They knew it was something that could not be understood by their children, or friends from a younger generation. You simply had to live through it—the humility, hunger, and long nights without hope, the dollar-a-day jobs, the lines for soup, the unheated rooms on winter nights—to understand what it did to people. A teacher in the 1930s, Olive was not paid in money; rather, at the end of her work period she was given a ration of scrip, which she would take to local farmers and redeem for food.

"It seemed to us that life just stopped during the Depression," said Olive. "It brought out the best and it brought out the worst in everybody." Given the times, was it not possible that Clyde could kill another man over food? Olive had thought about this question since the whispered stories of Clyde's awful past first came into town in mid-spring.

After much rumination, she had settled on an answer. She told about a rock in Saint Ignatius the size of a house, a remnant from an Ice Age glacier as it gouged its way north. Nobody asks about the rock or how it got there, said Olive Wehr. The neighborhood was built around it. Everybody accepts it for what it is.

BETTY BAMONTE was late for work and looking for something at home in Metaline Falls. She went downstairs to the first floor of the brick building and started rummaging through a stack of papers next to her husband's master's degree project. Looking at the completed thesis, she thought of how she had been left out of the recent triumphs. He used to talk nonstop about how excited he was to be stirring up the past. If she let him, he would jabber on till dawn. On many nights, even after she kissed him and told him to put the project out of his head and go to sleep, his mind kept racing, and she shared the thumping heart. The entire bedroom seemed to pulse with his restless mind. As the initial breakthroughs came, she was the first to know; Tony rushed the information to her like a kid running home from school with his best report card. She was a partner in discovery. But in recent weeks, she learned of developments—the existence of Clyde Ralstin, the complete story of Pearl Keogh—from reading the newspaper. She felt no closer to her husband than the average subscriber might feel.

A section of computer paper buried in a stack on Tony's desk caught her eye. Betty saw these words, in big letters spat out by the automated printer:

XXOO LINDA LOVES TONY

She stared at the paper in disbelief.

XXOO LINDA LOVES TONY

Was this what those Thursday nights in Spokane were all about? The reason he couldn't look her in the face without turning away? Why he no longer asked the basic questions about the structure of her day?

She caught her breath, forcing the air out slowly. Now she was gasping; the oxygen had left the room. She didn't care what happened to him now, if he ever came home or lived or died. If he returned to Metaline Falls today, she would not let him in this house. She would throw everything of his in a bag and tell him to be gone, off to some fleabag room down the road, where he belonged—out, out, out! When the flash of anger passed, she started to cry, alone with the hollowed-out feeling of the betrayed.

XXOO LINDA LOVES TONY

She threw the paper down. Work beckoned, but she could not move just yet. She sat, buried her head in her hands.

BAMONTE COULD FIND no one in Saint Ignatius who had heard Clyde Ralstin mention anything about the Conniff killing. Instead, he found himself nearly drowning in a reservoir of good feeling for the old man. And how dare the sheriff *insinuate* that he might have been mixed up with police corruption and a cop killing!

Mike Walrod, the undersheriff, was one of the few people in town who had seen another side to Clyde. The old man had a hot temper, he said, which caused some people—Indians, without money or options, who lived in his apartments—to fear him. Still, Walrod was confident that Ralstin would talk to the law. "He was a cop, he used to talk to me about it," said Walrod. "He would say, 'I sympathize with your job, 'cause I know how it works.' "

That night, staying in a small roadside motel outside town, Bamonte wondered if perhaps he was going after the wrong man. The last thing he wanted was to hound an innocent person to his grave. But as he sifted through the evidence, he arrived at the same conclusion as before: everything pointed to Ralstin. Even if he had lived somewhat of an exemplary life since the killing, he still had to answer for September 1935.

In the morning, Bamonte went to the Lake County sheriff's office; it was time to face Ralstin. Mike Walrod was planning to go with Bamonte to Ralstin's house. But just as the two cops were leaving, a phone call came.

"A lawyer on the line for you, Sheriff Bamonte."

Bamonte picked up the phone. An attorney, Philip J. Grainey, somewhat ubiquitous in western Montana, with offices in two towns and a practice that stretched over an area bigger than most states, identified himself as Clyde Ralstin's attorney, hired to represent him in the Conniff investigation.

"I didn't know he had a lawyer," Bamonte said.

"He does."

"We're on our way to Ralstin's house right now," the sheriff said. "Would you like to meet us there?"

"My client doesn't want to talk."

"Excuse me?"

"I said he doesn't want to talk. It wouldn't be right for him. Not now."

"What do you mean, he doesn't want to talk? He was a cop. I'm a small-town sheriff. Why shouldn't one cop help another? I'm just looking for a few answers."

"Can you come to my office?" Grainey asked.

"I'd rather talk to Clyde."

"What . . . exactly what have you got on him, Sheriff? What sort of case? Maybe we can talk about something."

"Let's talk to Clyde first."

"My client hired me . . . to represent his best interests. And his best interest now is that he would rather not discuss this case."

"Why not? If he's innocent, what's to hold him back?"

"He has the legal right to remain silent."

And as Bamonte heard the basic speech he'd heard hundreds of times, his doubts of the night before vanished. He wanted to sit face-to-face with Ralstin—close enough to see him sweat, to watch him quiver, to lock old eyes with young eyes—and ask him what happened to his .32 revolver, the one that he reported missing when he left the police department in 1937, and what he was doing at a roadblock one hour after the shooting, and why Acie Logan would have named Clyde as the shooter, and what Virgil Burch was talking about when he told Pearl Keogh the same thing in 1940.

"Come out to my office," said Grainey. "We can talk there."

Walrod could not believe Clyde was refusing to cooperate. "Let me call him." He dialed Ralstin at home, spoke to him for a few minutes, then hung up.

"He won't talk," said Walrod, greatly surprised. "Told me he had nothing to say. Said we should see his attorney. Makes you wonder."

BAMONTE DROVE twenty-five miles north to the town of Ronan, a hamlet that seemed, even more than Saint Ignatius, to be overwhelmed by the great wall of the Mission Mountains. He felt as if he had been squeezed among the ages and dropped between two curtains of granite.

Grainey was polite and to the point. He said Ralstin had hired him after the stories started coming out of Spokane. Clyde had no criminal record, the attorney said, and had lived a fine life, as far as he knew. He had very little time left on this earth. His family was deeply upset by this . . . encumbrance from the Pend Oreille. Why would the sheriff want to bother an old man?

For one thing, Bamonte explained, the marshal's murder remained an unsolved homicide, and he had a legal duty to investigate any leads. Secondly, even if the case never made it to a courtroom, Bamonte owed it to the Conniff family, Olive and Mary and George junior, to follow through with what he had started. Finally, he had a scholarly interest in the case.

Grainey nodded. The moral posturing concluded, the attorney cleared his throat. "Are you going to arrest him today?"

"Arrest him?"

"Yes. He thinks you're going to arrest him."

"Why is that? I mean . . . if he's done nothing wrong, why does he think I'm going to arrest him?"

"All this business in the papers."

"I want to talk to him," Bamonte said. "I've got a few questions."

"What have you got on him?" Grainey said.

Bamonte was not prepared to lay out his entire case, but he wanted to show the attorney enough to coax him into cooperating. The sheriff produced a copy of the two Sonnabend interviews, in which Acie Logan named Ralstin as the killer and the leader of the gang of butter thieves.

"Sonnabend—he's dead, isn't he?" Grainey asked.

"Yes, but—"

"Then what are we supposed to make of this? Hearsay."

Bamonte showed part of the transcript of an interview with Dan Mangan. "Mangan knew Clyde pretty well," said the sheriff. "Worked sixteen years at SPD. Left as a sergeant. Had a place not too far from here, at Hungry Horse. The Dam Town Tavern. Said Clyde used to come up for drinks."

"Yes . . ."

"Told me about the gun. Look." He showed Grainey a section of the transcript of the interview with Mangan. "Said they threw it over the bridge to cover for Clyde."

"And why would he do that?"

"Clyde had something on him. Had something on just about everybody in the department."

"Mangan—he's still alive?"

"He is."

"You didn't find the gun?"

"No, it's . . . We did not."

"This doesn't prove a thing. These are not sworn statements."

Bamonte opened his briefcase and took out a small tape recorder. He slapped a tape inside and pressed the play button. "Listen to this."

What Grainey heard was the scratchy voice of Pearl Keogh, recounting her days at Mother's Kitchen, finding butter wrappers from the Newport Creamery just days after it was robbed.

"And this." He sped the tape up to the part where Pearl recounted the dinner-table boast of Virgil Burch, the one in which he said Clyde Ralstin sprayed the marshal's body full of lead, and that their only regret was that they had to leave the creamery before picking up all the dairy products they wanted.

Grainey, accustomed to dealing with the banalities of small-town legal work in the late twentieth century—the divorces and wills, the petty crimes and drunk drivers, the trespasses and title disputes— had never heard a story so rustic and foreign.

"Sonnabend may be dead," said Bamonte. "But this lady, Pearl Keogh, is alive." He turned off the tape recorder. "And she'll testify if we ask her to."

"You don't have enough to charge Mr. Ralstin," Grainey said. "Do you?"

"That's not up to me," Bamonte said.

Grainey asked about physical evidence—fingerprints, butter wrappers, a weapon, anything to place the former detective at the crime scene.

"We have some loose ends," Bamonte said. "But if you let me see him, I'm sure he can clear everything up."

"Sheriff, this was fifty-four years ago. You can't expect him to remember."

"I just want to ask him a few things."

Grainey was adamant: His client would not discuss any part of the Conniff case with Sheriff Bamonte. It was, he reiterated, Ralstin's legal right to remain silent.

Now more than ever, Bamonte felt convinced Ralstin was his man. "Did you ask him about this?" Bamonte said.

"He's never heard of Conniff. Doesn't remember anything about the case."

"That's why I'm here," Bamonte said. "Memory."

"He doesn't have to talk to you, Sheriff."

"If he's innocent," Bamonte said, "he's got nothing to hide. He's supposed to be such a great supporter of the law. Just let me sit down with him. Straighten this thing out."

Grainey was insistent. "If you try to talk to him, it might kill him."

"I thought—"

"He is a frail old man. He has a bad heart. He suffers from internal bleeding. This whole matter has weakened him. I'm afraid an interrogation might just be too much for him."

"Too much?"

"Yes. You know what I mean."

"How sick is he?"

"He has trouble breathing. He can't exert himself for long without shortness of breath. He just wants all this to go away."

"It's not going to go away," Bamonte said.

"You don't have enough to charge him. And you say you're not here to arrest him. Well then, Sheriff, what do you want from this dying old man?"

Bamonte gathered up his papers and his tape recorder. He rose, thanked Grainey for his time, and made his way to the door.

"You tell him I know all about this," the sheriff said. "Tell him I know what he did. Make sure he understands you. Tell him I know."

20.

Retreat

THE SHERIFF left Montana in the afternoon, feeling frustrated. The friends and protectors of Clyde Ralstin had urged him to pack up his story and never return. The sky matched his mood: flat-bottomed clouds skidded across the top of the Mission Range, edging east. It had been bright and warm in the morning, but now the sun was gone, and Bamonte could see fresh snow near the summits. Occasionally, some shafts broke through the cloud cover, very dramatic, two-mile-long beams spotlighting parts of Saint Ignatius. For a few seconds, he saw the light sweep over the ancient brick sheathing of the church. Outside, a priest handed out copies of an Indian prayer to visitors. The last verse of the prayer, handed down by elders of the Flathead tribe, went like this:

> Oh, Great Spirit,
> Make me always ready to come to you
> With clean hands and straight eyes.
> So when life fades, as the fading sunset,
> My spirit may come to you without shame.

Inside the church, behind the main altar, were three panels, a triptych depicting visions that had changed the life of Saint Ignatius, the Spanish nobleman who founded the order of Catholic priests known for their intellect and political skills. Above the triptych was a mural of the Last Judgment, with the face of a benevolent-looking God staring down on those lesser beings awaiting his word.

Like those mortals in Brother Carignano's mural, Clyde Ralstin now sought redemption. His friends said the old man, never known as a very religious person, was evoking God of late. Ralstin told one visitor that it was not up to the sheriff from Pend Oreille to decide if he had lived a just life or should escape judgment for distant sins. "It is between God and I," he said.

Still, Bamonte wanted some lesser authorities in his county to have a chance at handing out earthly justice before Ralstin moved on. He felt alone, on a limb with the investigation. His prosecutor had not been much support of late. Bamonte wondered if he should drop it.

Driving west, Bamonte was troubled by one of Grainey's contentions, the notion that any further investigation—particularly an interrogation of the suspect—might cause too much stress, enough to kill Ralstin. The sheriff could be held responsible, Grainey had said, if something awful were to happen to his client, some sudden deterioration in his condition. What's more, if dredging up Clyde's past hastened his trip to the grave, the moral burden would be on Bamonte. Did the sheriff want that on his conscience? Bamonte considered this an odd transference of blame. What happened on September 14, 1935, belonged to Ralstin; Bamonte was a messenger from the other half of the century, late to collect.

While Bamonte had mixed feelings about the possibility of hastening Ralstin's death, he was clear on another concern: he did not want the liability on Pend Oreille County. As it was, the county barely had enough money to keep its police cars in gas and antifreeze. Bamonte's critics were growing. The media attention was a thrill, but when the spotlight passed, Pend Oreille County was left with all the old problems—no jobs, abusive husbands, drunk drivers on winding roads, and a sheriff who chased ghosts.

"Let this old man die in peace," Grainey had said. The words bounced along in the front seat with the sheriff as he chugged up pass through the Bitterroots. He had expected Clyde, his prisoner, to be sitting next to him. Instead, he rode home with doubts.

In all the nights when Bamonte had lain awake in Metaline Falls, his picture of Ralstin had changed very little. He was a tough-nutted, callous-hearted cop who dealt in other people's secrets, the worst sort of character merchant. The person he had just heard about in Saint Ignatius did not fit the bill. Shielded from the years, protected behind two great mountain walls, Clyde Ralstin was a man ready to have a street named after him, not a convict-in-waiting. He had never killed another human, let alone a cop, his defenders said. Bamonte was used to such dichotomies; the man who would set his family on fire, or lead a posse of neo-Nazis to kill a talk-show host for no other offense than having an opinion, or steal butter from a hungry community, was usually the best of fellows to those who professed to love him. Rare was the newly convicted felon who could not call on a friend or brother to hail him as a good man wronged by the law.

Still, Bamonte wondered, as he had the night before, if maybe he *was* pushing too hard. Years ago, the sheriff had risked his job defending a person who was wrongfully arrested by Bamonte's own deputies and convicted by a jury of the very people who kept Bamonte in office. Among cops in the inland Northwest, Bamonte's reputation was that of a contrarian, the outsider who had to wear a V-neck instead of a crew, who wouldn't so much as accept a cup of coffee from a friendly merchant. Some of his critics said he was soft on criminals, willing to give a guy a break when none was deserved. So his tracking of Ralstin was not the reflex motion of a cop who assumed all suspects were guilty until proven otherwise. He felt strongly about Ralstin. In his gut, there was no doubt.

AT HOME, when Bamonte walked inside, he was tired, his back muscles knotted and tense from the long drive. He knew immediately that something was wrong. Betty would not touch him. Arms folded, she pinned him down with her eyes.

"What is it, hon?" Tony asked.

She could not bring out the words she had rehearsed. When she tried to talk, tears came forth. Betty had gone to bed in grief, cried most of the night, and awoke feeling like she had slept in a mud puddle. Now, she took several slow breaths.

"I know . . ." she said, trembling, trying to find the courage, ". . . why you've been gone on Thursday nights."

"I told you—"

"Don't . . . lie . . . to . . . me," she said. "Don't, Tony!"

He sat down.

"Who's Linda?" she said.

"Linda?"

"Yes. Linda."

"A friend."

"And . . . ?"

"She's a friend. She . . . has some problems. We've been talking a lot."

"And you love her?"

"Why do you say that?"

"And she loves you?"

"What are you—"

"Don't . . . lie . . . to . . . me! I found the message on your desk. 'Linda loves Tony.' "

He was sinking. He didn't feel caught; he felt weak, and spineless, and miserable, and full of self-hatred. He was no better than his mother, quibbling and lying about the silver miners parading through as Bull worked underground.

"Did you sleep with her?"

"Betty. Please."

"Did you?"

At that instant, Betty knew they were through. It no longer mattered what the explanation was; the deed was done and confirmed. She was overwhelmed by tears, and he started to cry as well. Partners for twenty-three years, lovers for all but the last few months, they could do nothing now but weep at the collapse of their marriage, a union that had been sealed in years of mutual pain. The skinny kid just back from Vietnam and the waitress had vowed to live with each other for life. A few years into their marriage, they both had been stricken with hepatitis, but Tony had refused medical help. He took yellow roses to his wife's bedside, fell asleep with his head on her stomach. When he could walk no more, he entered the hospital, and then went twenty-one days without food. Betty recovered, but Tony continued to decline. His weight fell from 160 pounds to 120, and his fever held on for days. When at last he pulled out of it, they were joined by something stronger than their wedding vows: a shared defiance of death. From then on, the Bamontes felt they could whip anything. Bouts of near-bankruptcy, the harassment of the Newport newspaper, a crushing miscarriage—they remained strong.

She looked up, eyes clouded and puffy. "You betrayed me, Tony."

"Yes."

"Do you have any idea what that feels like?"

He did. Yes, he did. And couldn't Betty understand? Remember: his mother had betrayed the family when Tony was five, and he never forgot, or forgave. He was a victim for life. Which made it all the more tragic that he could repeat the very type of transgression that broke up the family.

"I'm . . . sorry," he said. "It's me. It's all my fault." When he started to see Linda, he did it almost without thought, following urges, floating with a current. Never did he foresee this moment when his wife would stare at him with the same barbed look he had fired at his mother.

"I can't explain. You know me. I get . . . so I feel like a failure. I was looking for something, and . . . with the stress of the Conniff case—"

"The Conniff case?" The mere mention of Tony's midlife obsession angered Betty. Shut out of the recent discoveries, Betty realized in the last few days that the recent moments of great good fortune probably had gone to Linda.

Betty did not doubt that Clyde Ralstin had killed George Conniff. Initially skeptical, she became convinced of Ralstin's guilt after going over the research which Tony had piled up downstairs. But his guilt or innocence was of secondary concern to her. What she had come to believe in the last few months was that Tony and Ralstin were very much alike. Her husband—compulsive, tough, a loner, stubborn—and the Conniff killer shared more than a Spokane police background.

Betty saw her husband, like Clyde Ralstin, as a victim of his past. And when it caught up with him, he refused to recognize it.

She had one bag already packed. Moving through a closet, she started to stuff another. "I'm leaving, Tony."

He was stunned. Yet he could not bring himself to stop her, or even try to touch her. All he could do was watch her slow-motion exit out of his life.

HUNGRY AND RESTLESS, Bamonte could not eat or sleep. He went outside for a walk. Metaline Falls seemed emptier and more abandoned than ever, the factory wheezing its last breaths, the streets empty. Though it was still early, only a few lights distinguished the village from the shroud of dark that engulfed the valley. Bamonte walked toward the river, unthinking, following an internal compass. At the edge of town, he dropped down a hill, then followed a muddy and deep-rutted road to a point where it disappeared. In a small clearing he found the cabin built in haste by Bull Bamonte nearly forty-five years before. His father's ashes were across the river on a flank of Mount Linton, but his ghost resided here, in the one-room log pile where Tony used to sleep on a cot, listening to Bull's labored breath. This was the home they had lived in before moving to the Red Rooster dance hall. When Bull dragged his broken body down from the mine shaft in time for dinner with Tony, he checked his gloom at the threshold. They were going to make it, he told Tony, because he worked hard, relentlessly, and life owed him a break. The mine would produce—it had to—and then Bull would have more time to spend with his boy.

Heavy with runoff, the Pend Oreille rushed through the canyon, just below the cabin—a sound so familiar it carried Bamonte back to the days when he lived in the hut. He could hear his father again, his lungs kicking up mining dust, straining for every breath. He always feared the stuttered breathing would end, without warning, and he would be left by himself. He felt that way now—deserted. With Betty's departure, the family was gone, and he alone remained in Metaline Falls. It wasn't likely that Tony's son would stay in town.

The boy and his father were so far apart; and that was his fault as well, Tony felt.

Abandoned long ago, the cabin smelled of rat shit and mildew; its roof sagged and leaked, and its walls were shredded of the chink that kept drafts at bay. Bull used to hang venison outside; inside, he kept his collection of Great Books and his Sunday clothes. Now the cabin was such a foul, decaying rot that even the kids from the village would not play inside it. Like the town of Metaline Falls, it was dying; and going down with it, he felt on this black night, was Tony Bamonte himself.

21.

Character Colors

IN LATE SPRING the rains stopped falling and the huckleberry bushes leafed out suddenly in the lower flanks of the mountains. A few weeks into May, the Pend Oreille receded and cleared up, free of silt, and the Spokane River also shrank and returned to its seasonal color. By June, the ground was dry enough that hay fields needed irrigation water to keep from browning. The first big fire of the season came early, started by a lightning strike, and flames jumped across the pine boughs of the big trees until the winds died down. Throughout the Pend Oreille country, people had the summer of 1989 figured out even before it formally arrived—it was going to be miserable hot, a skin cracker, well into fall.

Across the state of Washington, on the north coast of the Olympic Peninsula, a former Spokane police chief was telling Bamonte about another dry season, 1935, when the pine forests were aflame and the city was full of smoke. A few Indians still kept stick homes in the river valley that year, the old man told the sheriff, competing for space with migrants pouring in from Oklahoma, Texas, Arkansas, Nebraska, Kansas, and parched pockets of the Midwest. "You couldn't look down the street without seeing a fight," said Clyde E. Phelps. The great army of Civilian Conservation Corps workers, uniformed and hungry, made a lot of people in Spokane uncomfortable.

Of course, a fight is what Phelps, a cop for most of his working life, and his interviewer, Sheriff Bamonte, would likely see first when they looked down the street.

Phelps was eighty-six years old, an appliance-sized man with a generous spillover around the middle and a mouse-colored Colonel Sanders beard growing from his chin. His upper body was enormous, the shoulders broad as framing timbers. Bamonte, on his day off, was in Phelps's living room, in the peninsula town of Sequim, looking for character references on Clyde Ralstin. His prosecutor had lost interest in the case. His few remaining sources at the Spokane Police Department said he could expect nothing to come from headquarters. Candidates for Bamonte's job, including several from his own office, were plotting strategy to beat the sheriff in the next election. But while he was losing support in his county, he was gaining a trio of admirers in the Conniffs. The sheriff had not backed down from his promise to follow every lead until he came to a cliff. With Betty gone, Bamonte spent nights, weekends, and his days off chasing tips and going over scraps of evidence. He knew every word of every document by heart. But maybe he had missed something. Maybe he hadn't asked the right question. Maybe a conscience had yet to spill.

Phelps had a strong memory and good credentials, but he was guarded with details. He went to work for the Spokane Police Department in 1929, five months before the October crash of the stock market, and retired in 1957, serving his last eight years as chief of police. In the early days, he patrolled the Hotel de Gink, the old brewery, where he could usually count on finding somebody passed out from sucking too much applejack, or dead from a blast of wood alcohol. He was enlisted for riot duty when a mob of CCC workers shed their uniforms and shovels and vented a bit of steam in the city. Federal troops from Fort George Wright on the bluff above the Spokane River were also called in to keep order against the New Deal workers.

"We had to knock 'em down first and then talk sense to 'em after they were on the ground," said Phelps. "They were mostly blacks, those CCC workers, from Harlem or someplace, or immigrants. They just didn't get along with the town."

Hearing about a cop's duty in 1935, Bamonte winced. They were basically bagmen for bootleggers, and enforcers of the status quo. His father, the vagabond Italian who arrived in the inland Northwest during the Depression, might have been one of those whose scalps were bruised by the batons of Spokane's finest. 'Most everything Phelps told the sheriff about police work of half-a-century ago seemed foreign to Bamonte; it made him wonder about the kind of people attracted to his profession.

Warming up to Bamonte, the former chief explained about a policy of tolerance for bootlegging, gambling, and whoring. "Spokane was wide-open back then," said Phelps. "One place was called Chink Alley, and that's where the gambling was. Close by were the cathouses and all the private clubs, where you could get liquor by the glass. Every now and then some cleanup-minded commissioner would come into office and we'd have to do something, but then things went back to normal, as usual."

With the tolerance policy came payoffs to police officers. "That's just how the system worked," said Phelps. "People always took money."

Bamonte asked if any police officers reported the patrolmen who were on the take.

Phelps looked at him like he was dim. "You said you were in the department when?"

"Nineteen sixty-six to seventy-three."

"Go to college?"

"Afterward, yeah. Once I was already on the force."

"Working on a . . . master's degree, is it?"

"Yes."

"Now?"

"Yes."

"And that's where you came up with some of this stuff about Clyde Ralstin?"

"Yes."

Phelps said he wouldn't hire college graduates when he was chief of police. Wouldn't do it now. "It's my opinion that higher education is not important to police work." A cop does need an education, he said, but not one from a classroom.

"You never—I mean never—would turn on a fellow officer," he said. What was needed in law enforcement, he said, was "horse sense." And horse strength to back it up.

"Nowadays, you got so many restraints, so many people going around concerned about hurting somebody's feelings or stomping on their rights, that a cop can't do his job. Back then, we had authority. You don't have any authority now—not as a cop or a supervisor. In all the years I worked as a policeman, I never once had a kid talk back to me. Never once. Bet you can't say the same."

Bamonte said nothing, for he had been the kind of police officer who was always getting in trouble for doing exactly what Phelps deplored. The main rap against Bamonte when he was a rookie on the Spokane Police Department was that he talked back too much.

The sheriff went through his list of characters from the 1930s. Phelps knew them all.

"Logan? Hell, yes, I remember Acie Logan. I booked him and fingerprinted him when we brought him in for . . . what was it?"

"Robbery? Burglary? The creamery thefts?"

"Whatever. He was your basic con."

"What about Mangan? Dan Mangan?"

Phelps shook his head. "He was a goddamn thief."

"How do you know?"

"All you had to do was watch him. We worked the same beat a few times. He told me about this little candy store at the State Theatre that he was stealing from. Said if you put your hand in just right, the door would pop open. He could also open a slot machine quicker than you could close your mouth. Another time, he burglarized a butcher shop, and I remember seeing him leaving the station house with a turkey neck hanging down to his feet. He worked with another guy, Hacker Cox, most of the time. Cox and Mangan were quite a pair. When Cox died, I know somebody who went to his funeral just to make sure he was dead."

"Bill Parsons. You remember him?"

Parsons, the rookie in 1935, rose to become chief of police, like Phelps, but he had not made much of an impression on the older man. "Barely remember him," Phelps said.

"Clyde Ralstin. You remember him, though?"

"Of course."

"And?"

"I read about what you said in the papers, Sheriff."

"Yes?"

"I think you got Clyde all wrong."

"How's that?"

"He was a skookum man, Clyde Ralstin. A skookum man."

Bamonte wasn't sure how to take the characterization. "Skookum" was a bit of Chinook Indian jargon: in one part of the Northwest, it meant "evil spirit"; in another part, "strong and excellent man." Somebody could be a skookum man and possess both qualities.

Phelps remembered Clyde as large-framed like himself, good-looking, tough. Beyond that, the former police chief did not volunteer much about his former colleague.

"Do you remember the Conniff killing?" Bamonte asked.

"The marshal?"

"Yes. Shot September 14, 1935—"

"I know what you're talking about. That's your case. That's the story in the papers."

"Well? What do you know? What do you remember, Mr. Phelps?"

Phelps didn't say a word for a few minutes, and then he looked the sheriff in the eye.

"I have a lapse in memory on that one. And that's the truth."

BACK IN METALINE FALLS, the house was empty, Betty's drawers flung open. It was hot and stuffy upstairs, the stale air trapped inside the brick walls. Bamonte felt alone and dispirited. Without his wife, the big, fortified building was something of a prison. Bamonte had hoped she might appear, and then he would tell her that never again would he seek somebody else. They would start another quarter-century together, and this time—he had the speech rehearsed—he would learn from his mistakes. There would be less work, fewer obsessions to keep him up all night, more time with the love of his life. She would forgive him, they would romp around on the brass bed, and then he would tell her all about the trip to Sequim, and ask for her advice. Just like old times.

He opened the windows and looked around for something to eat. Phelps had proved to be nearly useless on the killing, a big disappointment. But he left Bamonte with one intriguing tip.

"You go back and check Ralstin's records, just take a look at them, and you might find something," Phelps had said. "I'm not saying he wasn't a skookum man, because he was. But there was something he was tied up in back then. I can't remember exactly what. You take a look."

The trouble was, Ralstin's personnel file had disappeared, or so the Spokane Police Department had reported in April. Had it vanished with Clyde, at the same time he left the department? Or did it get thrown out in the move from the Stone Fortress to the new police headquarters across the river? Or did somebody deliberately bury it, one old friend doing a favor for another?

KEITH HENDRICK was surprised to hear that his mentor, the pillar of Lapwai, Idaho, had hired an attorney and refused to talk with Bamonte. He had predicted that Ralstin would sit down with the sheriff and clear it all up, one cop to another. Surely, the old man had some answers.

"And his attorney says if I try to talk to him, ask him about the shooting, the stress might be enough to kill him," Bamonte said over the phone.

"You sure?" Frail and feeble—it didn't sound like Clyde.

"His attorney, Grainey, makes him out like he's just going to fall over any minute," the sheriff said.

"Not the Clyde Ralstin I know."

Hendrick told about a few dustups Ralstin had been involved with since he turned eighty. "He is not a man to be trifled with, no matter his age," said the Lapwai police chief. "He came back to town a few years ago, riding a bus here from Montana for a funeral. Buddy of his. So on the bus, he got in a fight."

"Ralstin did?"

"Yes. Clyde. Didn't start it without just cause, though. Couple of guys were drinking. Making a ruckus. Causing a scene on the bus, from what I hear. Clyde gets up and goes after 'em. One of the guys was forty years old—and Clyde knocked him out. The other fellow, a twenty-five-year-old, he wouldn't have any part of him after he seen what he did to his friend."

"How do you know about this?"

"Clyde told me. Heard from somebody else, too. He banged his knee up during the fight—but that was nothing compared to what Clyde did to the other guy."

That was more like it, Bamonte thought—the Ralstin who had smashed his son-in-law's head into the sidewalk, the cop who took on all comers in the police gym, the master of Mother's Kitchen.

"Got himself in another fight, just a few years ago," Hendrick continued.

"When he was what—eighty-four, eighty-five years old?"

"Yeah. Must've been. This time, he's in Spokane, driving around, doing I don't know what. So he bumps somebody's fender, by accident, and the guy gets real hot. He chases after Clyde, catches up with him. The guy reaches inside Ralstin's car and grabs his wife. Then he starts calling Clyde a son of a bitch. That was all it took. Clyde nailed him right there."

"He tell you that story, too?"

"Yes, he did. He said, 'You know, I must be losing my punch.' I said, 'Why's that, Clyde?' He says, 'I hit him three or four times and I couldn't put him down.' "

TALKING TO a Lake County sheriff's deputy in Montana, Bamonte was wondering what Ralstin had been up to since his visit to Saint Ignatius. The deputy said Ralstin had been traveling. Just after Bamonte's visit, he went to southern California to see his son, who was in the navy, stationed in San Diego.

"I thought he was too sick to get around?"

"No, sir."

Another source—anonymous, a onetime friend of Clyde's, he said—told Bamonte that Ralstin had been back in Lapwai, visiting relatives. It appeared to the sheriff that he was taking care of loose ends, rushing to see family members before he died or was arrested, whichever came first.

The picture of a peripatetic octogenarian, making peace and shoring up old stories, did not match the image presented in a letter Bamonte had just received from Phil Grainey. It was addressed to the sheriff and Thomas Metzger, the Pend Oreille prosecutor. The letter read:

As you know, I represent Clyde Ralstin of St. Ignatius, Montana.

In my previous conferences with Sheriff Bamonte, I have expressed my very strong concern that Mr. Ralstin, because of his advanced age and deteriorating health, would be unable to withstand the ordeal of being charged with the 1935 murder of George Conniff. Since my last conversation with Sheriff Bamonte, I have obtained a medical report from Mr. Ralstin's physician, Dr. Clancy Cone, which I am enclosing herewith. The letter speaks for itself but clearly gives strong support for my concern.

Mr. Ralstin has a history of internal bleeding and significant heart disease together with a number of other physical problems which place him at high risk. The process alone, and the resulting stress of being faced with criminal charges, would place him in serious jeopardy and perhaps even lead to his death, regardless of its outcome.

I have discussed in detail with Mr. Ralstin the accusations set forth in the newspaper articles and the additional information supplied to me by Sheriff Bamonte. Mr. Ralstin absolutely denies any involvement in a burglary ring and the slaying of George Conniff. He says that he is innocent and I am convinced that he will maintain his innocence to the end.

I certainly sympathize with the family of Mr. Conniff and recognize their desire to receive some form of retribution for the loss of their father. If the evidence was sufficient to lead a jury to conclude beyond a reasonable doubt that Mr. Ralstin was involved, then no one could fault them for wanting to press for a jury verdict. However, in this instance, there is clearly insufficient evidence to lead to a conviction and more importantly the accused would probably not live to the end of a trial. Since a verdict of any sort is unlikely, the only result would be the loss of Mr. Ralstin's life and the destruction of his family.

Hopefully, some sense of humanity and compassion will prevail over the desire to close this case, and Mr. Ralstin and his wife will be allowed to live out their few remaining years in peace.

> Very truly yours,
> French, Mercer & Grainey
> Attorneys-at-Law
> Philip J. Grainey

Enclosed was a two-page medical summary from Dr. Clancy L. Cone of Missoula. Dr. Cone explained that Ralstin suffered from heart disease, which the doctor treated by a valvularplasty procedure. Ralstin's memory was diminished and his speech slurred after the valvularplasty. His arteries were narrowing. He had a peptic ulcer, gout, anemia, and occasional internal bleeding. Dr. Cone ended his letter with this conclusion:

I see Mr. Ralstin's health status at this point as very fragile, in part because of his advanced age, although he has been a remarkable physical specimen. In addition the problems of two causes for intestinal hemorrhage and a known tight narrowing of the coronary artery which may set the stage for symptoms of angina or conceivably heart damage. I feel it very risky for him to be subjected to a prolonged episode of emotional stress, fatigue, interruption in his current life routine to the point that I doubt seriously that Clyde could be put through a lengthy trial without the high risk of medical complications.

* * *

TOM METZGER, the prosecutor, ran into Bamonte in Newport and asked him what he was working on. The sheriff rattled off a few drunk-driving cases and a robbery and told of an investigation into the latest cult to discover the far reaches of the Pend Oreille.

"Anything else?"

Bamonte looked to the ground. "Still chasing a few loose ends on Conniff."

"Conniff? Jeez, Tony. When are you going to give it up?"

"Got a few things left to check. You haven't been much help, Tom."

"Just where the hell do you think you're going with this thing?"

"Till the end. Till there's nothing left to check. I'm running out of time, too."

"Why's that?"

"He's going to die. Ralstin is."

"So what do you think I'm going to do—drag some old codger back here and then put him away for life?"

"It's not my job to determine punishment, Tom. I started this, and I intend to see it through, with or without your help."

SICK AND BEDRIDDEN, Sarah Schultz had sent her son to fetch the sheriff. She was ninety-one years old and had known Clyde Ralstin since the 1920s, when they were neighbors in the Nez Percé country of Idaho, which her father had homesteaded. She never liked Clyde. The man seemed to run over people, Indians and whites alike. She had been following Bamonte's case in the Spokane papers. When the name Ralstin first appeared, it touched in her memory a forgotten episode from a nearly forgotten decade.

The summer air settled in the Spokane Valley, gathering smog, and made life uncomfortable for anyone stuck indoors without air-conditioning. Mrs. Schultz lived by herself in a two-story house in the city. She moved to Spokane in the early 1930s, after losing everything—the family farm, her life savings—in the Depression. She seemed very weak, a woman with little control over anything in her life. Before another day passed, she wanted to make sure that

Sheriff Bamonte was aware of something about the man he was pursuing.

"He's killed before, you know," she said.

"I did not know. Tell me, please."

"'Long about the same time. In the 1930s, I'm sure."

"What happened?"

"He shot and killed a boy. The son of a friend of mine. I'm not sure how old, but he was just a kid. And then, Ralstin got away with it."

"Why? I don't follow."

"Well, he was a policeman. Killed the boy in the line of duty, or so he said. Ralstin used to brag about it, from what I heard."

"Do you know the boy's name?"

"Roger . . . Roger . . . something. His mother was Mrs. Clifford. Docia Clifford. But the boy's last name was different, because she had remarried."

"And the year—you don't remember what year?"

"No. In the 1930s, some time then."

"Here in Spokane?"

"Yes. In Hillyard."

"I'll find a record of it."

"They had this hearing, afterward. Some kind of inquest. I sat through it with Mrs. Clifford, and it was a total sham. They covered up what Ralstin had done, and protected him. That's what it was all about. My friend lost her son, who was a fine boy, a good student who had never done anything wrong. Her other son went on to become a judge, so you can imagine how Roger might have turned out. And Ralstin, he . . . he . . . he got away with it."

Bamonte stood, jolted by the tip, anxious to dash out the door. "I can't thank you enough, Mrs. Schultz."

"Is this helpful?"

"In a big way."

"Can I tell you something else?"

"Certainly."

"It's just my opinion. This other thing I told, that really happened."

"Go ahead."

"Clyde Ralstin wasn't a policeman. He was a criminal who put on a uniform."

THE STORY of Ralstin shooting a kid, if true, fit the image Bamonte had been trying to flesh out—not the frail former judge trying to live the last days of his life in peace. Bamonte felt that he understood a few things about killers. Usually, somebody who could kill another human craves excitement, a blood lust of sorts. Often, the killer is weak and insecure, looking for power or assurance in desperate acts. To snuff a life satisfied both needs. Little things became standoffs, to be settled only by one man in absolute triumph, the other on the ground, crushed.

Bamonte asked his friend Bill Morlin, the reporter for the *Spokesman-Review*, to search his newspaper morgue for the killing. Morlin, as intrigued as Bamonte about the true character of Clyde Ralstin, found nothing in the paper's files, under Ralstin, about a shooting. Nothing under homicides. He went to the coroner's office, asking about inquests from the 1930s. Bingo—something came up on an Officer Ralstin. They gave him the date. He went back to the paper and discovered a packet of pastry-flaked yellow clips that the librarian said had been taken from an envelope marked "Police— Shootings By" and put under a general crime category.

Among the clips was a story from April 4, 1937, inside the paper, wedged between a piece on "Midget Dancers United by Cupid" and an account of firebombing and rioting in Nelson, British Columbia. The article was headlined BOY OF 15 SHOT TO DEATH IN FLIGHT FROM POLICEMAN. The six-paragraph story told of Roger Irvine, age fifteen, a student at John Rogers High School in the Hillyard section of Spokane, who was killed by a bullet which pierced his heart from behind. The boy was joyriding, along with two companions, in a 1937 Plymouth coupe they had stolen. The patrolmen were in pursuit when Irvine, the driver, slammed on the brakes, which caused the police car to smash into it. The boys then fled and were fired on as they tried to run away from the officers.

"The bullet that ended young Irvine's life was fired by Prowl Car Officer Clyde Ralstin," the story said.

In the same file, Morlin found several follow-up pieces and a copy of Ralstin's resignation. He showed these to Bamonte. The second story, dated April 5, 1937, not only confirmed what the old woman had said but elaborated on it:

> Irvine, described as a bright and orderly student, who enrolled at the Rogers school from Kellogg, Idaho, the first of this year, was shot as he and his two companions jumped from the stolen car and ran down an embankment. The course of the bullet, which entered the lower part of the youth's back and ranged upward near his neck, showed Officer Ralstin had shot low in an effort to hit the boy's leg, Prosecutor Ralph E. Foley said at an informal coroner's hearing.
>
> The youth evidently stumbled while running down the embankment, Prosecutor Foley said, and received the bullet in a most vital part of his body.

This account assured Bamonte of several things. First, despite the official fuzziness from the Spokane Police Department, and the void of formal records on him, Ralstin worked for the department. Second, he had been demoted from detective—as he was in the last stories Bamonte had seen on him, from 1935—to prowl car officer, as he was called in 1937. Third, and most important, he shot the kid in the back. Joyriding was hardly a capital crime, and the fleeing boys were not exactly threatening the officers' lives. The kid had stolen a car, smashed it up, and then ran away when chased by policemen. For that, he was shot in the back. A marksman like Ralstin, the best shooter in the department, a man who could split a duck's beak from fifty yards, would not aim for the legs and hit the spine. He shot to kill.

In recounting the boy's short life, the paper wrote:

> Roger had never been in trouble before. He possessed many awards of honor certificates from public schools to show excellence in scholastics. Active in virtually all athletics, he captained

the Logan grade school baseball team in Spokane and had turned out for track at John Rogers High School. Teachers acclaimed him as always a gentleman. At Kellogg high school the youth starred in football and showed all-American promise.

While in Kellogg, he lived with his brother and sister-in-law, Mr. and Mrs. Joseph Irvine, saved the money he made while attending school and visited his mother regularly.

"Roger was at all times a gentleman, studied and worked hard," said his mother, Mrs. Docia Clifford. "I have been assured of this again and again by his teachers, his pastor and his friends. He and I were the closest of pals and he always brought his problems to me.

"I hold no malice toward that Officer Ralstin. He has my sympathy. It might have been his boy. I do not feel that Roger was a criminal and I know that those who knew him do not believe so.

"My trust in God makes me believe that whatever is done is done for the best. I am not able to feel just now that Roger's death is for the best, but I know that later I will realize that. As I see it now, it was just a mistake, not a sin, but a mistake. Roger was not a criminal, and I know that he took that car just for a thrill."

A third story, dated April 6, 1937, told of a coroner's probe and mentioned deep in the story that "police said there is little likelihood of charges being brought against Officer Ralstin, whose duty it is, they explained, to stop any escaping felons." Later that night, a six-member coroner's jury followed the prosecutor's recommendation and absolved Ralstin. The killing was justified, they said, because "Roger Irvine was fleeing from justice after the commission of a felony, to wit: the unlawful taking of an automobile."

Included in the packet was a letter of resignation from Ralstin, dated three months after he killed the boy. The notice, and a small newspaper clip, did not say precisely why he left the police force, but referred to a dispute when Ralstin failed to show up for work. No mention was made of previous suspensions or demotions, just a hint of the contentious nature of a man who seldom did anything without a fight.

"Upon acceptance of my resignation, you are hereby authorized and directed to disregard my notice of appeal from that certain order of suspension dated June 7th, 1937, and signed by Commissioner A. B. Colburn," Ralstin wrote. "It is understood that with the acceptance of my resignation that the records of the Civil Service Commission and the Spokane Police Department will show that I resigned as a member of the Spokane Police Department."

In the accompanying newspaper story—a three-paragraph notice —Ralstin was asked about the resignation. "I asked for a six-month leave of absence because I had a chance to get a better job—one I always wanted," Ralstin was quoted as saying. "When my request was denied, there was nothing else to do but resign."

FROM THAT DAY in July 1937 on, there was no mention of Ralstin in any story in the paper's morgue. In the file marked "Police— Shootings By," no stories appeared for more than thirty years. Then, a clip from the late 1960s carried an account of a shooting by a young patrolman who fired on an armed robber as he was fleeing a department-store holdup in downtown Spokane. The robber, hit with a single shot between his eyes, was left in a vegetative state afterward, severely brain-damaged by the wound. An inquest found that the shooting was justified.

Of course, Bamonte recognized the story instantly. The patrolman was Bamonte himself.

22.

The River

ALONE ON the Pend Oreille River, Bamonte guided his boat downstream, following the slow current, no particular direction in mind. It was a Saturday morning in late July; the sky was smeared to a faded yellow from forest fire smoke and lazy air. Another drought, perhaps the worst in twenty years, made people cranky and less tolerant, a behavior pattern the sheriff could chart along with the high temperature readings. Soon as it got hot, and the winds disappeared, the men of the Pend Oreille lapsed into their mean streak, draining six-packs every few hours, bashing their wives, smashing up cars. The sheriff had his hands full chasing calls in the distant corners of the county.

And it was not much better at home, at the end of those summer days when the light held to the sky till nearly ten p.m. Bamonte was trying to reconcile with his wife, a trial return.

"Just move back, and see what happens," he had asked Betty. "We don't have to do anything. No conditions. We'll be like . . . roommates, if you want."

The words between them were barbed—small informational exchanges sent as a form of reconnaissance, but received like a lance. Tony slept on the first floor, Betty on the third. But of course he didn't sleep; the heat alone was enough to keep him awake. He wanted to strip himself of the bark of pride, tell Betty what a mess he was, and what she meant to him. But when he tried to explain himself, it all came out like clumps of gravy. He felt stubborn and inarticulate, the curse of the physical man, trapped in the code of manhood handed down by his father. Men stood for action over contemplation, aggression over mediation, work over family. Afterward, he thought of what he should have said, and it seemed so simple. Watching his family slip away, he knew he was failing, but still he could not act. There was no manual for such repair.

On the river, he passed ospreys diving for river rats, and fishermen with sunburned backs and slack lines. Irrigation sprinklers spit water over rusty hay fields. With the boat engine at low idle, he coursed with the flush of the river, his thoughts trailing along with him. He was trying to find a way to get at Ralstin. The discovery that Clyde had killed a boy and then left the police department under cryptic circumstances had refired Bamonte's outrage. The kid was unarmed. He posed no threat to the officers. He was scared. He ran, like any fifteen year old, and Ralstin knocked him dead. It was legal, of course, and all justified, because the shooter wore a badge. In Bamonte's mind, Clyde Ralstin had killed at least two people, then sailed through more than half a century of life without answering for his crimes. Worse, Bamonte believed Ralstin had killed for excitement—a hunter of animals who shot humans with the same disregard, firing on one person before he could see him, shooting the other one in the back. It was all turkey shoot. After twenty-three years as a cop, Bamonte knew why some people, otherwise rational, hated policemen. There were just enough Ralstins in uniform to make every other officer pay for it.

All this talk about the benevolent judge of Lapwai and the helping neighbor of Saint Ignatius made the sheriff sick with cynicism. But with every character tidbit brought forth by Bamonte, Ralstin's position also hardened, and his supporters closed ranks around him. Bamonte was on a self-serving and irresponsible crusade, they charged—a sentiment echoed by top brass in the Spokane Police Department.

"Don't you have anything better to do?" one officer in Spokane asked Bamonte. And, of course, he did. Summer was the worst time to be a rural sheriff—everybody was outside, riding boats, or RVs, or souped-up vans, or dirt bikes, doing the same awful things they did indoors, except in public view. His shift sometimes lasted as long as daylight.

In Saint Ignatius, the friends of Clyde Ralstin repeated what Phil Grainey had said: Clyde was too frail to spend an afternoon with an interrogator, and had nothing to say anyway. When pressed by the sheriff, Grainey finally issued a challenge to Bamonte: "Put up or shut up." He said, "If you got enough to prosecute him, charge him. If you don't, drop the case."

Bamonte knew he did not have enough. Not yet. Nor did he feel he had much time left to come up with something. The sheriff could hear the clock; not a statutory timer but the slowing tick of life. He did not want Ralstin to die before the full story caught up with him.

One hope, a slim one, was the Spokane River. As Bamonte was constantly reminded, he lacked physical evidence. All he had, the critics said, were overripe consciences, memories stained by the years. Bamonte thought if he could find the gun, it would corroborate the best evidence from his strongest living witness. Dan Mangan had pointed to the rock walls in a pool between tiers of Spokane Falls and said his partner had tossed the gun there to cover for Clyde. If Mangan was telling the truth, the gun might still be under the river. But even if the sheriff found the gun, Mangan was fast deteriorating, his blood slowing through his hardened veins. He could barely talk. The case would fall apart if either of Bamonte's two best sources, Pearl Keogh and Dan Mangan, died before he finished the investigation.

THROUGHOUT THE SUMMER, Bamonte had kept the Conniff family informed of developments. After going a lifetime without hearing the slightest word from the authorities about who might have killed their father, feeling snubbed and ignored, the Conniffs now had been privy to one astonishing break after another. They encouraged Bamonte, inspired him during his low points. George Conniff in particular was full of ideas, some of which conveyed the outrage he carried on behalf of his father. But when Bamonte shared with the Conniffs his thought about searching for the gun, George was less than enthusiastic. "It's a longshot," he said. "Your chances of finding something are a hundred to one."

In the early part of the summer, Conniff was not sure exactly what drove Bamonte. Did he want revenge against the old cops and the old ways? Glory? A political plum for his next election campaign? But as he came to know him, talking late nights with the sheriff, and he saw the investigation go from a glamour hunt to a political liability, he was convinced that Bamonte wanted nothing more than justice for the death of the marshal. Sometimes, the way the sheriff spoke about it sounded a little spooky. "I'm the voice of the dead, I'm all they have," he told Conniff.

The Spokane Police Department did not seem any more receptive to Bamonte's latest idea than they had been to his previous requests. But the sheriff never gave up hope that somebody in uniform would do the right thing. He asked the department to provide him with a few officers to help search the river, two blocks from their headquarters.

"You can't be serious," an assistant to the chief said over the phone.

"Look, you've got—what?—two hundred and fifty officers sitting within a stone's throw of the river. Just let me borrow a few men for an hour or so," Bamonte said.

If the drought kept up, the Spokane River would continue to shrink, presenting a rare opportunity to sift through the secrets that had been buried underwater, Bamonte explained. "It could be years before the river conditions are ever just right again."

Usually, the river ran at better than ten thousand cubic feet of water per second; by early August, it was a tenth of that force. But Spokane police refused to provide any assistance, in manpower or equipment. Not even a police metal detector was offered. A vital piece of evidence in a first-degree murder investigation might be at the bottom of a river in the middle of the Spokane Police Department's jurisdiction. Why no cooperation? Bamonte asked. Back-channel, department officials explained that they had more urgent things to do than pursue a case that could tarnish the institution.

Bamonte then contacted the Washington Water Power Company, whose dams pinch the river for most of its length, and asked for assistance. It also expressed astonishment.

"The water's getting so low," Bamonte said. "Isn't there any time when I can just get out and walk on the riverbed?"

The company was planning to remodel its big Monroe Street Dam, below the site where Mangan said the gun had been dropped, and needed to do some survey work at low-water point before the project could proceed. Sometime in August, it planned to draw the water down to a trickle.

"You'll let me know?"

The company said it would take his offer under consideration. There were some legal problems. And it did not want to appear at odds with the Spokane police.

A more direct way to close the investigation—equally farfetched, but the only other choice—would be to force a confession from Ralstin. Maybe the old man, so near death, could be shamed into telling his secret. The Conniffs offered to write Ralstin a letter, an appeal to his heart. Bamonte did not think Clyde would soften; still, the letter was worth a try.

On August 8, the Conniffs composed their note, carefully considering each word, trying to keep their anger off the page. Like Bamonte, they believed that Clyde Ralstin had killed their father in 1935—shot him for butter, and then put the last bullet inside him to make sure the marshal would not live to tell what he'd seen. But venom would not serve their purpose. The letter, mailed to Saint Ignatius on the same day it was written, read as follows:

Mr. Ralstin:

We are the son and two daughters of George Conniff. As you know, we have been concerned for many years about the exact circumstances of our father's tragic death.

When we learned in March of this year about your possible

involvement in this event, we were both saddened and relieved. We were saddened because it brought up again the most painful experience of our lives. We were relieved because we finally had a chance to learn how our father was murdered.

After some conversations with Pend Oreille Sheriff Tony Bamonte, we wanted very much to get to the truth of this matter.

We have received letters from Attorney Philip Grainey and Physician Clancy Cone. Please be assured we can sympathize with your medical condition and are sensitive to what a trial could do to your health. We have thought about our actions very carefully and have prayed about this matter at length.

Mr. Ralstin, words cannot convey the deep sense of loss we have felt over the years because of the death of our father. He meant the world to us and to our mother. His murder robbed her of a devoted husband. Theirs was one of the happiest of marriages.

Our six children and nine grandchildren have been deprived of a wonderful man who was gunned down in the prime of his life. Our father's death has hung over us for many years and has been a source of continuing pain.

Our primary concern is to find the truth and to achieve some kind of justice for what happened. We are not vindictive people, but we have suffered a great deal over our father's death. We appeal to your sense of humanity to tell us what really happened. We look forward to hearing from you at your earliest convenience.

Sincerely,

George Conniff, Olive Pearce and Mary Pearce

A week passed, and they heard nothing. When another week went by with no response, the Conniffs knew they would never hear from him. Instead, they received a letter from Grainey, explaining that his client had nothing to say. If Ralstin were truly innocent, as he and his supporters claimed, surely he would have the decency to explain, the Conniffs reasoned. It was no mystery to them that Ralstin did not send so much as a word. A killer hides. A killer denies. A killer does not explain his actions.

Every week, Bamonte called the Washington Water Power Company.

"Just checking to see how that river's doing," he would say. "See what your schedule is."

In the third week of August, the company was ready to stop down the flow so that there was a window of time, no more than a few hours, when no water would come through the valley.

"I'll take it," Bamonte said.

Without aid from Spokane police, the sheriff needed somebody with searching expertise. He called the Treasure Hunters Club, a group whose members are well acquainted with metal detectors, and asked if they could help him look for a gun. Several members volunteered. He then contacted the Conniffs, advising them not to get their hopes up.

Word also spread to a local television station, which broadcast news of the sheriff's plan. In the hamlets of the Pend Oreille, in Spokane, in police departments throughout the inland Northwest, people said, "There he goes again." Some of Bamonte's political opponents saw the river search as their gain. The sight of the sheriff slopping around in the mud, looking for a gun from 1935, while kids whacked out on PCP raced up the backroads of the Pend Oreille, was political dynamite.

THE SKY WAS DARK with thunderheads on the afternoon of August 21; the collision of stale, suffocating air with cooler, westerly breezes produced a gnashing of electricity. At home, Tony was full of turbulence. Betty was gone, lazing away the last days of summer at a cabin. She had asked her husband if he wanted to join her. He shrugged—work. "I've got to see this through," he said.

"But that doesn't mean you can't take a day off."

"I will."

"When?"

The next morning, it rained, a dawn of warm drizzle. A few hours into daylight Bamonte met his team at the Post Street Bridge, above the river in the heart of Spokane. He had with him the Treasure Hunters, an odd party of informally deputized assistants who usually spent their free days searching for silver dollars and quarters on beaches. Their metal detectors were charged and ready to go. A few bystanders had gathered. And an older man—he looked to be in his eighties—seemed to be spying, watching the sheriff's every move through binoculars. He moved around on a cliff atop the river. The Conniffs arrived, taking up a position above the river.

The Post Street Bridge, built in 1917, is 340 feet long, and spans the midsection of the falls. Mangan had been very specific in pointing out where the gun had been dropped by his partner. He said they stood at the north end of the bridge, above a point where the water crashed into the high, hard-edged cliffs of basalt, and let the weapon fall to its grave. Now, the riverbed was naked, drained of water. Without the cover of the swift Spokane, the channel looked ugly, embarrassed to show itself. A chocolate water line was plastered against the rock banks. Thick, greased pilings ran across the mud and stone bottom. The floor was littered with wires and cables and metal rods and garbage cans and batteries and cement blocks. Fat river rats, a type of marmot, dragged pieces of scrap onto the shore.

In the short time since white men had driven out the Indians, another sweep of history had passed through this channel. Ghosts of defeated people and surging salmon runs, relics of industries that hitched their future to the brute force of the river—all the shouts and grunts of ancient vitality had drained through the chasm. A few fragments of animal bone, preserved in layered silt, might still be found, evidence of Colonel Wright's crime of 1858, when he slaughtered the horses upriver. It took all day to kill the eight hundred horses; some had to be lassoed, dragged out, shot twice in the head. After killing the animals, Wright had said to Garry, chief of the Spokanes, "You have been badly whipped. You must come to me with your arms, your women and children, and everything you have, and lay them at my feet. If you do this, I will dictate the terms upon which I will grant you the peace." A second, perhaps more lethal blow to Garry's band came forty-two years later, when Washington Water Power began work on its first big hydroelectric dam, a few feet from the place where Bamonte now stood. That dam blocked the returning chinook salmon, which had been the source of native prosperity for thousands of years. Very few clues remained from those great runs, unless one believed, as the natives did, that the salmon were gods, temporarily inhabiting the skins of fish as a way to return inland from the sea. If so, the salmon were all around. Downstream, on rock faces hidden behind wire fences to keep vandals out, the earlier inhabitants had left a few paintings—drawings of the sun, lizards, small buffalo.

As if to mark the change from one band of people living around the falls to another, an enormous fire had engulfed the new town of Spokane Falls in 1889, burning virtually the entire downtown area, thirty-two blocks, to the ground. The fire broke out exactly one hundred years earlier than Bamonte's search, in August. It started in a cafe kitchen, spread to the wood-frame buildings lining the river, and then swallowed the city. Firemen arrived, tapped into the hydrants, but nothing came through their hoses. The water system failed completely, and with it went the city. To those broken members of Spokane Garry's band living without salmon in shacks downriver, the fire must have seemed like fitting revenge on the people who had established their will over this land by slaughtering horses and destroying salmon runs.

What mattered to the river now was whatever the Washington Water Power Company commanded. David Thompson, the first white man to see the Spokane, had called it "one of the wildest and least navigable streams in the world," but it was now tame and well-mannered. The power company's founders had purchased Post Falls—once the summer gathering site of a band of the Coeur d'Alene led by Chief Seltice—in order to provide power for the mines in the mountains of northern Idaho. In drawing down that dam, twenty-eight miles upriver from Spokane Falls, they dried up the riverbed that Bamonte wanted to search, an area that had never been disturbed. Most of the riverbed except the place Mangan had pointed to had been stirred up in the 1970s, when the utility was doing extensive repair work on the Monroe Street power station, a few feet downstream from Post Street.

Down the banks of the river the sheriff went. He walked out among the mud-tarred rocks, under a drizzle, to a place not far from shore, in what would have been a pool of frenzied water at least ten feet deep, directly behind the big dam. Some of the rocks were polished; others were caked with sticky clay and mud. Bamonte believed Mangan was telling the truth, because the place he had pointed to was so precise, an odd spot to bury a gun. Why not throw it in the middle of the river? But he doubted if they would find anything; he prepared himself for another round of ridicule and scorn from the police department up on the bank, and from his constituents. Bamonte tracked a site line from the bridge to the river bottom, and then began kicking over rocks at the place where the weapon was most likely to be.

"Found something!" came a shout from one of the treasure hunters. He pulled a sawed-off shotgun, lightly rusted, no more than a few years old, from the river.

"Set it aside," Bamonte said. "We'll turn it over to SPD."

From atop the bridge, George Conniff watched, shaking his head. Bamonte was obsessed, clambering over the rocks.

Five minutes into the search, Bamonte spotted an irregular-looking shank of mud wedged tightly against the rocks.

"What's this?" he said, calling a few people over. "Look. . . ." He stooped down, ran his fingers through the goo. It was hard. He picked it up and let the water drain away; it was heavy. Outer layers of mud fell off, but the core did not break. In the misty light, it revealed itself as cinnamon-colored, a precious fossil in the shape of an L. Bamonte lifted it up, a handful of rust and silt, and wondered if what he held had been clutched by Clyde Ralstin on the night of September 14, 1935.

"I'd say that's a pistol," said one of the treasure hunters.

There was no doubt—it looked like a small handgun, but the rust was so heavy that parts of it were indistinguishable.

"Mangan was telling the truth," Bamonte said. "It's right where he said it would be."

He searched the bridge for the Conniffs, then held his find aloft, making sure they saw it.

"My . . . God—he's done it!" George Conniff said. His sister Olive was near tears; she sensed a miracle.

The man who had been watching Bamonte from the cliff was now spying down from the bridge. When the sheriff looked up at him, he turned away. Later, when everyone had left the river, the man dropped a metal object, about the size and weight of a pistol, from the bridge to see if it could, in fact, land where Bamonte had made his discovery. Bamonte found out the man was a former bootlegger, one of Ralstin's best friends in the 1930s, an intimate of the Mother's Kitchen circle that included Virgil Burch and Acie Logan. When questioned by a friend of Bamonte's, he said he was there looking out for Clyde's best interests.

The gun appeared to be precisely the weapon they were looking for. It was six and a half inches long, the barrel rusted shut, the trigger missing, and the handle hollowed-out in the center, where a hardwood core would have been grafted to the metal. Reporters gathered around Bamonte; the fool was a genius. He was momentarily stunned into silence. He felt vindication. He felt like he had Clyde Ralstin at last. He wanted to say, "God damn, I got the asshole cornered." He wanted to shout, to wave the gun in front of Ralstin's face, and say, "Remember this? Remember!"

But instead of gloating, he gave a measured response, the autopilot reply of a baseball player after he's won the game with a late-inning homer. "This is extremely good circumstantial evidence," he said. Asked about his next move, Bamonte said he was going to send the gun to the state crime lab for verification of its make and year. "This investigation is far from over."

Like the years of cover-up and deceit, the river itself had been peeled away, and what it revealed backed up the words from all those lanced consciences. The news of Bamonte's great find, carried in newspapers and television accounts around the world, brought a flood of inquiries and a rash of tips. Reporters from Australia, Europe, Mexico, and throughout the United States called about the story.

Bamonte was overwhelmed by the reaction; he had been so wrapped up in the case that he had lost a sense of perspective. He just wanted to catch up with Ralstin, to see it through for the Conniffs, to prove that Charley Sonnabend and Pearl Keogh—and yes, Bamonte himself—were not crazy. In a way, it mattered less and less what the sheriff said about who killed George Conniff in 1935. Bamonte the graduate student had awakened history; Bamonte the sheriff had forced it from the academic attic. Once free, it took on a life of its own.

23.

Last Gathering

THE GUEST OF HONOR sat in front of the room, next to his wife, surrounded by more than a hundred admirers, friends, and curious acquaintances. On his ninetieth birthday, Clyde Ralstin was the toast of Saint Ignatius. Judging by the turnout, it did not seem to matter that he was the lead suspect in a first-degree murder case, or that news about the discovery of a rusty handgun had joined his name to murder and spread the word to cities half a world away from Montana. To many of those gathered inside the senior center, all the evidence they needed was before them: entering his tenth decade, Ralstin still had his legs and his arms, his sight and his hearing, most of his hair, some of his teeth, and could raise his hand-carved willow cane high enough to threaten a much younger man. Would God preserve a killer for so long, in such mint condition? In the fight against time, as with most other struggles, people love a winner. And so on this evening in mid-September, the cottonwoods of the Mission Valley showing a blush of color, fifty-four years to the week after George Conniff had his life taken from him, the man said to be his executioner was hailed for his perseverance and applauded for his fine life.

Beyond the usual accolades that come with reaching a certain age, what Clyde Ralstin heard on his birthday was a strain of congratulations not unlike the kind he and Virgil Burch used to share with each other at Mother's Kitchen after a particularly successful butter heist. Several men of varying ages approached Ralstin, bellowed "Happy birthday," and then whispered into one of his flappy ears. "The bastards didn't lay a hand on you," one man was heard to say as he walked away. "You did it," said another. "You goddamn well pulled it off."

They chuckled, slapped his back, poked his ribs, raised a glass. He attempted a smile, but the old confidence wasn't there; the eyes were dimmed.

Few people mentioned, to his face, the name Conniff or the word "killer," or brought up the gun that had been resurrected from the bottom of the river. Bamonte's name was heard once, tailing on a snarl. "Vindictive," he was called—which was progress of sorts: no longer did the people of Saint Ignatius say the sheriff from the Pend Oreille was making it up. Too many things were falling in place. Now they said, so what? Let it rest. What more do you want to do to the guy?

Clyde's wife, Marie, was her husband's best defender. She tried to keep quiet, but it grated on her. She could see how the investigation was draining life from her husband. "Even if he did do it—which I don't think he did—what difference does it make?" she said. "I was only eleven years old when that happened. It's done. It's dead. Let it stay dead."

Her friends had urged her not to get too worked up.

"It's not fair!" Marie said, angered. "That man the sheriff is talking about—that's not the man I know. I love Clyde for the man he is today, not for what he may have done before."

A woman stirred the crowd. "Let's go, everybody! Gather round. One, two, three—'Happy birthday to you. . . .' "

AFTER FINDING THE GUN, Bamonte sent it to the Washington State Crime Laboratory in Seattle. Because rust had penetrated the pistol, the only way to determine the make was to examine its shape and compare it with similar weapons. A serial number, usually stamped on the side of the frame under the grip, was long gone. The barrel was sealed, foreclosing any examination of the groovings in comparison to bullet size. Still, there was no mistaking that the L-shaped piece of decomposed metal was a .32-caliber handgun, from a vintage of fifty to a hundred years ago. Frank Lee, the crime lab's firearms supervisor, concluded that the gun was likely an Iver Johnson .32-caliber Smith & Wesson, a pistol introduced around the turn of the century. Conniff was killed with a .32. At the time, most police detectives in Spokane carried the same kind of gun—a breast-pocket special, easily concealed. Bamonte already knew from a previous document that Ralstin, when he was forced out of the police department in 1937, had reported his .32 missing. Closing out nine years of demotions, suspensions, and warnings, Ralstin said at the time that he wasn't sure what had become of his gun, but he thought it was stolen. There was a grain of truth in the assertion, Bamonte felt, if you considered who did the stealing.

As corroded and ancient as the gun was, it gave credence to the sheriff's long investigation, an artifact to back the tiers of the tale. Doubters at the Spokane Police Department all but disappeared— at least in public—grousing less about the cop who was bad-mouthing their shop and more about the need to get on with other things. The odds against finding the weapon had been great; the odds against finding in the exact spot pointed to by Mangan a gun other than the one dumped by the pair of Spokane policemen were enormous. Ralstin's old buddy, the spy who stood atop the bridge, had spread a story that Bamonte had planted the gun. But he knew as well as anybody that the sheriff's search of the river was conducted in public, in front of numerous witnesses and a television camera.

Rusted shank and lab report in hand, Bamonte went back to his prosecutor, Tom Metzger. He wondered what more he would have to do before an arrest warrant would be issued. Metzger was cautious, but the sheriff pressed his case. Any fair-minded person, he said, could not doubt that he had found the gun disposed of by Spokane police. Fine. Next question: What were the police doing burying a murder weapon in the falls? Ladies and gentlemen of the jury, the People call Dan Mangan.

"Ralstin's in trouble," the old sergeant recalls being told as he's handed a loose-wrapped package by his superior. "Get rid of this."

Follow that with Pearl Keogh, her testimony of Virgil Burch and his boast about Clyde's performance on the night of September 14, 1935—"Ralstin just blowed his brains out. Said 'It was us or him.' "

Hearsay, strike it.

All right. Then enter into evidence the police reports from 1955 and 1957, the summaries of two visits with Detective Sonnabend, who told of arresting Acie Logan in 1935, and Logan spilling his guts, after three days of interrogation, about the black-market butter gang, naming Detective Ralstin as the leader and the shooter. Charley Sonnabend, whose integrity had never been questioned, twice summoned a passel of lawmen to his bedside to recount this confession. His life at ebb, he insisted that one fact be passed on before he died: the Conniff killer was a cop named Ralstin.

"Well," the defense attorney and a skeptical juror might ask, "is this man Ralstin—the chief of security at the place where America made plutonium for the first nuclear bomb, the judge of Lapwai, the civil servant, everybody's favorite neighbor, the father of a fine young son, grandfather by marriage to five, great-grandfather of six—really the kind of man who would kill another human—not to mention another cop?"

He is indeed. Ladies and gentlemen of the jury, he killed a fifteen-year-old boy two years after he gunned down the marshal. Shot the kid in the back.

Objection. Inadmissable. The kid killing was not part of the court record.

Back and forth went Metzger and Bamonte, kicking around what they had. The prosecutor had been down the lane of long odds before with his hyperactive sheriff, a man who once had helped to spring a felon convicted on evidence gathered by his own men, because new information pointed the other way; a man who had written Attorney General Edwin Meese that "justice was not served" and actually expected Meese, who spent most of his official years fending off personal ethics charges, to investigate the Forest Service for its role in the accidental death of a convict killed in a fire (a *con!*). Metzger looked at Pend Oreille County's best-known windmill chaser and shook his head. As dramatic, compelling, and thorough as Bamonte's investigation had been, helped by luck and fate, a convergence of mildewed guilt and quirky river currents, the prosecutor still was not satisfied with the package.

"Not quite there yet, Tony."

"But the witnesses, the statements, the gun . . ."

"Not enough. Sorry."

What was needed before Ralstin could be charged with murder in the nation's oldest active homicide investigation, Metzger said, was somebody who had heard him confess. His wife. A best friend. A relative. A neighbor. Somebody who could come forth, point to the old man in court, and say, "He did it. I know because he told me."

Even then, there was another problem, Metzger explained. Ralstin might insist on calling certain people to his defense—acquaintances, say, who could provide alibis. But the most significant ones were dead. Thus, while there was no statute of limitations on murder, the law also provided that if a person could not get a fair trial because key witnesses were missing or dead, the case could be dismissed. Such a situation was sometimes known as the passage-of-time defense.

"You've done a hell of a job," Metzger told the sheriff. "I don't think anybody expected you to get this far. I know I didn't."

For Bamonte, it was not enough. Yes, he had gone back to the past, erased one set of facts about a man and an institution and replaced them with something else. To change the content of years laid to rest—that in itself was a sensation even the best historians rarely experience. In those last days of a drawn and dry summer, Bamonte knew the exhilaration of resuscitating a long-buried personal history, but he also knew the grief. His own family had fallen apart. After failing to find some sign that her husband was ready to change, Betty left for good. They filed for divorce; nearly a quarter-century of marriage was handed over to the lawyers.

IT WAS EASIER to roust demons from the other man's closet. After the prosecutor poured water on his case, Bamonte talked to George Conniff.

"I imagine you're going to fold the tent," George said.

No, he would not quit. He had worked on a dozen murder cases in his entire career as a cop; every case had been solved. He would chase Ralstin until the sheriff's voice was many voices—the Conniffs', Pearl Keogh's, the Lapwai police chief's, those of the family of the murdered fifteen-year-old and the doubters in Saint Ignatius—whispering, then speaking aloud: You can't hide. We know what you did. We know.

LATE ONE NIGHT, Bamonte emptied out his files, panning for a last break. Sonnabend, Logan, Burch, Cox, Hinton, Black, Ralstin —say something! Going back through the scraps of paper, the jottings on side margins and familiar reports, he found the name of one retired Spokane policeman with whom he had yet to speak—Bill Parsons. The top brass, committed to preserving a flattering view of the institution they represented, had generally been the least helpful to Bamonte, and he did not expect much from Parsons, now approaching his eightieth birthday. From police records, the sheriff knew Parsons had been around the Stone Fortress in 1935, his rookie year. In 1966, when Bamonte joined the Spokane Police Department, Parsons was its chief.

The sheriff phoned Parsons, who said he did not remember Bamonte from his days at the department, but he knew all about him. Parsons had been following every step of the investigation. After the gun was found, Parsons figured it was inevitable his name would come up; the pistol had forced his past to the surface. The only question left was whether Bamonte would make it out to see him before he died. Bamonte explained that he wanted to talk about the gun, the police cover-up, Ralstin, and Mangan. They arranged to meet at Parsons's home.

Before he hung up, Parsons startled the sheriff. "You know Mangan's lying about that gun."

"What?"

"Says his partner, Cox, threw it off the bridge. Cox wasn't his partner that day."

"Who was?"

"Me."

ON THE MORNING of September 5, Bamonte sat in the kitchen of Parsons's home, facing his former boss. Parsons still had his bush of silver hair, the creaseless face, but he seemed to have very little life left in him. Emphysema was wearing him down. He was barely able to sit, sucking oxygen from a container.

The key to understanding why Ralstin was never questioned or arrested for the killing was with the department itself, Parsons said.

"Was Dan Mangan an honest person?" Bamonte asked.

"No."

"What kind of stuff was he into, Bill?"

"Anything he could get his hands on."

"Was Ralstin an honest man at that time? Do you remember him being honest?"

"Any story I heard was just the opposite," Parsons said.

"What kind of stuff did you hear about him, Bill?"

"Chippy . . . burglary . . ."

"What kind of burglaries?"

"I have forgotten what kind they were. There is . . . Some of the guys called him Slippery Dick."

Parsons had not seen or spoken to Ralstin since 1937, five years before Bamonte was born. The last time he encountered Mangan was in the late 1940s, when he used to go to his annual summer bash at the bar in Hungry Horse. Mangan, now living in a nursing home in north Spokane, had just been through another stroke—his third.

"What do you remember about Dan Mangan dropping this pistol off?" Bamonte asked Parsons.

"Dan and me were riding in the car, and in the station, Dan said, 'C'mon.' Went up to the Hacker Cox house and got a package and come back down to the bridge. Dan got out and tossed it over the side."

"Who was driving, Bill?"

"Dan was."

"Did you guys take turns driving?"

"Yeah."

"Where did he live?"

"I can't tell you."

"Did you have radios in your cars then?"

"Oh, yeah."

"Did you get a call over the radio to go up and get it?"

"No. In the station the captain told Dan to destroy it."

"What captain was that?"

"Captain Hinton. He's dead now."

"Do you remember what the date was on that? Was it one or two days after the murder?"

"It was shortly after. I wouldn't say it was one or two days. . . . I know it was shortly after because the next day I heard something that Captain Hinton was talking about a cover-up."

"What did he say about that, Bill?"

"I don't know. Just double-talk. . . ."

"Where did Cox live?"

"Mainly northwest. That's all I can tell you."

"And then Dan Mangan drove to his house?"

"Yeah."

At Cox's house, they received a package, wrapped in newspaper. Parsons asked what it was, but Mangan wouldn't answer him. They drove to the bridge.

"He threw it," Parsons said. "I never got to see the damn thing good till he threw it."

"Did he throw it or drop it?"

"No, he threw it."

"Do you remember how far he threw it?"

"He just threw it over the side of the bridge . . . a short distance."

"What did he say after he threw it?"

"He wouldn't answer me for a while." Later, Parsons said, Mangan told him they were tossing the gun to help Ralstin—a departmental favor.

Parsons added that he'd heard of another courtesy done for Clyde, during a roadblock on the night of the killing. Ralstin had appeared in a car, running hot, on the road out of Newport leading into Spokane, and two Spokane police officers let him by. Parsons knew because one of the officers at the roadblock, now dead, had told him.

This was the third account Bamonte had heard of the roadblock. The first had come from the Sonnabend memo, the second was from Pearl Keogh, who said Virgil Burch had bragged that Logan, Clyde, and he—under a tarp in the back—had breezed through a roadblock set up by Spokane police.

Parsons's story differed significantly from Mangan's on the question of who actually disposed of the gun. Mangan had pinned it on Cox, his long-dead former partner. Parsons was sure Mangan had it wrong. The image he held—the rookie watching the veteran dump a pistol in a murder case—was clear.

"Why do you think Mangan is not telling the truth right now?" Bamonte asked.

"Mangan's getting pretty feeble-minded," he said.

If the sheriff was ever to get these old cops in court, he needed to have their stories converge. Somebody was lying. They would have to decide who. Bamonte explained his dilemma to Parsons. The chief said nothing. Bamonte left him with a choice: do nothing, or help out the law.

A few days later, Bamonte called Rosemary Miller, Dan Mangan's daughter. She wasn't surprised that her father might have misled Bamonte about a key detail. His whole life had been a dodge from responsibility. So, he was lying to protect himself, putting the sin on a dead man while painting himself as a passive participant. What else was new?

Was it possible, Bamonte wondered, to get the old boys together? As it turned out, Jerie Parsons had called with the same request; in recent days, her husband had started talking about the case, sharing details with his wife. He wanted to make up for his role in a crime he had concealed for half a century. He wanted to help the sheriff —"to settle it," as he said.

* * *

MOST PEOPLE check into the Regency Plaza knowing it will likely be the last place they will ever call home. Sprawling over a plateau that used to hold bunchgrass and fields of camas bulbs, it has a vaguely colonial look, with its white columns and faded brick facade. But the Plaza is new, and its facade came from a factory. Faces, pale from too many days indoors, stare out windows that look at the parking lot and beyond, at the bald top of Mount Spokane. The Plaza is surrounded by warehouse shopping outlets and new apartments, a dormitory for the dying amidst the urgency of young adults busy with their first years away from home.

Dan Mangan was waiting for the chief on a couch in the sitting room just off the Plaza's entrance doors. He wore the prosthesis, and it itched, as usual. Parsons arrived, with his wife, and sat down next to Mangan. Jerie joined Rosemary Miller on a couch. No pleasantries were exchanged. The chief didn't like Mangan; never cared for him. The two men were drawn together now by the events of a single shift. It was only when Parsons came to shed himself of the event he shared with Mangan that he found company—that of a man he considered a liar and a thief. And so for this one afternoon in the last days of his life, Bill Parsons did not feel the loneliness.

"Dad," Rose said in a very loud voice, "you remember Bill Parsons?"

Mangan leaned over and whispered something into the other man's ear. Neither woman heard what was said. Then the soft voices fell away and the two old men looked at each other in silence, slowly gathering memories, forcing themselves to think of a time they had tried to forget.

"Who did throw that gun off the bridge?" Mangan asked abruptly.

"You did," Parsons replied. "I was your partner that afternoon. It was you and me that got called in to get rid of the gun. And it was you—" he coughed, raised a finger, and pointed at Mangan—"who threw that gun in the river."

He started another sentence, but couldn't force the words out with his deflated lungs. He took a long pull of oxygen.

"The hell!" Mangan replied, a burst of acknowledgment. He searched the couch for the eyes of his daughter. "I'll be damned."

Parsons motioned for Jerie. It was done. The record was clear. She helped him up, and they walked down the corridor of the Regency Plaza to a restroom.

Rose went up to her father. She wanted to be sure. "Dad . . . do you realize what you just said?"

She had never seen her father, the brute, so broken and helpless, an eighty-six-year-old man shorn of a major deception. He started crying.

"Yeah," he said to Rosemary. "I realize."

"Can you actually say to yourself that you did it?" she asked him.

"Yes. I can."

PARSONS AND MANGAN never spoke again. Mangan suffered another stroke, which left him unable to talk. Parsons died one month later, in his wife's arms. The funeral drew a large crowd of policemen, in uniform.

THE MEETING at the Regency Plaza probably helped both men more than it helped Bamonte. Yes, they got their stories straight. But Bamonte was still without the one person, or detail, he needed to convince his prosecutor that a ninety-year-old man should be dragged over the mountains to face a crime from 1935. He was running out of time, and the bank of potential witnesses was empty. It was down to Bamonte and Ralstin, the accuser and the accused.

Bamonte did not have any strong desire to see Ralstin in jail. In practical terms, a life sentence for a man his age could amount to no more than a few months. Clyde had lived a life since the killing. What would it accomplish to take away his last days on earth and put him behind bars? The medical expenses alone would be enough of a drain on Pend Oreille County's paltry finances to make incarceration unpopular. Justice would have to be extracted in some fashion other than the courts and jail. There had to be some way to take from Ralstin what Ralstin had taken from others.

Since Clyde had refused to answer any questions from Bamonte, the sheriff thought of using a surrogate. Bill Morlin, the Spokane newspaperman, came to mind. The reporter was already thinking of paying a visit to Ralstin's house when Bamonte suggested it. Morlin would get a story, Bamonte would get a few more answers.

Ten days after Bamonte found the gun, Morlin arrived in Saint Ignatius, camera and notebook in hand, and knocked on the door at 365 First Avenue. A woman in her early sixties answered the door. His strategy was to be low-key and homey, a neighborly visit. Morlin's twelve-year-old boy, Jeff, was waiting for him in the car. The reporter introduced himself—"just came by to say hello, that's all."

"We're not talking to reporters."

"I know, I know," Morlin replied. "My boy and I—that's him in the car, Jeff—we were in the neighborhood. Just wanted to say hi."

Peeking inside the house, Morlin saw an old framed picture of a younger Clyde Ralstin and his bride, Marie.

"Nice picture," he said. "Would you mind if I took a picture of it myself? Just for the record, you know. We want something that shows you at your best."

"Well . . . I guess."

"Is Clyde around?"

"He's inside. You can't disturb him. He's not feeling well. The stress of all this is . . . killing him."

"I understand. He's quite an energetic guy, from everything I've heard. Built a house not far from here?"

"Yes."

He handed the picture back to Mrs. Ralstin. Looked inside again.

"Uh . . . would you like to meet my son, Jeff? Yeah? Hold on a minute." He called out for his boy. "Jeeeeeff!"

Jeff emerged from the car, holding his skateboard.

"Meet Mrs. Clyde Ralstin, son. This is Jeff."

They exchanged polite words. Mrs. Ralstin would not let the reporter and his son go any further.

"Guess I better be going now," Morlin said. "Nice meeting you." He turned, walked away, then stopped halfway.

"Say, would you mind if I just shake your husband's hand?"

"Shake his hand?"

"Before I leave, I'd just like to shake his hand."

"I suppose it wouldn't hurt anything. . . . But don't you get him riled up. He has a terrible heart problem."

Morlin followed her past the threshold, into a small house stuffed with guns and animal skins and knickknacks from nearly 160 combined years of living. In a corner, embedded in a chair, was a chalk-faced man, shoeless, with sunken cheeks and clamshell ears. He had on a string tie, suspenders, and he clutched his willow cane. Morlin introduced himself.

"I'm from Spokane," he said. "Just wanted to say hi." His notebook, and small portable tape recorder, were concealed. Ralstin said he had a lot of friends in Spokane. Morlin let him ramble for a few minutes. On the advice of his attorney, Ralstin had turned down all interview requests from reporters. Clyde said he had nothing to say about the Conniff case.

"I understand," Morlin said. "But you know what the sheriff says. . . ." He went through Bamonte's accusations in rapid-fire bursts, trying to goad Ralstin into responding. Ralstin snapped a few answers back—Clyde speaks!—and Morlin had his story.

"Let me just turn this on for a second, so I don't misquote you," he said, showing the tape recorder.

Ralstin talked for about eight minutes. Then Morlin asked him if he could step out into the daylight for a picture. Just one shot. Clutching his cane, snarling in defiance, Ralstin moved slowly to his doorstep and faced the world.

THE REPORTER'S STORY ran on page one of the September 4 edition of the *Spokesman-Review*, under the headline EX-OFFICER DENIES ROLE IN MURDER.

Not only did Ralstin deny killing Conniff, but he said he could not remember the crime and had never been to the town of Newport.

"It's all hogwash," he said. "This whole thing is just hearsay from guys that stray from the truth so easy."

On a few points he was adamant. "The Lord and I know that I never was ever in that town of Newport, that I never set foot there," he said.

Why did he leave the police department?

"I had woman trouble," Ralstin explained. The Conniff killing, and the shooting of the fifteen-year-old boy, had nothing to do with his resignation. "The pay was so low it was pitiful," he said.

But he could not deny his friendship with Burch and Logan, a pair of cons, whose roles in the Conniff killing and the creamery heists seemed beyond doubt, detailed in the public record, newspaper accounts, police reports.

"They criticize me mainly for, they say, hobnobbing with crooks. How do they think I found out who all these crooks were that I sent to the penitentiary?"

He would not be more specific. Then he repeated an earlier statement. "I never set foot in that town, and the Lord knows it," he said. "Twixt him and I, why, I'm not worried too much about it."

While the interview produced no jackpot for Bamonte, the sheriff was encouraged, and found several useful bits in Morlin's account. For one thing, Ralstin's answers showed him to be a liar. Woman trouble? By his own boasts, as well as the accounts of those who knew him well, Ralstin was an incurable skirt chaser. But there was no evidence that his resignation, three months after he shot the kid, a month after he missed days of work without explanation, had anything to do with his philandering. Couldn't remember the Conniff case? That claim also jarred with the facts: he was suspended for six days without pay, directly after the Conniff killing, for leaking information about the murder investigation to his cronies at Mother's Kitchen. Then he was demoted from detective to a lowly foot patrolman. Two career-busting actions because of his role in the killing—and he couldn't remember the case? As for his claim that he'd never set foot in Newport, three men who knew him well had said otherwise. There was a whorehouse just across the Idaho border in Priest River—a favorite destination of Clyde's, his friends said. The most direct way to Priest River, from Spokane, was through Newport. Finally, he said he hung out with crooks as a way to send them to the penitentiary.

If so he certainly never acted against his buddy Virgil Burch, a man with a lengthy criminal record, or Acie Logan, a career convict. When both men were arrested for stealing and fencing creamery products, it wasn't Clyde Ralstin who came forth to testify. In fact, Ralstin was nearly charged along with them. What protected him was his own leverage within the department.

"... HAPPY BIRTHDAY, dear Cliiiiiiyde ... Happy birthday to you!"

The Saint Ignatius Senior Center filled with applause, a sound that spilled out the door. The guest of honor acknowledged the crowd with a wave of his hand, and then most everyone went back to talking, laughing, and sharing stories. But amid the good cheer was an undercurrent of harsh gossip and whispered innuendos.

"He knows that I know," Bamonte had said, and so, now, did a lot of other people.

Some guests came to the party not to fete Clyde Ralstin but to judge him, to look him in the eyes and see for themselves if he had the face of a killer, to try and size up the man who had lived many lives, and every day of the twentieth century. The spy from the Post Street bridge, Ralstin's buddy since 1929, could taste the poison in the air. He told Clyde he never should have talked to that reporter, Morlin. "That's the worst mistake you made," he said. "You shouldn't have told him anything, Clyde."

At least one longtime friend of Ralstin's had made up his mind after reading Clyde's comments in the newspaper. Keith Hendrick, the Lapwai police chief, had been at Ralstin's eightieth birthday party, and he was invited to his ninetieth. But he did not show up. Hendrick's doubts about his mentor had been growing all summer. He was particularly bothered that Ralstin—"a cop to his dying day," he always called him—would not talk to Bamonte. It looked like he was hiding something. Still, he wasn't sure one way or the other until Clyde told Morlin he could not even remember the Conniff case. "I don't buy that," Hendrick said. "Clyde has a mind like a steel trap. He wouldn't say something like that unless he was lying."

Something else had helped to turn Hendrick. Clyde had come back to the Nez Percé country late that summer. He visited a few relatives, old friends, and his brother Chub. Later, when a visitor asked Chub about the killing, he conceded that Clyde may have helped organize the creamery robbery, but he could not have been the one who shot Conniff because he was pheasant hunting with him in the fields around Lapwai. A check of the 1935 records showed that the season for shooting pheasant in Idaho, Washington, and Oregon did not begin until October—at least two weeks after the killing. That Chub, in his last days, would cover for his brother with a story that wouldn't hold up did not surprise Hendrick. Blood, of course, was thicker than loyalty to the law.

But what bothered Hendrick more than that was that Clyde never came to see him. "He couldn't face me," the chief said. "If he was innocent, he would have come and talked to me, and told me his story."

So while Hendrick, Mangan, Parsons, Pearl Keogh, the Conniffs, and Bamonte were not at the party, their collective presence was felt in the senior center at Saint Ignatius. Under the big sky of Montana, Clyde Ralstin was without shelter from his past.

"That sheriff is killing him," said Marie. "Why doesn't he just let him alone? Why? Why?"

Despite his outward appearance of vigor, Ralstin *was* dying, the internal bleeding worse than ever, the joints inflamed, the stomach, most of which was ulcerated and then cut out in surgery, tight and queasy. He was in pain all day, and, more recently, at night as well. No longer could he take refuge in sleep; the sheriff had robbed him of this last hideout.

In his day, Ralstin could break bodies and intimidate those around him. He could live by his own laws. He was enforcer and judge. Over time, he could hide in the folds of the Bitterroot Mountains, or blend among relatives in the high plateau above the Snake River, or tuck himself into the crease of the Mission Valley. But the land could no longer swallow people in the last days of the twentieth century, and its great bounty was disappearing. In 1989, only a single sockeye salmon returned to spawn in the upper reaches of the Salmon River, in the Nez Percé country over which Ralstin once ruled. The land kicked back more than it took in; a rusted pistol was more likely to come from a river than a fish that had spawned there for more than ten thousand years.

OVER THE AUTUMN, Bamonte worked on the finishing touches of his master's thesis. He was alone, his marriage heading toward dissolution in court, his son living in an apartment. He wanted to finish his small history of the Pend Oreille, and then put the graduate project to rest. But he was full of doubt, as usual, about whether his five hundred pages on crime and punishment in the wilderness of northeastern Washington added up to anything worthwhile. Would the professor laugh at the final product, poke fun at his writing, ridicule his thesis? At the same time, a television producer from an NBC network show on crime "Unsolved Mysteries," contacted him. He wanted to do a piece on the Conniff case. At first, Bamonte wasn't sure. But then he saw it as a chance to throw the net out one last time, and to send another psychic blast across the mountains at Clyde.

In December, with the ground covered with snow and the edge of the Spokane River iced up, Bamonte went to Gonzaga University to orally present his master's thesis to Professor Carey and four students. It was not a give-and-take academic session; instead, Bamonte told a story. In the eye blink of time since Pend Oreille had been a county, people had been murdered for silver and for butter, for a few hundred dollars, over wives and pickup trucks, in fits of rage and patterns of cool calculation. The men charged with tracking down those killers were not great detectives or skilled investigators; they were somebody's neighbor, a George Conniff or an Elmer Black, who had been handed a badge and a gun and told to seek justice. Sometimes, as in the Conniff case, the bad guys wore a uniform.

Carey was impressed by Bamonte's passion and his sincerity. "He truly believes," Carey said later, "that a policeman should be somebody special, that they should live up to something like a code of chivalry. What he found out, of course, was that policemen have a feudal loyalty to each other."

The professor gave the sheriff high marks for his thesis; listening to Bamonte's presentation was one of the most fascinating experiences he has had as a teacher. He urged his student to avoid bitterness, to learn from his project, to expand his world view.

A few days later, NBC broadcast the segment on the Ralstin case. Clyde's friends called the sheriff "a jackal" for cooperating with the television crew. How could he deprive Ralstin of peace during his final days? After the broadcast, dozens of tips came into the sheriff's office. It seemed that American cities were full of people who believed their neighbors could be killers. None of the tips panned out, though.

Ralstin was so upset by the broadcast that he could not eat. He coughed at night, brooded in the day, and cursed the sheriff for bringing this upon him. He would sit alone in his chair, the window shades closed, the snow piling up outside, sobbing to himself. The days were short, less than eight hours of light, and they seemed so dark to Clyde, like he was in a cave.

"Why won't he let me alone?" he said to Marie. "Everybody in that damn police department was crooked! All the way to the top! Why single me out? I don't deserve this."

She wiped the tears away from his eyes. "You've got to put this out of your mind, Dad," she told her husband.

"I can't," he said, weeping like an infant, choking between words. "He's killing me."

She would not let him answer the phone. It could be a reporter, or somebody calling to scold him. Try as Marie did to shield him, her husband was surrounded.

The internal bleeding became so bad Clyde entered the hospital. One of his veins was cracked, leaking like a hose with a slit. On the nineteenth of January, 1990, one day after Tony and Betty Bamonte filed for divorce, Clyde came down with a severe chill, his body trembling, his hands clammy, his breathing short. He was put under intensive care at the Community Medical Center in Missoula, a town that got its start as a hideout for outlaws on the lam. Four days later, he died—of natural causes, the doctors said. His wife said he never mentioned the Conniff killing in his final hours. After his body was cremated, and the ashes scattered over the Mission Valley, the sheriff of Pend Oreille County said the murder investigation of George Conniff was over, the case closed with the death of the only living suspect.

Marie thought her husband could have lived another five years if Bamonte had not hung the noose from 1935 around his neck. Clyde's attorney felt the same way. He said the stress from the sheriff's investigation had squeezed the last bit of life out of Ralstin. The assertion did not bother Bamonte; some people, he pointed out, dig their own graves.

EPILOGUE

MAY 1990

Commencement

A FEW MINUTES before the 103rd commencement of Gonzaga University, families gathered for pictures around the most popular landmark on the Jesuit campus: the statue of Bing Crosby. Golf bag at his feet, the bronze Crosby was without his pipe; as usual, somebody had stolen it. He had never been much of a student, preferring to drink and croon under a late moon with his pub band than study history or spar in Latin with the priests. The few people on hand today in Spokane who had actually known Crosby remembered him as something of a screw-off. Of course, it didn't matter what he did in the 1920s. His years in college were recast in light of what happened to him later—a C student who became a statue.

The lilacs had opened on the campus grounds, and their scent was intoxicating. You could walk along the Spokane River, take in the perfume of spring, and daydream about the future. But this graduation day, a Saturday in the second week of May, was too cold for final strolls under flowering trees. At ten o'clock, when the band summoned everyone into the basketball auditorium, it was only thirty-nine degrees outside, and raining. Children scratched and fussed inside their new clothes, the boys tugging at clip-on ties, the girls adjusting patent-leather shoes with straps one notch too tight. The gym was packed, a cross-section of the people of the inland Northwest:

Indians from British Columbia, cowboys from Montana, wheat farmers from the Palouse, third-generation Spokane families sending another graduate out to work. The procession started, and everyone rose. The graduates came in like a conquering army, all smiles, waving, a serpentine line of blue and black gowns. In the midst of the procession was the sheriff of Pend Oreille County; Bamonte strode in, one among hundreds, and took his seat.

After the national anthem, Father Bernard J. Coughlin, the school president, went to the podium, on a stage above the sea of caps, and the audience fell quiet. The priest made a few light remarks about a fiftieth-reunion class in attendance—"They've been out bar-hopping," he said. Then he switched to his serious comments. The graduating class of 1990 might well remember, years from now, how much the world had changed in the last few months: the Berlin Wall had come down, heralding the end of communism and the demise of the cold war, and Americans were talking about a peace dividend, a time when people could go through their days without worrying that some diplomatic dustup would lead to world annihilation. More likely, the priest said, what the graduates would carry with them from this ancient Jesuit campus on the river was the Christian ethic—at least, that was his hope. He did not mention religion.

"The full human being is someone who can commit to something beyond himself," he said.

Bamonte looked tired. He had spent the night at an inn next to the river, upstream from Spokane Falls, and he was troubled. Something was missing; his mood did not match his expectations. He had cap and gown and a hole in his stomach. Professor Carey noticed that his student seemed depressed, and he could not understand why. The young man who had flunked his senior year in high school had grown into an adult student who wrote a master's project that changed a small plank of history. He had shown remarkable intellectual growth, the professor said. He had started his studies with a view of the world that was largely black and white. "Now he's begun to see something bigger, a truth that goes beyond one or two dimensions."

Setting a goal, getting a grade—it seemed simple, by comparison, to so many other things.

Epilogue

"Respect your own intelligence," Father Coughlin said, finishing his remarks. "The mind is really all we have to work with."

ACROSS TOWN, at the same time Bamonte was going to the podium to receive his master's degree, another ceremony was under way, a memorial. On the rain-swept plaza in front of Spokane police headquarters, a Salvation Army band shivered, then pressed blue lips to brass, forcing out the first, wobbly notes of "Faith of Our Fathers." The service, an annual event, was a tribute to every police officer in the state of Washington killed in the line of duty. Their names were engraved in granite on the police steps. At least one name had been missing from all the years of the memorial—that of George Edwin Conniff, the Newport marshal. It was a simple oversight, the police brass said. So today Conniff would be added to the list, along with five others, his name carved into the base of the institution that had allowed the person who most likely killed him to get away with it.

Seated near the front in folding chairs were the Conniffs, the son and daughters of the marshal, there to see the circle closed. They had mixed feelings. To them, the tribute was just, and fitting, and long overdue; but it felt awkward that this vault of secrets and cover-up, with its black slate roof and its Gothic tower, could now honor the slain marshal.

An icy drizzle fell from cement skies. The band played "Taps," and everyone stood in the cold, heads bowed.

As the music faded away, Donald C. Brockett, the Spokane County prosecutor, began his remarks. A small, ageless man, he looked like Jack Nicholson without the potential for mischief. Next to him was Spokane's police chief, Terry Mangan, and dozens of uniformed officers.

"Aren't we all victims when someone close to us dies?" the prosecutor said. A few heads nodded. George Conniff looked straight at the podium, unblinking, his face hard. Brockett hit all the right notes, talking about duty and order, justice and fair play. To George, it was a blend of solemnity and hypocrisy.

"The streets would become a jungle," Brockett concluded, "if everyone carried out their own form of justice."

A benediction followed. Then the Salvation Army band played "Amazing Grace." The ceremony over, the small crowd dispersed. Afterward, when all the pictures were taken, when the band had packed up its instruments and left, when the dignitaries had gone off to Saturday-afternoon softball games, the Conniffs remained behind on the plaza in front of police headquarters, lingering in the cold rain to spend a few final moments with the memory of their father. They wept.

IN THE EVENING, Bamonte met his ex-wife for a drink at the inn along the Spokane River. They sat next to a window, his diploma at his side. She was happy for Tony, and her being there made him feel better. They talked about the past, their early days in Spokane. The city was changing, growing for the first time in half a century. The shell of Mother's Kitchen, which had passed through many hands after Virgil Burch sold it, had just been torn down. Soon, the place where Clyde Ralstin had held court and cut deals would be a parking lot. Nobody marked the occasion. They talked about the future, what would come of Metaline Falls, the little border town where they had spent so much of their life together. As expected, the cement factory closed down, and some residents of the village thought the town might well fold up and return to nature, a valley of larch trees and grizzly bears at the river junction. The high school put on a play about racists, called *The Foreigner*. Such a production, in the town that gave birth to a group of violent neo-Nazis, was inappropriate, said the mayor: "It's over. It's done. Nobody cares. They've forgotten about it." But the teacher who put on the play said it was a necessary reminder. She recalled what Abraham Lincoln said: "We cannot escape history."

Bamonte clutched Betty's hand, recalling the good times they had been through together, and how much hell he had caused her. He was still seeing Linda, and he was in love with Betty—a seeming contradiction that he could not explain. He looked out at the river.

She brought up the Conniff memorial, a service that never would have been held had it not been for Tony's persistence.

"You made a difference," she said. "My God, you made a difference!"

But he had lost the enthusiasm for talking about the history he had changed. He looked at Betty, and then they talked into the night about things that are much harder to recast.

Darkness came. The Conniffs went home. Graduates went off to parties, families, jobs, and disappointments. The river coursed through the town that hid the secrets of Billy Tipton and Butch Cassidy and Clyde Ralstin.

In September, Bamonte faced a primary election to keep his job. He ran his usual campaign—a few yard signs, talking to people in cafes and on the street. He worked other cases, including a murder in his county that bore striking similarities to one in Spokane. When Bamonte alerted Spokane police about his findings, they said their case was closed; they had a conviction.

As the election neared, the Spokane police chief called three press conferences at which he specifically criticized Bamonte. Some reporters were baffled. What was the chief of the biggest police department in the region trying to do? They had never seen one cop bring the press together to ridicule another lawman.

On primary day, September 18, Sheriff Bamonte lost his job, by thirty-four votes.

A reporter asked why he had been defeated. He thought he knew the answer, but he kept it to himself. After more than twenty years as a cop, he still did not belong.

A NOTE ABOUT THE AUTHOR

Timothy Egan is the Pacific Northwest correspondent for the *New York Times*. His last book, *The Good Rain*, was published in 1990 and received the Pacific Northwest Booksellers Award and the Governor's Writing Award. He lives in Seattle with his wife, Joni Balter, and their two children.

A NOTE ON THE TYPE

This book was set in Caledonia, a typeface designed by W. A. Dwiggins (1880–1956). It belongs to the family of printing types called "modern face" by printers—a term used to mark the change in style of type that occurred about 1800. Caledonia borders on the general design of Scotch Roman, but is more freely drawn than that letter.

Composed by PennSet, Inc., Bloomsburg, Pennsylvania.
Printed and bound by R. R. Donnelley & Sons,
Harrisonburg, Virginia.

Designed by Peter A. Andersen